THREE DAYS IN MARCH

THE EVENTS IN 1952 THAT MARKED THE BEGINNING OF
THE END OF THE REPUBLIC OF CUBA

COLECCIÓN CUBA Y SUS JUECES

FULGENCIO BATISTA, GREETED BY THE TROOPS AS HE ARRIVED AT CAMP COLUMBIA ON MARCH 10, 1952. HE DRESSED AS A CIVILIAN TO GIVE THE *COUP D'ÉTAT* THE APPEARANCE OF A POPULAR UPRISING. UNDER HIS LEATHER JACKET BATISTA WAS WELL ARMED AND PREPARED FOR THE WORSE.

EDICIONES UNIVERSAL, Miami, Florida, 2014

FROM THE SAME AUTHOR:

HISTORIA DE LA QUÍMICA INDUSTRIAL
TOTAL QUALITY AND PRODUCTIVITY MANAGEMENT
PERFORMANCE MANAGEMENT
STRATEGIC PLANNING
MANAGEMENT DEVELOPMENT
PROCESS IMPROVEMENT TEAMS
QUALITY STRATEGIES
GESTIÓN DE FUTURO
ONCE UPON A TIME (CO-AUTHOR)
CONTRAMAESTRE
BARAGUÁ
POETAS Y MEMORIAS DE CUBA
JIMAGUAYÚ
FREEDOM EMBATTLED (CO-AUTHOR)
REPUBLICAN CUBA
EXILED CUBA
THREE DAYS IN MARCH
GUÁIMARO
COLONIAL CUBA

RAÚL EDUARDO CHAO

THREE DAYS IN MARCH

THE EVENTS IN 1952 THAT MARKED THE BEGINNING OF THE END
OF THE REPUBLIC OF CUBA

Copyright © 2014 by Raúl Eduardo Chao

First Edition, 2014

EDICIONES UNIVERSAL
P.O. Box 450353 (Shenandoah Station)
Miami, FL 33245-0353. USA
Tel: (305) 642-3234   Fax: (305) 642-7978
e-mail: ediciones@ediciones.com
http://www.ediciones.com

Library of Congress Catalog Card No.: 2014956166
ISBN-10: 1-59388-266-1
ISBN-13: 978-1-59388-266-2

Chao, Raúl Eduardo, 1939-
THREE DAYS IN MARCH / Raúl Eduardo Chao

Front Cover:
The Cuban National flag
Back Cover:
A collection of photos from the personalities surrounding the events of March 10, 1952. See page 264

Todos los derechos son reservados. Ninguna parte de este libro puede ser reproducida o transmitida en ninguna forma o por ningún medio electrónico o mecánico, incluyendo fotocopiadoras, grabadoras o sistemas computarizados, sin el permiso por escrito del autor, excepto en el caso de breves citas incorporadas en artículos críticos o en revistas. Para obtener información diríjase a Ediciones Universal.

In Honor of
hundreds of
patriotic Cubans of all races,
young and old, civilian
and military, men and women,
in the cities and
the countryside,
in all corners of the island,
who supported
Constitutional
Government in Cuba
in 1952.

In Memoriam:
Johnny Clark

Table of Contents

Prologue   11

I   The Preliminaries   13

1. Cuba, a Land of Intrigues and Conspiracies (1)   15
2. Cuba, a Land of Intrigues and Conspiracies (2)   22
3. The Fosters' Apartment at 525 Escobar Street   29
4. US Ambassador to Cuba Mr. Beulah   34
5. A Man Named Batista   39
6. Carlos Prío, the "President Cordial"   43
7. A Report from Havana's top CIA man.   47
8. Cuba's top Communist Gossips with the CIA   50
9. The Persuadable Mr. Mujal   53
10. The Incorruptible General Quinino Uría   58
11. The Store at Neptune 621   65
12. Close Encounters of the First Kind   73
13. The CIA tries to Save the Prío Government   79
14. Prior's good Works were not Good Enough   85
15. Was Eduardo Chibás Prior's Rasputin?   94
16. Comments and Arguments from Kuquine   99
17. The Last CIA Report from Democratic Cuba   106

II   The Consummation   113

A Telex to Secretary of State Dean Acheson   115

18. Columbia, where Cuba began to Break Apart   117
19. The Wolf comes out of its Lair   123
20. The Last Carnival in a Free Cuba   128
21. Batista seeks the Advice of his Grand Paê (1)   134
22. Batista seeks the Advice of his Grand Paê (2)   140
23. The Start of the *Madrugonazo*   145
24. March 10 outside Columbia Camp   152
25. The Whereabouts of Prío during the Coup d'État   158
26. Prío could not get Support from his Followers   164
27. All Resistance to the Coup d'État Collapses   172

III	**The Aftermath**	**177**
28	The March 10th Coup and the Press	179
29	The CIA knew things that Prío Didn't	186
30	Money and Loyalties flowing after March 10th	192
31	The Final Withering Away of the Republic	198
32	The Final Meeting of the Tertulia at 621 Neptuno	209
33	Were there ever any Good Politicians in Cuba?	215

Epilogue	**231**
Appendices	**237**

Appendices

I – The Presidential Cabinets before and after March 10, 1952	238
II - Arguments before the US Department of State by Supporters and Opponents of the March 10 *Coup d'État*	239
III – Important World Events during the Year 1952	241
IV – Cuban Military participating or leading in the 1952 Coup	242
V — *Consejo Consultivo* 1952	243
VI – Main Characters at the time of the March 10, 1952 *Coup d'État*	245
VII — Alphabetical Index	260

Prologue

Three Days in March contains an insightful lesson and a sad story. It documents the events in 1952 that resulted in the final demise of the Cuban republic, half a century after its founding. The penetrating lesson is that nations cannot remain indifferent to recurring events that undermine the moral firmness of their principles. The sad story is of events that destroyed the dreams and efforts of thousands of Cubans that conceived, fought for and laid their lives to establish a new nation of their own.

Were all Cubans guilty, in varying degrees of responsibility? It was so suggested by a notorious journalist some years after March of 1952. This book intends to show that they were not.

True, there were reporters and commentators who filled the newspapers and the radio waves with devastating articles, speeches and proclamations, attacking all politicians. There were vicious demagogues seeking approval and applause from barren and ignorant crowds. There were uninformed crowds returning felons, crooks and malefactors to public positions, ignoring honest politicians that were doing admirable things for Cuba. There were also inhumane, wicked and unpatriotic opportunists that impeded many efforts of honorable governance in Cuba. The republic, unfortunately, did not lack unworthy politicians who sacked its coffers or placed expediency above principle.

But, coexisting with these unfortunate happenings, there were hundreds of Cubans —and no few politicians— fully engaged in building up a sterling republic, modern, progressive, downright honorable, virtuous, free from fraud, guile or duplicity. They were making great strides in that direction when the *Three Days in March* interrupted their worthy efforts.

Now it is all in the past. Cubans have had more time without a republic than the years they were living in one. Many of them are in exile; others remain in the captive island. In exile, all accounts have started from zero. Cubans from the Diaspora have reconstructed their lives and have long forsaken the painful emotions of inherited shame or guilt. The children of those who had the misfortune of having acted improperly in Cuba have found no reason in exile to feel degraded in the estimation of their peers. To a certain extent, their honest and trustworthy lives of today have redeemed Cuba's errors of the past and have proven that integrity, truthfulness, and straightforwardness are at the core of the Cuban soul. In their hearts they have wished —for half a century— they could deliver all those Cubans that were left behind. But life is never that simple and justice and righteousness not always prevail.

In that sense, for Cubans and for all citizens of the free world, *Three Days in March* bears an upright and opportune lesson: democracy is fragile and brittle. Their defenders have to be alert to the misuses and the mistreatments of liberty; otherwise an outbreak of demagoguery and folly could prevail. Politicians, newspapers, teachers and journalists should not sanctify what wild and uncultivated mobs would like them to say. They should rather not be an echo of the charismatic and the seductive, but a beacon of guidance for the thoughtful and the enlightened. The physical and moral integrity of a nation collapses when sowers of hatred and infamy are tolerated rather than repudiated, and when people are blinded and victimized by hate, bias, jealousy, ignorance and lack of knowledge and pride in their own virtues.

RAÚL EDUARDO CHAO
CORAL GABLES, MARCH 2013

I The Preliminaries

«There is a movement of young officers in the Army towards the impeachment of President Prío and his replacement by the Vice President. They feel I am the political figure that could give a key historical perspective to their movement. If we ignore their feelings, the Republic runs the risk of their acting on their own; this would be very serious because the military have no sense of political orientation.»

WORDS FROM EX-PRESIDENT **FULGENCIO BATISTA** TO CUBAN VICE-PRESIDENT **GUILLERMO ALONSO PUJOL** AT A SECRET MEETING IN MARCH OF 1951; ALONSO PUJOL RELATED THIS CONVERSATION IN AN ARTICLE THAT APPEARED IN BOHEMIA MAGAZINE EARLY IN 1952.

«There are reports of an insubordination in the Cuban Army. An article in the opposition paper Alerta alleges that Cuban troops of the 7th Regiment at La Cabaña revolted because their reluctance to serve with the UN forces in Korea. Prío has denied Alerta's story. The paper is sticking to its original account.»

CONFIDENTIAL REPORT FROM **BURKE ELBRICK**, US CHARGÉ D'AFFAIRES IN HAVANA TO THE US DEPARTMENT OF STATE IN WASHINGTON, DC, ON MARCH 15, 1951.

«Explain to me, Carlos Prío, how did you acquire the central "Ophelia"; how did you acquire, the property "La Chata" in Arroyo Naranjo; how did you purchase the 1,500-acre farm "Galera" in Calabazar; how did you acquire recently the "Lage" farm from the Benítez brothers, and the "La Altura" farm, in Bahía Honda; why are you using trucks, tractors, cranes and materials owned by the Ministry of Public Works to build private roads, a private dock, an airport tarmac, an artificial lake and two royal palaces for your exclusive use. Explain that to me, Carlos Prío, if you can!»

OPEN LETTER TO CARLOS PRÍO FROM EDUARDO CHIBÁS, BOHEMIA MAGAZINE, MAY 8, 1949.

1

Cuba, a Land of Intrigues and Conspiracies (1)
August 1949

MORE THAN ONE DAY can be identified as the date when General Batista's *Coup d'État* of March 10, 1952, began to breed and be hatched. Perhaps one the best and most likely indications of what the military were brewing in Cuba was contained in a confidential CIA report to Dean Acheson, US Secretary of State. It was sent to Washington by Earl T. Crane, first secretary of the US embassy in Havana on August 26, 1949. It was accompanied by documents from General Genovevo Pérez Dámera, dated August 25th of that year, requesting a visa on an emergency basis for the General and his entire family. The documents —including the corresponding diplomatic passports— had been carried to the embassy by a young naval officer in civilian clothes, who presented a hand-written letter by the General. The young officer explained that the General was at his home in Camagüey and would wait there for the visas; the embassy informed the young courier that former government officials were not entitled to such courtesies and the General and all members of his family had to show up in person to be photographed and fingerprinted.

A day later, the embassy received a phone call from the General, stating that the family would visit the US for only 29 days as tourists. Under those conditions, the embassy informed him they did not need visas or passports. The only member of the family excluded from this was Genovevo Pérez Valdés, the General's son, who was already in the US as a student at Valley Forge Military Academy in Pennsylvania. Young Genovevo, however, had never applied for a student visa and was informed he would have to return to Havana with his parents unless he produced a birth certificate, photographs, a medical clearance (X-Ray and Blood tests) and a $10 fee.

Needless to say, General Pérez was very upset and began to realize how much his personal stock had lost value; months earlier —when he was Chief of Staff of the Cuban Army— he had been feted and honored in Washington by obliging and openhearted US military officials.

The bad luck of Genovevo, he presumed, came after he had been replaced at the top position in the Cuban Army by General Ruperto Cabrera. The decision had been President Prío's need to dispose of the last left-overs of Grau's team in the executive branch. Unfortunately for Genovevo, his demise was used by his enemies to rabidly attack him, particularly those in the press who had lost certain privileges upon the unexpected confirmation of the new General by the Prío government.

Most of the misfortunes of Genovevo, however, came after the Havana newspaper *El Crisol* published an article under the title "Genovevo conspired. He sold himself to Trujillo," subtitled "He was going to simulate an attempt on his life to blame President Prío and provoke a revolt." The article included declarations about General Pérez such as,

«In shameful connivance with the Jackal Trujillo, after pretending to collaborate with those trying to liberate the people of Santo Domingo, he sent military planes there as a vulgar stool pigeon would do, and exchanged information with the dictator in order to build up a story that Prío planned his death. He betrayed the confidence of his friends.»

The article was anonymous, signed only "Active member of *Acción Revolucionaria Guiteras (ARG)*." [1] The only person mentioned in the article was Eufemio Fernández, a former revolutionary leader, a mortal enemy of Genovevo Pérez and at the

---

[1] ***Acción Revolucionaria Guiteras*** *(ARG)* was formerly called ***Joven Cuba*** in the 1930s, and had been founded by Antonio Guiteras.

time, Chief of the Cuban Secret Police.[2]

Officially, Genovevo Pérez was removed from his charge because «he had attempted to create a barrier between the President and the Army and had engaged in numerous acts of indiscipline.» Some examples were his appointments of military aides without consultation with *Palacio*, his refusal to assign funds for "assistance" to the press and his poor example of low discipline when it came to his own physical fitness.

The press reacted very favorably to the removal of Genovevo.[3] Sergio Carbó, in *Prensa Libre*, editorialized «All Cuba rejoices. The President has recovered his constitutional authority.» *El Mundo* newspaper said «President Prío acted in defense of civil institutions and has contributed to the strengthening of democracy against the menace of destructive forces.» The *Diario de la Marina* editorial said «The probable international repercussion to Pérez removal was accentuated by the positive reaction of two US military attachés that congratulated the President upon seeing him.» [4] The newspaper *Alerta*, whose director was Minister without Portfolio Ramón Vasconcelos, presented an editorial saying «The situation was intolerable because many Colonels had been without effective contact with the General in Chief and felt excluded from military influence by a monopolistic boss.» *Alerta*, however, was the only paper

---

[2] **Eufemio Fernández Ortega, MD**, had been involved in the *Cayo Confites Affair*, the presumed invasion to *República Dominicana* that General Genovevo had wiped out at the request of the US Department of State. See page 59. The US embassy in Havana paid no credence to the story in *El Crisol*. In a CIA document dated August 22, 1949, the Chief of the Havana office stated «*The content of this article does not appear to justify the lurid headlines published by the paper.*» The CIA agreed, however, that General Genovevo Pérez had sent a military plane —with a Colonel Chávez— to Port-au-Prince via Santo Domingo, and that the trip had taken place. Curiously, Chávez was demoted to Inspector of the *Regimiento Número 9* in Holguín, a meaningless position, after the defenestration of Genovevo Pérez. Eufemio Fernández Ortega was executed by the Castro regime in Cuba in April of 1961.

[3] Genovevo did away with a tradition to **sequester** half the funds assigned for school breakfasts for military children to use them for "assistance" to the national press — which involved handouts regularly paid to several well accredited newsmen.

[4] It was false information. The presence of these two military attachés at Palacio —an Air Force attaché called Glenn and a US Army attaché called Schaffer— had nothing to do with General Pérez dismissal.

recognizing the unusual honesty, integrity and honor of General Pérez Dámera.

In the end, Genovevo was partially responsible for his own demise. He had been appointed to his position of Chief of the Army by President Grau and Prío inherited him. Prío felt very insecure when he assumed the presidency, since he had been elected by a plurality of votes and not a clear majority. He hesitated to name his own Chief of the Army because he needed Grau to be content and not create problems. Genovevo was initially very popular but he lost his luster very fast, due to his sense of no-compromise and aggressiveness. When he lost his appeal, Prío did not remove him before taking precautions: the police was called to quarters; the guards in the Presidential Palace were reinforced; Mrs. Prío and their two daughters left the capital for the family's country home *La Chata*, in Arroyo Naranjo; Genovevo was well protected in Columbia, but not in his farm in Camagüey, where he had almost no protective escort. Only then Prío made his move, attributing its urgency to the pressure from Quirino Uría and other high officers of the army, which was not true. Prío's timing was impeccable and precise. Most armed services and public opinion were elated at the news of Genovevo's fall. Luckily for Prío, Genovevo ungrudgingly accepted his demise and told the press that from there on he would be "raising chickens" at his farm in Camagüey.

The fall of Genovevo, long accused by his enemies of having been in Batista's army in the 1940s and having opposed many "revolutionary works," explains clearly how Cuba was ready in the early 1950s for a fatal disruption of its democratic path.

In 1949, Jesús González Cartas [5] (aka *el Extraño* – the freak), was expelled from the position of Lieutenant of the Naval Police, presumably under pressure from General Genovevo Pérez. González Cartas had access to President Grau and accused

---

[5] After an alleged lifetime of crimes and gangsterism in Cuba as a member of *Acción Revolucionaria Guiteras (ARG)* since the 1940s, **el Extraño** was murdered in Miami on May 29, 1976.

Genovevo of multiple abuses of power; Grau responded with a laconic: «Take your proofs to any competent tribunal.»

An additional reason for *el Extraño* to be so aggressive in his attacks to Genovevo was the General's investigations on the assassination of Enrique Enríquez Ravena, [6] the chief of Cuba's secret police in 1945, who apparently had been murdered for his opposition to the release of a member of *ARG* that had been imprisoned by Batista and who had been shot dead later as he tried to escape. Enríquez Ravena had been a close friend of Genovevo, who was determined to avenge his murder.

Eufemio Fernández and *el Extraño* more that simple revolutionaries or gangsters, were serious "investors" in Cuba's business world. Not known by many people, the *ARG* owned a prosperous and superbly located building and automotive garage at Carlos III and Infanta streets, a flourishing business, Cross Electric, at Compostela and Obrapía Streets and the very cash-generous *Ruta 58* (Puentes Grandes to San Lázaro), a roaringly profitable bus company affiliated with the *Cooperativa de Omnibus Aliados (COA)*.[7] Of far less economic importance was their ownership of the newspaper *La Voz* and its printing presses, located at 75 San Ignacio Street in Havana.

For months Eufemio and *el Extraño* tirelessly followed Genovevo's path, day in and day out. They knew Genovevo visited the *Almendares* home of a famous Cuban singer and would sit in the porch with her. Gallantly, they declined to murder Genovevo in the presence of a lady. One member of their gang, known as *el Ñato* (pug nose), found that Genovevo often visited the home of a Hilda Codina, an employee of the Ministry of Health, but violence was again rejected by the presence of a lady in the venue. *El Ñato* also found that Genovevo

---

[6] **Enrique Enríquez Ravena** had been born in the Dominican Republic but raised in Cuba. He was married to Carlos Prío's sister and was a member of the *Movimiento Socialista Revolucionario*, a nationalistic group of Marxist taint, to which Fidel Castro and Rolando Masferrer also belonged.

[7] It was valued in $300 thousand and was the main headquarters of **Eufemio** and **el Extraño**. It was said at the time that the cash generated by *Ruta 58* made possible the revolution that brought **José Figueres** to the presidency of Costa Rica.

had a brother called Justo, who owned a *panadería* —*La Guardia*— at the corner of Angeles and Estrella Streets in Havana. They planned to kidnap Justo to flush Genovevo from his secure grounds in Columbia; unfortunately for them, the General was distanced from his brother and seldom visited his brother's business. Finally they learned that the General liked to drive along 23rd Street often. *El Extraño* had one of his lieutenants, Bienvenido Girú, aka *el Chiquitico* (the little one), rent an apartment in the second floor of a building at 311 26th Street, where he would have a clear shot to every car driving down 23rd Street. While Eufemio spotted Genovevo's car from a phone booth at 23rd and 22nd Streets, on the west side of Colón Cemetery, *el Extraño* tried to kill the General from his apartment balcony. Luckily for the Chief of the Army, his car speed exceeded the skills of *el Extraño* and a *Wolf MC 308 Full Metal Jacket 168 grain bullet* bounced off 23rd Street, without anyone getting hurt.[8]

Photo above:
General **Genovevo Pérez Dámera** with a group of Veterans in 1949.

---

[8] Two rarely reported facts were that both Eufemio Fernández and *el Extraño* moved all over the city using official police cars provided by Colonel **José M. Caramés**, Havana's Chief of Police; also, Minister **Rubén de León**, presumably under official orders from the presidency, supplied IDs to Eufemio Fernández and *el Extraño* with no names entered on the assigned spaces; they could identify themselves under any name, any time they wanted.

Photos, left to right, top to bottom:

Genovevo Pérez Dámera, on the day in 1948 when he was confirmed by Prío as Chief of the Cuban Armed Forces. On their right, Prío's VP Guillermo Alonso Pujol. Genovevo was deposed by Prío on August 24 of 1949. In 1954 he was elected Senator for Pinar del Rio —although he had been born in Matanzas and lived in Camagüey. In 1958 he was re-elected to the Senate. In 1959 he left Cuba as an exile and died poor in Plantation, Florida, in 1970;

One of the few photos of **Eufemio Fernández Ortega,** aka **el Extraño.**

Prensa Libre's front page news on the day of the "*Prío's hat on the floor affair.*"

The *Prensa Libre* photo by reporter Narciso Baez Sosa that Genovevo disliked. Observe Prío's hat on the floor. To Genovevo it suggested a lack of concern in the Army for the comfort of Prío, its Commander in Chief. He ordered the reporter out of his sight.

2

Cuba, a Land of Intrigues and Conspiracies (2)
February, 1952.

MONTHS LATER ON FEBRUARY 8, 1952, former President Ramón Grau San Martín, founder of the *Partido Revolucionario Cubano (Auténtico), PRC (A)*, and later leader of the *Cubanidad* political group, made a reconciliation pact with his rival President Carlos Prío Socarrás, natural leader of the *PRC (A)*, with much flourish and ostentation. It presumably reunited the two rival *Auténtico* forces and —they thought— almost guaranteed victory for Carlos Hevia, the party's candidate in the 1952 elections. Roberto Agramonte, the Ortodoxo candidate, declared that «uniting these two individuals will bring together the two politicians most responsible for corruption and graft in government in Cuban history.»

Two months earlier, on November 25, 1951, Policarpo Soler Cué (aka Domingo Herrera, among other names), the notorious Cuban gangster, had broken loose from the *El Príncipe* prison in Havana. The escape had been organized by Orlando León Lemus (*el Colorado*).[9] Joining Policarpo in his adventure was José Fallat (*el Turquito*), the man who had allegedly assassinated Emilio Tró and Aurora Soler, the wife of Morín Dopico, at *Orfila*. See pages 23, 59. Four days later, on February 12, Alejo Cossio del Pino, ex Interior Minister and owner of the radio station *Radio Cadena Habana*, was murdered as he was having

---
[9] When ***el Colorado*** was captured and killed in February 1955, police occupied in his house seventy sub-machine guns, forty M1 carabines, four .45 caliber pistols, two dozen hand grenades and fifty bottles of Nitroglycerine to be used for bomb manufacture.

breakfast at a café in downtown Havana. Cuba had become a paradise for gangsters, mobsters, racketeers, felons, murderers and criminals.

The origin of gangsterism in Cuba can be traced to the period between 1933 and 1944, when Fulgencio Batista was the strong man in the country. Specifically, it could be said that violent political assassinations were first perpetrated in June 17, 1934, under the presidency of Carlos Mendieta, when a group of *ABC* party members were murdered by persons unknown, who later attempted to take the life of President Mendieta himself. When Grau San Martín was elected president, he began to undo most of what Batista had accomplished: the Cuban Army and the Police Force were reorganized, many public employees were fired, work at *Topes de Collantes*, the enormous hospital that Batista had started in the Escambray mountains, near Trinidad, was discontinued.

Grau believed that revolutionary groups turned into gangster mobs did not have to be controlled, only set to fight each other. It was at this time that *Unión Insurrectional Revolucionaria (UIR)*, led by Emilio Tró, *Acción Revolucionaria Guiteras (ARG)* under Eufemio Fernández and Jesús González Cartas (*El Extraño*) and *Movimiento Socialista Revolucionario (MSR)*, controlled by Rolando Masferrer, Manolo Castro and Mario Salabarría[10], took control of the public space in Cuba. One immediate consequence was the *Battle of Reparto Orfila* [11], named after a neighborhood of Marianao, west of Havana, where the *UIR* and the *MSR* battled each other with a balance of six fatalities. [12]

---

[10] Ramón Grau San Martín, hoping that these gangsters would be civilized if they had a good source of funds, appointed **Manolo Castro** as National Sports Director, **Mario Salabarría** as Chief of the Bureau of Investigations and **Emilio Tró** as head of the Police Cadet School.

[11] September 15, 1947.

[12] There were 37 known **political assassinations** due to "action groups" during the Batista regime (1933-1944), 64 during Grau's (1944-1948), and 31 during Carlos Prío's (1948-1952).

At the same time, government corruption became rampart. There were extortions, intimidations, blackmails, shakedowns, killings, abductions and rampart dishonesty and moral decay. Four extreme examples were the alleged plunder of $100 million by Education Minister José M. Alemán during the Grau government; [13] the swindle of $47 million in worn-out Cuban currency not incinerated but returned to circulation, [14] presumably by Antonio Prío, Minister of Finance during the government of his brother Carlos Prío; the looting of $42 million from the Sugar Workers Pension Fund, and the murder of a son of Joaquín Martínez Sáenz, founder of the ABC party, by Abelardo Fernández (*el Manquito*), as the youngster was exiting the Miramar Yacht Club.

It was not uncommon in the Cuba of the 1940s and 1950s that candidates with honest and incorruptible reputations would become crooks and felons as soon as they accessed public office. It was also sad to recognize that someone with a reputation of an embezzler or a convicted criminal could run for the House or the Senate and be elected. Such were the cases, for instance, of Casimiro Eugenio Rodríguez Cartas and Benito Remedios Langaney.

In 1951, Rodríguez Cartas was serving a sentence for the May 3, 1950 murder of Representative Rafael Frayle Goldarás in the lobby of the *Edificio América* in Galiano and Neptuno Streets, in downtown Havana. Prior to that, in 1911, he had been sentenced to 10 years by the *Audiencia* of Santa Clara for an assassination and in 1917 he had been convicted for the murder of Florencio Guerra, mayor of Cienfuegos. In 1944, however, Rodríguez Cartas was elected to the lower legislative chamber in Cuba and reelected in 1948. It was in 1951 that

---

[13] It was said that on October 10, 1948, Minister **Alemán**, using four trucks from the Department of Education, retired several suitcases full of currency from the Cuban Treasury building, and took them by air to his own office at the DuPont Building in Miami.

[14] What was incinerated in front of witnessing officials and inspectors were old newspapers cut to the right size, some of which were plainly visible as the flames were undoing the packages, according to reports at the time.

Rodríguez Cartas shot his lover, María Teresa Zayas, daughter of former president Alfredo Zayas, inside the office of Senator Armando Dalama in Havana. As he exited the building, a policeman tried to arrest him but he invoqued his parliamentary immunity and left the scene. A ruling depriving him of parliamentary immunity was argued at a closed session of the Chamber of Deputies in Cuba and only four deputies voted to strip his immunity: Radio Cremata (*Liberal*), Manuel Bisbé (*Ortodoxo*), Teodoro Tejada (*Auténtico*) and Anibal Escalante (*Comunista*). The Chamber saw fit to turn immunity into impunity. Years later Rodríguez Cartas died and, by his expressed last will, he was buried standing up, with a pistol on each hand, a $100 bill in his vest pocket and a note saying:

«*A man that has always lived on his feet should be given the opportunity to fall into hell standing up.*»

Remedios Langaney was a member of the lower chamber in Cuba for many years. Only once in all those years he stood up to address his colleagues. He had made a fortune in the sugar business (owner of Rio Cauto Sugar Mill, producing over a million tons of cane per year, 100 farms all over the island and the Adelaida Livestock Corporation; he was the largest producer and exporter of pineapples in the island through his *La Cubanita* Corporation). With his money, Benito Remedios bought elective positions for his entire family, his wife, sister, brother-in-law and his son. His campaign slogan was

«*I will double the best offer you have for your vote.*»

It was said that in the 1950s, electoral votes in the provinces were easily purchased for $10. Remedios changed parties many times, depending on the fortunes of the political organizations. At one time or another, he was affiliated with the *Partido Conservador*, the *Conjunto Nacional Cubano*, the *Coalición Socialista Democrática*, the *ABC*, and the *Partido Republicano*. In spite of his fortune and his audacity, Remedios was not too smart. His death was a pathetic colophon to his life. On January 15, 1952, he told his driver to park in a "restricted zone" in the corner of Reina and Aguila Streets. A policeman asked the driver to move the car and threatened him with a ticket. Benito returned to the car claiming he was a member of Congress and could park anywhere. The policeman insisted that the car had to be moved. Benito became angry and drew his gun, but the policeman was faster. One of the richest and most corrupt politicians in Cuba was dead as he tried to evade a traffic ticket.

Photos above, top to bottom, left to right:

The Mausoleum of **Casimiro Eugenio Rodríguez Cartas** at the *Cristobal Colón Cemetery* in Havana, designed to accommodate his corpse in a vertical position. It soon became a tourist attraction in Havana; a rare photo of President **Ramón Grau San Martín** with **Pelayo Cuervo Navarro** in the background. Cuervo Navarro was assassinated on the *Country Club* neighborhood in Havana in 1957; **Orlando León Lemus (el Colorado),** reading about his own racketeering record in the newspaper *El Tiempo*; the **Principe Garrison** on a small hill in western Havana.

A Gallery of Rogues in Cuba during the 1950s

Photos, top to bottom, left to right:
Policarpo Soler, who tried to get elected to Congress in Cuba in 1952;
José M. Alemán, the Education Minister who presumably stole $100 million from the public treasury and bought half of Key Biscayne in Miami;
Rolando Masferrer, a mobster who reached the position of Senator of the Republic;
Policarpo Soler with **Orlando León Lemus (el Colorado).** Lemus liberated Policarpo and José Fallat (*el Turquito*) from *El Principe* on November 25, 1951;
Fidel Castro Ruz, a known gangster at the University of Havana. Chibás rejected his request to be part of the *Ortodoxos* and only accepted him at the insistence of José Pardo Llada;
Abelardo Fernández (el Manquito) as he was entering the courthouse accused of the murder of Martínez Sáenz' son;
Manolo Castro, former FEU President, appointed by Grau as Cuba's *Secretary of Sports*, gunned down on February 22, 1948 as he was lured out of a movie theater.

A Gallery of Victims in Cuba during the 1950s

Photos, top to bottom, left to right:

At *top left*, the tragic scene at the neighborhood of *Orfila* in Marianao. The photo captures the moment when **José Fallat** (*el Turquito*) shoots across the hedge at Emilio Tró and Aurora Soler, wife of Antonio Morín Dopico, head of police at Marianao, in front of Dopico's residence.

Top right: **Joaquín Martínez Sáenz**, former Senator, Minister of the Treasury and Agriculture and President of the Cuban National Bank, who had been the founder of the *ABC* party with Carlos Saladrigas and Jorge Mañach in 1932. Taking advantage of the chaos in Cuba, Luis Joaquín, Martínez Sáenz son, was murdered by Cuban Mafiosi on September 6, 1946, allegedly by orders of rival millionaire land owner Enrique Sánchez del Monte.

Bottom left, **Alejo Cossio del Pino**, former Minister of the Interior, owner of *Radio Cadena Habana*, murdered by some of the "trigger happy boys."

Bottom center: former head of the Armed Forces, **Genovevo Pérez** after a failed attempt against his life.

3

The Fosters' Apartment at 525 Escobar Street
Months earlier, 1951

THE MAN WHOSE NAME was redacted at the bottom of the Telex on page 115 of this book was **Albert Foster**, the top CIA chief in Havana (no kin to US Secretary of State John Foster Dulles). Other than retired General *Genovevo Pérez Dámera* and Army General Inspector General *Quirino Uría*, he was the best informed person about the plans and whereabouts of Cuban former President General *Fulgencio Batista y Zaldivar* in 1952.

The CIA began to be active in Cuba in 1948. Truman had created the Central Intelligence Group (CIG) in 1946, within a year of his being elected president. Its purpose was to provide him with reports on international affairs in a timely manner. In September of 1947 the name of the group was changed to Central Intelligence Agency (CIA). Cuba and Guatemala began to be included in the reports the following year. Albert Foster, together with Walter Bedell Smith (CIA director) and CIA Officer Meredith Davidson, were the men in charge of briefing Truman every Friday. "Beedle" Smith, a former US Ambassador to Moscow, was the man that turned the CIA into the arm of government primarily responsible for covert operations; Albert Foster was the only CIA Officer that had warned the CIA about the North Korean invasion of South Korea in June 1950, an event that —had it not been for Foster— would have taken the administration entirely by surprise and would have been the agency's first intelligence failure. Assigning Foster to Cuban operations was a measure of the importance the Truman administration was ascribing to Cuba in the postwar years.

Albert Foster was a graduate of Columbia University in New York, where he met and later married Cuban-born Ruby Alonso in the summer of 1943. They spend their honeymoon at the *Hotel Nacional* in Havana, moved to an apartment in NE Washington, DC and agreed to relocate to Cuba when the Agency assigned Albert to head its intelligence work in Cuba. Recommended by the US Embassy in Havana, Ruby was hired as a bilingual secretary-stenographer in the Cuban Presidential Palace in 1951, and soon became a secretary to Cuban President Carlos Prío Socarrás.

The Fosters first residence in Havana was an interior studio apartment at a four story building at 525 Escobar Street, near the *Calzada de Zanja*; from its rooftop, Albert could easily access by radio the CIA offices at the old American Embassy in the *Edificio Horter* (No. 7, Obispo Street), in Havana. [15]

Coincidentally (or not), Juan Marinello, the intellectual leader of Cuba's Communist party (Partido Socialista Popular, PSP) lived on an apartment on the second floor of the building at 525 Escobar Street. Very skillfully, Foster looked for chance encounters with Marinello; their first meeting was provided by a gas company inspector who knocked at Marinello's door when Foster was climbing the stairs on his way to the fourth floor [16]. A good friendship ensued and on many occasions Marinello would look forward to talk to Foster as he returned from his work at the end of the day.

Albert Foster's day work was teaching English as a second language to cadets at the *Escuela Cívico-Militar de Ceiba del Agua*.

---

[15] After the completion of the new American Embassy building in the *Paseo de Malecón* in 1952, the CIA kept its offices on the third floor of the *Edificio Horter*, next to the American Chamber of Commerce offices in the same floor.

[16] There is no written evidence or anecdotal recollections that Foster's moving in the same building as Marinello had been planned. It was perhaps a happy circumstance that Foster knew how to manipulate to his advantage.

Schools like these were created by Colonel Fulgencio Batista some years before he became president in 1940. Interestingly, one of the students of such school in Oriente province (School No. 107 in Birán) was Raúl Castro; he was photographed (proudly wearing the military uniform of his *Escuela*) during an anniversary of the birth of José Martí in 1938. The ceremony took place in the Cívico-Military School in *Ceiba del Agua*; in the photo (see page 32), Raúl Castro is in the arms of Batista himself, next to Cuba's president Federico Laredo Brú. [17] Neither six-year old Raúl Castro nor Colonel Batista suspected at the time they would become a nightmare to each other within the next 20 years.

Also living in the fourth floor of the building at 525 Escobar was a young couple, Tomás Fernández and Engracia Acebo, with their two very young sons. Tomás was a refugee from the Spanish Civil War, a self-taught and self-made man and an avid reader and enthusiastic political aficionado [18]. Foster shared many conversations with Fernández, whose point of view as a non-Communist progressive observer of Cuban life was of special interest to him to get to know the Cuban ethos thoroughly.

Photo on the left:
The Military School opened at *Ceiba del Agua* by Colonel Fulgencio Batista in 1937. **Albert Foster** was an English teacher there. It was his main cover as the CIA top man in Havana in 1952.

---

[17] In 2001, Fidel Castro, in an interview with Rodolfo Medina, Assistant Director of *UnoMasUno*, the Mexican newspaper, attested to the authenticity of this photo.

[18] **Tomás Fernández** had immigrated to Cuba at age 16 as a "*sobrin*," a young man sponsored by a family member who had taken residency in Cuba and had achieved economic success. For over 14 years he worked for his backer and ended up buying his business when the man retired. By 1952, almost 40 years later, Tomás was the very successful owner of three furniture stores on Neptuno Street in Havana.

Photo on the left:
Cuba's CIA head agent **Albert Foster** and his wife **Ruby Alonso** (also a CIA operative) at a café facing *Parque Central* in Havana, in 1952.

Photo on the right:
The *US Embassy* in 1951, three floors on the Horter Building at 7 Obispo Street, in old Havana.

Photo on the left:
Front page of newspaper *Avance* on August 12, 1960, showing Colonel **Fulgencio Batista** holding six-year old **Raúl Castro** in his arms during a 1938 celebration of José Martí's birthday at the *Instituto Cívico-Militar de Ceiba del Agua*, with President **Laredo Brú** at his side.

When Albert Foster took command of the CIA operations in Cuba, the agency had infiltrated almost every organization of any consequence in Cuban affairs. They routinely gathered news and opinions from the Cuban Army and Navy, the National Police force, the executive and legislative branches, every political party, including the Communists, and the Chambers of Commerce and provincial governments. From its position at the 525 Escobar apartments, Foster would regularly receive radio transmissions from his agents, would filter them and report to the American Embassy in Havana or directly to Langley, Virginia. His orders were to secure access to Washington only through Williard Leon Beaulac, the US Ambassador to Cuba.

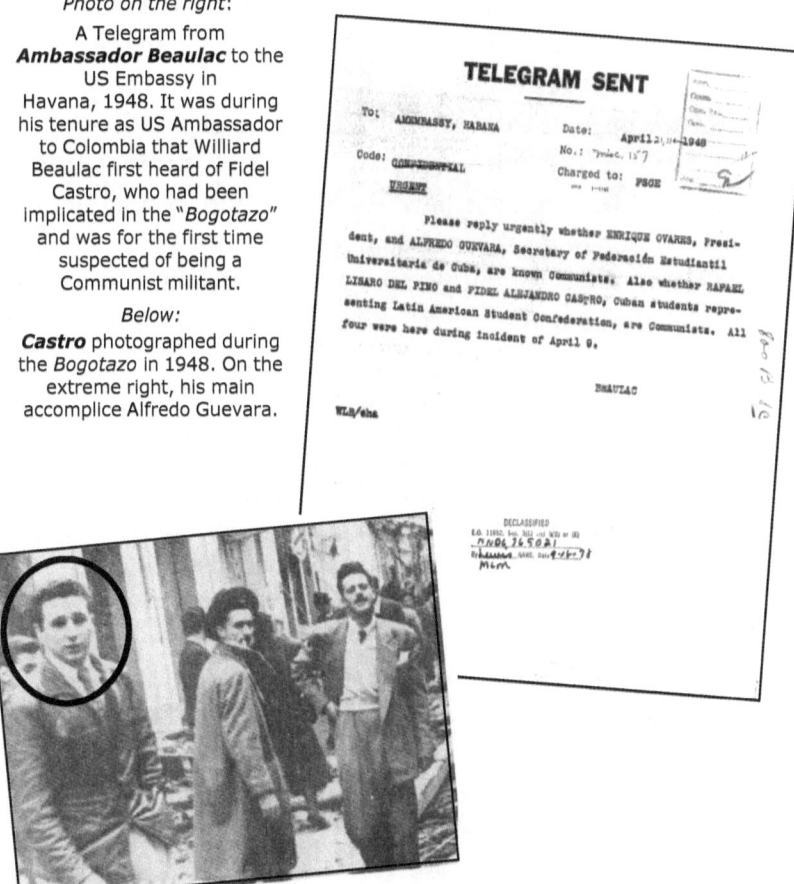

Photo on the right:
A Telegram from **Ambassador Beaulac** to the US Embassy in Havana, 1948. It was during his tenure as US Ambassador to Colombia that Williard Beaulac first heard of Fidel Castro, who had been implicated in the "*Bogotazo*" and was for the first time suspected of being a Communist militant.

Below:
Castro photographed during the *Bogotazo* in 1948. On the extreme right, his main accomplice Alfredo Guevara.

4
US Ambassador to Cuba Mr. Beaulac
February 1951

WILLARD LEON BEAULAC, a Georgetown University graduate, was a professional diplomat, having served as US Ambassador to Paraguay (1944-1947) and Colombia (1947-1951). When he was appointed to the Embassy in Havana in 1951, his experience also included former positions at the embassies in Mexico, Honduras, Haiti, Nicaragua, San Salvador and Spain. Beaulac attended Brown University before serving in the Navy during World War I. In 1921 he graduated in the first class of Georgetown new Foreign Service School and was the first person to receive a diploma from that school.

At the time he was appointed to the Havana post, Beaulac was briefed about the most critical issues in the relations between the US and Cuba:

1. The negotiations between the government of Cuban President Carlos Prío Socarrás and the Rockefeller Group *vis á vis* the exploitation of Cuba's nickel mines in Oriente province (considered for an imminent start-up in the early 1950s) were getting nowhere; these agreements had reached a standstill after the insistence of Prío that Cuba should receive a minimum of 20% of the net profits; [19]
2. The US was interested in reviving the issue of Cuba sending a battalion as a token cooperation in the Korean War. Carlos Prío

---

[19] Years later, some political analysts felt that the coup had been instigated by the Rockefeller Group in reaction to the obstructions of the Prío government to their plans to exploit Cuban nickel mines. No evidence of such instigation was found by this writer.

was reluctant to hold new conversations after his initial negative to participate in the war in late 1950.

3. There were numerous difficulties with Cuba on trade matters, [20] on maintaining clear channels for radio broadcasting, on the US having intervened in the Cuban War of Independence against Spain, on the US questioning the contributions of Cuban warriors in gaining their independence, as well as resentment towards the US for having used the right to intervene in their domestic affairs under the Platt Amendment. [21]

Photos above:
1951-1953 US Ambassador to Cuba **Willard Leon Beaulac** and his wife Catherine (Caroll) at a reception in the Cuban Presidential Palace in 1952.

4. The Cuban government had adopted very restrictive [22] and nationalistic labor laws that seriously jeopardized American businesses. Cuba had failed to meet important longstanding claims by US citizens and corporations, even though they had been recognized in Cuban courts. This had caused reluctance on the part of the US to make additional loans to Cuba until the Cuban government made a substantial effort to liquidate such claims. This

---

[20] Cuba had signed the **General Agreement on Tariffs and Trade** (GATT) in Geneva in October of 1947 and had frequently violated its provisions, according to the US.

[21] Even though the **Platt Amendment** had already been repealed in 1934.

[22] Examples: forcing the utilization of more workers than necessary; regulations limiting the percentages of non-Cubans in the workforce; the transfer of imported merchandise to Cuban railroad cars at the time of Custom inspections.

issue became critical in 1951 after the authorization by the Cuban Congress to negotiate a $200 million loan from the US.

5. Because of its successful opposition and elimination of the Machado dictatorship in 1933, the party in government (the *Auténticos*) in 1951 had shown a *"democratic zeal"* that inclined Cuba to provide sympathetic assistance to what they considered *"repressed and struggling peoples,"* such as Puertorricans (pro-independence efforts by Pedro Albizu Campos' Nationalists), Dominicans (Cuban-supported Juan Bosch struggle against Rafael Leónidas Trujillo), Costarricans (José Figueres' successful 1948 revolution) and Nicaraguans (help to the opponents to Anastasio "Tacho" Somoza's election in 1950).

6. Cuba, on the other hand, supported the US during World War II, and then became rather impatient when asking for the elimination of US Air Bases in Cuba. It also supported the US on the question of Chinese representation (Taiwan rather than Continental China, during the two years of Cuba's membership in the UN Security Council). That support was sometimes obscured by Cuba's insistence of granting independence to colonial peoples, whether or not they were adequately prepared. It was also jeopardized when Cuba was sympathetic to the attempted assassination of Luis Muñoz Marín by followers of Pedro Albizu Campos on October 30, 1950.

An additional intriguing issue was transmitted to Ambassador Beaulac by Secretary of State Dean Acheson at a private meeting before the Ambassador departed for Havana. On August 12, 1950, President Prío and General Ruperto Cabrera had shown up in Ciudad Guatemala on a very unheralded and secret visit to President Juan José Arévalo. Having landed in the capital of Guatemala at 10:00 am in a Cuban military plane, Prío met with President Arévalo and Colonel Jacobo Arbenz, Minister of National Defense, until noon, at which time he returned to Havana after a brief luncheon with several Guatemalan military chiefs and other ministers. Upon inquiring by Milton Wells, US Embassy *Chargé d'Affaires* in Guatemala, Colonel Arbenz insisted that only President Arévalo had the right to divulge the nature of President Prío's visit. He intimated, how ever, that Prío had encouraged Arévalo to curb current Communist influences in his government, given that they were damaging Guatemala's reputation. Dean Acheson urged Beaulac to ascertain —once in Havana— the nature of these conversations, which were evidently more than ordinarily important.

Photos above, top to bottom, left to right:

Left, Juan José Arévalo (1904-1990), President of Guatemala from 1945 to 1951. His administration was marked by an unprecedented relatively free political life throughout his six year term.

Right, Jacobo Arbenz (1913-1971), the son of a Swiss pharmacist relocated to Guatemala, served as defense minister in the government of Juan José Arévalo and was elected President of Guatemala in 1951. He ended his life in Mexico by his own hand.

The **Nicaro Nickel Plant** in Oriente. It was built by US investors in 1942, interrupted production in 1947, after the war, and restarted operations in 1952. At one time it employed 5,000 workers. It was confiscated in 1960 and renamed Rene Ramos Latour Plant. The plant was finally scheduled to be closed in 2009. See page 85.

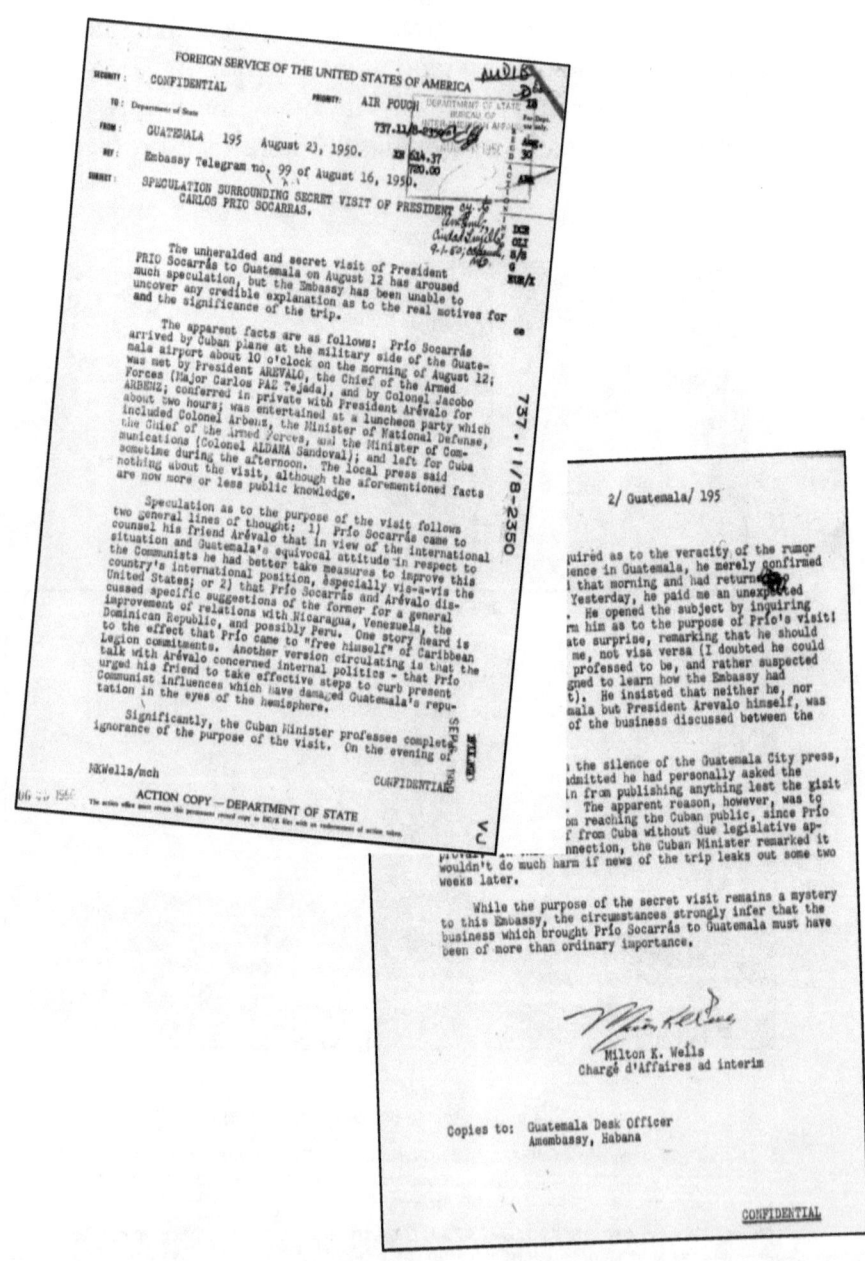

Photo above:
The Telex from Milton Wells (US Embassy in Guatemala) to the US Department of State in reference to President Prío's secret meeting in 1950 with President Arévalo of Guatemala and his Defense Minister Jacobo Arbenz.

5

A Man Named Batista
Years before 1952

FULGENCIO BATISTA Y ZALDIVAR (1901-1973) was born in the neighborhood of Veguitas, municipality of Banes, in the province of Oriente, Cuba. Of humble origin, from an early age he worked in menial jobs to sustain himself as a farm *retranquero*, railroad switchman, fire-man, truck conductor, manual worker on a sugar mill warehouse and timekeeper.

On April 15, 1921, he enlisted as a soldier with the Cuban National Army at Camp Columbia,[23] in Havana. In 1923 he was discharged and later that same year, was again ready to enter definitively into military life. Four years later he was promoted to Staff. After a year as a Sergeant, he studied and obtained a position of army stenographer. This final climb allowed him to serve on the Sixth Military District in Columbia, where he began to stand out for his condition, character and personal attractiveness, features that enabled him to occupy a certain

---

[23] Following the end of the Hispano-Cuban-American war of 1895, during the US occupation of Cuba in 1898, **General Fitzhugh Lee**, the U.S. consul general in Havana, established his headquarters outside Marianao, a town on the West of Havana, and called it **Camp Columbia**; in 1933 the *Campamento Columbia* became headquarters for Batista's army. It was from Columbia that Retired General Batista accomplished his *golpe* in 1952.

leadership position within sub-officers and soldiers of that district.

The economic, political and social situation in Cuba after the fall of the government of General Gerardo Machado Morales, on August 12, 1933, gave Batista the opportunity of joining a student-military movement and displace the true leaders through subtle methods; he soon became the leader of the military side of the conspiracy on September 4, 1933.

After stripping from power the interim government headed by Dr. Carlos Manuel de Céspedes del Castillo, Batista was promoted to Colonel and appointed Chief of the General Staff. He exercised absolute military control and deposed and changed seven successive presidents. He left active service on December 4, 1939, and became president of the Republic for the period 1940-1944.

During his presidency, in January 1942, he promoted himself to the rank of Major General, and as such, once he completed his mandate, he retired to a luxurious residence in Daytona Beach, Florida. He went into self-proclaimed political exile for four years but in April 1949 returned to Cuba as a Senator elected *in absentia* and organized the *Partido Acción Unitaria (PAU)*, a vehicle to promote his candidacy for president in the 1952 general elections. The *PAU* later changed its name to *Partido Acción Progresista (PAP)*.

For 11 years (1933 to 1944) he exercised a strong influence on the Cuban Army. The deep impressions he left in the institution facilitated his return in 1952, when he led the movement that toppled President Prío; on that year Batista, proclaiming himself head of state, started a ruthless and eventually criminal dictatorship.

Ramón Grau San Martín and **Fulgencio Batista**, the two men that dominated Cuban political life from 1933 to the end of the Republic in 1959.

Photos left to right:
Fulgencio Batista at age 16, in 1917. He was proud of the fact that, even under conditions of severe poverty, he was able to follow the fantasy of getting his portrait taken as a successful gentleman; Batista in real life at that age, working as a railroad *retranquero* (switchman).

Photo above,:
Fulgencio Batista in 1935, showing the condecorations imposed on him by **Colonel Carlos Mandieta y Montefur (1873-1960)**, a president he had appointed in January 1934, which he would depose in December of 1935.

Photos above, left to right, top to bottom:

Fulgencio Batista honored at a parade in Daytona Beach during his self-exile in 1949.

The US public was fascinated with **Fulgencio Batista** from the 1930s to the 1950s. He was considered a friend of the US and a man who had pulled himself by his bootstraps. His picture often appeared in US news magazines.

6

Carlos Prío, the "Presidente Cordial"
Early 1951

CARLOS PRIO SOCARRAS (1903–1977) was born in Bahía Honda, Cuba. He became involved in politics while a law student at the University of Havana and spent two years in prison for his anti-government activism. In 1933, as leader of the Cuban Federation of University Students (*FEU*) he took part in the revolution that deposed Gerardo Machado's dictatorship. The 1933 revolution was a joint student-military movement. Prío was the main student leader; his military counterpart was Sergeant Fulgencio Batista. After the 1933 events, Prío helped organize the *Partido Revolucionario Cubano (Auténtico)*, while Batista became the "strong man" in the government of Cuba.

According to Encyclopædia Britannica:

"Prío went into exile in the United States when this party was outlawed, returned to Cuba in 1939, and was elected to the National Assembly. In 1940 he became leader of his party and was elected senator in that year and again in 1944. He served as prime minister from 1945 to 1947 and Minister of Labor from 1947 to 1948. In the latter position he opposed the Communists, ending their control of the unions.

«Elected president in 1948, Prío continued the centrist policies of his predecessor, Ramón Grau San Martín, and pursued programs of agrarian reform and establishment of low-cost housing; he established a National Bank, regulated civil service, and formalized Labor Courts. In spite of vigorous efforts to increase foreign trade and restore public order, Prío was unable to solve Cuba's economic problems. In the face of growing labor unrest, he was not able to combat corruption and gang violence.»

Prío was deposed by the military coup led by his nemesis, General Fulgencio Batista, on March 10, 1952.

Photos, top to bottom, left to right:

President Prío with **President Truman** in *Washington* in 1948;

The top leadership of the Auténtico Party in 1948: **Carlos Prío, Ramón Grau San Martín** and **Carlos Hevia**.

President Prío during the inauguration of the Martí Mausoleum in the *Cemetery of Santa Ifigenia*, in Santiago de Cuba.

Photos above, left to right, top to bottom:

Carlos Prío Socarrás on a balcony of the Presidential Palace in Havana in 1933. On his left is **Ramón Grau San Martín**, followed by Army Chief **Fulgencio Batista** and **Sergio Carbó**, director of the newspaper *Prensa Libre*.

Carlos Prío (circled) campaigning for president in 1948.

Carlos Prío Socarrás in 1949, with **Guillermo Alonso Pujol,** his Vice President. Alonso Pujol was the leader of the *Republican Party*, which had made a political alliance with Prío's *Auténticos*. The pact, which had endured since 1944, came to an end on January of 1950. The rift occurred when Prío supported his brother Antonio for Mayor of Havana, instead of Republican Nicolás Castellanos, who was elected in June, 1950.

Photos above, left to right, top to bottom:

Two posters offered by *El Pais* newspaper, announcing the inauguration of what turned out to be the last democratically elected government of Cuba in 1948:
On the top, President **Carlos Prío Socarrás** with **Guillermo Alonso Pujol,** his Vice President, for the Executive Branch; **Lincoln Rodón** as President of the House of Representatives and **Miguel Suárez Fernández** as President of the Senate, for the Legislative Branch;

Below, President **Carlos Prío** entering the Capitolio Nacional to deliver his first Message to Congress. On his right, **Lincoln Rodón** and on his left, **Miguel Suárez**.

7

A Report from Havana's top CIA man.
Late 1951

ALBERT FOSTER, CHIEF CIA AGENT in Cuba, having been vetted by US Ambassador to Havana Willard Beaulac, addressed the following report to US Secretary of State Dean Acheson via Earl T. Crain, First Secretary of the US Embassy in Havana:

1) Once the pact *Auténticos-Republicanos* has been cancelled, the following members of the Republican Party have resigned their positions in Dr. Prío's Cabinet: Dr. Ramón Corona as Minister of Justice; Dr. Arturo Illias Cuza as Minister of Communications; Guillermo Alonso Bermúdez (the Vice President's son) as Sub-Minister of National Defense.
2) A new political reality exists now. New parties and new alliances are likely to be formed. As of today, the only confirmed alliance is the Prío forces with the Liberal party.
3) The Prío faction of the *Auténticos* will likely increase its participation in government, as warned by Prime Minister Manuel Antonio de Varona. It is also likely that the Liberal party will join the *Auténticos*. They have supported Antonio Prío's candidacy for Mayor of Havana.
4) Alonso Pujol's Republicans are likely to make an alliance with the Grau San Martín faction of the *Auténticos*. There are rumors that even Batista will join this anti-Prío opposition. He has already inferred that his brother Panchín will not run for Mayor of Havana and will defer to Nicolás Castellanos, the Republican candidate.
5) The PSP (Communists) have retired Anibal Escalante as candidate for Havana Mayor and announced their desire to join the anti-Prío

coalition.

6) The Ortodoxo party candidate for Havana Mayor will be Manuel Bisbé, a Chibás follower with very remote chances of succeeding.

7) We do not know at this point if Grau is ready to form another party of if he is simply putting pressure on Prío to be restored as president of the *Auténtico* party. Alonso Pujol is also unpredictable. What is clear is that Batista and Grau will not be rooting for the same candidates.

8) It is likely that incumbent Nicolás Castellanos, [24] the *Auténtico* politician turned *Republican*, will be elected as Mayor of Havana. It will be a hard blow to Prío's influence and prestige.

9) It is taken for granted that Cuba will vote YES to outlaw Communist parties throughout the hemisphere at the March meeting of the American Foreign Ministers.

10) Pepín Bosch, Finance Minister, has resigned and Auxiliary Minister Alvarez Díaz is now the acting Minister. The president of the *Cooperativa de Omnibus Aliados (COA)*, Menelao Mora, has resigned, alleging that the COOP has lost $100,000 per month since the government intervened it.

11) All 161 Cuban sugar mills are in operation, with an average yield of 12.23%. Molasses will surpass last year's production by at least 10%.

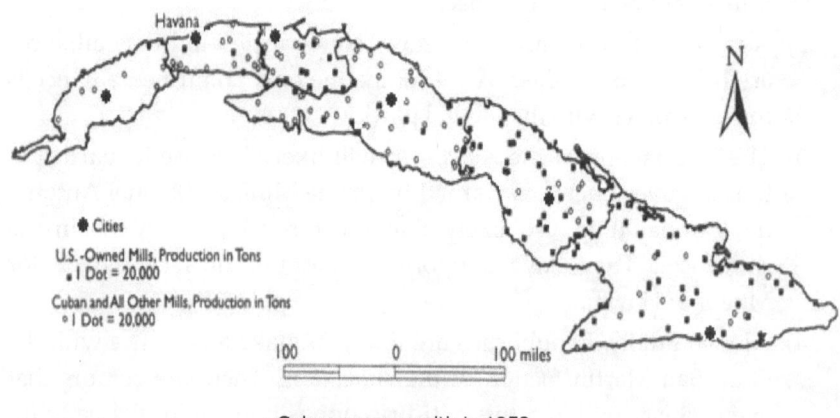

Cuban sugar wealth in 1952.

---

[24] **Nicolás Castellanos**, as President of the *Havana City Council*, succeeded **Manuel Fernández Supervielle** as Mayor of Havana after the elected Mayor committed suicide in May of 1947. See page 218.

Photos above, top to bottom, left to right:

On top, **Antonio (Tony) Varona** and **José A. (Pepín) Bosch**;

Below, the four candidates for Mayor of Havana (the second most important elective position in Cuba) in 1950:

Nicolás Castellanos, the incumbent Mayor, from the *Partido Republicano,* who had the backing of Batista and Grau; he was reelected with 52% of the vote.

Antonio Prío, from the governing *Partido Revolucionario Cubano (Auténtico),* who only obtained 37% of the popular vote.

Manuel Bisbé, from the *Partido del Pueblo Cubano (Ortodoxo),* who got 11% of the vote.

Finally, **Anibal Escalante**, the candidate from the *Partido Socialista Popular* (*Communists*), who was retired as a candidate at the last minute. It was the last free election in Cuba.

8

Cuba's top Communist Gossips with the CIA
March 14, 1951, in the AM

IN MID MARCH 1951, Albert Foster and Juan Marinello had a long meeting on Marinello's apartment in Escobar Street, to exchange views about current happenings in Cuba. They had developed a cordial but cautious friendship after many casual encounters on the staircase of the building they shared. Over a small cup of hot Cuban coffee, they both tried to induce their interlocutor to inadvertently disclose some secrets that would help their cause. By then Marinello had been made aware that Foster was the top CIA man in Havana; the information had come from ***Francis Xavier Waldron*** (aka Eugene Dennis, 1905-1961), a reliable and regular source at the US Board of the US Communist Party (CPUSA). Waldron had joined the Party in 1926, fled to the USSR in 1929 and in 1935 returned to the US. By orders from Comintern leader ***Dmitry Manuilsky***, his son had been kept hostage in Moscow to insure his continued cooperation with the Soviets.

Marinello informed Foster that Cuba had had a tough time denying rumors that Cuban troops would not be sent to Korea. The rumors had started when Minister of Defense ***Rubén de León*** had announced that the authorization for such a decision had to be cleared with the Cuban Congress, thus weakening statements by President Prío that «Cuba will comply absolutely with her obligations as a UN member.» Marinello also made it known that Prío was about to repeal Decree 2273, which granted all citizens the "right of reply" to slanders broadcasted over the radio. Such derogation would save Orthodox Senator *Eduardo Chibás* from embarrassment, as he had termed **Rolando Masferrer** (Congressman from the *PRC-Auténticos*) a "gangster." What Prío was trying to do was to avoid a serious —and possibly armed— confrontation, since Chibás had declared that Masferrer would be granted the right to reply during his Sunday CMQ radio program «over my dead body.»

Foster shared with Marinello his information (obtained from Ruby, his wife) that Nicolás Castellanos was in conversations with Prío to jump fences and join Prío and the Liberals. Rumor ws that Prío had said

«We have been weaning them away from the opposition with promises of succulent jobs and patronage.»

Grau, on the other hand, was running into "insurmountable" money problems organizing his *Cubanidad* party.»

On a more serious matter, Foster suggested to Marinello that the lives of some of the PSP leaders were in peril, particularly since they were insisting in a new drive to organize a "popular front" to oppose the *Auténticos*. At that point, Marinello agreed that the chances for a popular front were "minuscule," in the always professorial and learned terminology of the learned Communist leader.

Before they parted company, Marinello and Foster spoke about the renewed rivalries between Angel Cofiño, Secretary General of the Federation of Electrical Workers (who favored joining the electrical union members to the *Confederación de Trabajadores de Cuba, CTC)*, and Vicente Rubiera, Secretary General of the Telephone Workers Federation, *FTT* (who remained committed to stay away from the CTC until their leaders renounced to all political ambitions).

Waiting for Foster as he got to his apartment was a note on his door signed EU, asking the CIA man to join him "at the same time and place as usual." A few hours later, at the bar of *Cafetería Siglo XX*, in the corner of Belascoaín and Neptuno

Streets, Colonel *Eulogio Cantillo*, Chief of the Cuban Army Air Corps, was waiting for him.

Photos, top to bottom, left to right:

Juan Marinello at the *Cuban Embassy in Paris* in the early 1950s. *From left to right*: Alejandro Otero, Nicolás Guillén, Paul Eluard, María Josefa Vidaurreta, José Gómez Sicre, Pablo Neruda, Marinello, Delia del Carril and Luis Cardoza y Aragón;

On the right, **Colonel Eulogio Cantillo** as head of the Cuban Air Force during the presidency of Carlos Prío. He supported the Batista *Coup d'État* in 1952. Seven years later Batista left him in charge when he fled the island. *On the left*, Cantillo trying to organize a government on January 1st 1959, after Batista ran away;

On the center, **Juan Marinello**, incarcerated in 1935 and exiled in Mexico for his Communist conspiratorial activities. Years later, in 1962, he was appointed by Castro as President of the *University of Havana*.

9

The Persuadable Mr. Mujal
May 14, 1951, in the PM

THE SAME DAY COLONEL CANTILLO was meeting Albert Foster at the café *Siglo XX*, *Eusebio Mujal* was meeting with Fulgencio Batista and other labor leaders at *Kuquine*, the countryside home of General Batista (at the time, Senator from Las Villas province) near the town of Arroyo Naranjo. Accompanying Mujal were *Modesto Barbeito,* Organization Secretary of the CTC, *Facundo Pomar,* Secretary General of the Transportation Union and *José Luis Martínez,* Secretary General of the *Federación Nacional de Trabajadores Azucareros (FNTA)*; all had been frisked upon entering the house by Army Sergeants Fonticoba and Clausel, two security men in Batista's total trust and reliability that Prío had generously provided to the General as bodyguards.

Eusebio Mujal Barniol (1915-1985), Secretary General of the *Cuban Confederation of Labor (CTC),* had been first elected to this position in 1947. After a youthful affiliation with the Communists, he became a rabid anti-Communist and a member of the Constituent Assembly that drafted the 1940 Cuban Constitution.[25] The CTC had been founded in January of 1939, when 1500 delegates from 789 labor organizations (organized across the island since the 1850s) met in Havana to form a national labor union. The CTC was never free from Communist influ-

---

[25] It was at that Constitutional Assembly that Mujal became known nationally for his passionate defense of some 27 articles of the new Constitution that guaranteed the right to strike, 8-hour working days, minimum wage for sugar workers, stable employment, vacations, sick leaves and maternity pay.

ence, however. Before its founding, the Communist-leaning *Central Nacional Obrera de Cuba (CNOC)* had been actively organizing workers since 1925; by 1933, hundreds of sugar mills were paralyzed by strikes, and Cuba saw for the first time "Soviets" [26] of workers and *campesinos*.

The ostensible purpose of the meeting with Batista was to discuss reports from reliable sources that Mujal and other *CTC* leaders knew (and did not oppose) the conversations of Communist labor groups with the *Bloque Obrero Progresista (BOP)*, an informal labor organization within the *CTC* sympathetic but not yet under the control of Batista. General Batista, wanting to dispel any notions of connections with the Communists, wanted assurances from the *CTC* leadership that they would resist any alliances of the *BOP* with the Communist party. Mujal gave assurances that he had no inclination to seek out or tolerate Communist activities within the *CTC*.

Very soon, however, the meeting drifted into exploring Mujal's possible support of Batista's ascension to the presidency. In a passionate and lucid presentation, Batista stressed his opposition to bulk-loading sugar for exports, [27] one of the hot buttons of the CTC and the FNTA (the sugar workers union) at the time. Neither Mujal nor Barbeito, however, showed any enthusiasm for Batista's seductive approach; in fact, Mujal and Barbeito had shared their feelings many times and felt that if Batista was allowed again to reach power in Cuba, his ambition would be to enrich himself like Rafael Leónidas Trujillo had done in the Dominican Republic and Anastasio (Tacho) Somoza in Nicaragua, i.e., securing a share in every legitimate and profitable business in the country.

---

[26] The *Soviets* were groups of self appointed activists, inspired by the Russian Revolution of 1905, organized to coordinate local revolutionary activities. The Bolsheviks gained a dominant position in Russia by gradually controlling the *Soviets*.

[27] Sugar bulk loading (*a granel*) instead of bagging was a demand of the British in the 1950s. Great Britain at the time was the second largest market for Cuban sugar. The *CTC* was diametrically opposed, even if there were assurances that no labor would be displaced, an unlikely and not credible guarantee by the government.

Facing that tepid reaction from Mujal, Batista reminded him he was the politician with historically the best ties to the labor movement and doubled down on his enticements suggesting that Mujal would be an appropriate Minister of Agriculture. [28] The reaction from Mujal was a strong repudiation of the idea, which took the General by surprise.

Mujal recognized that Batista, through Decrees 2605 of 1933 and 1123 of 1943 had been the first president that permitted only one central syndicate organization, the *CTC*; furthermore, he knew that Batista had prevented Soviet infiltration into public service companies. But somehow, after years of loyalty to the *Auténticos*, Mujal felt it would be difficult to explain a new loyalty to a man who was sure to lose by a large margin in the presidential elections of 1952.

Less than a week after the meeting of the labor leaders with General Batista in *Kuquine*, Eusebio Mujal (*CTC*), José Luis Martínez (*FNTA*) and Marcos Hirigoyen (Secretary General of the National Federation of Transport Workers), were asked by Ray H. Crane, Assistant Attaché of the US Embassy in Havana, to attend a meeting at an Embassy private house in G Street in the tony neighborhood of *El Vedado*. Present at the meeting were Albert Foster, the top CIA man in Havana and Donald R. Mann, Public Affairs Officer of the US Embassy in representation of the Ambassador.

Eusebio Mujal Barniol

Foster first questioned the labor leaders about President Prío's nationalization of *Autobuses Modernos, S.A.*; he particularly wanted to know if such a move represented the first step of the Cuban state taking control of transportation and other pub-

---

[28] At the time Mujal had established a dairy farm and had great interest in rural education. He was also seriously thinking of becoming a gentleman-farmer. It was also said that he had already chosen his successor: **Jesús Artigas Carbonell**, a somber and, according to his enemies, a rather sour individual. Word at the time was that, upon knowing of his selection, Artigas turned into a happy warrior, and began to show a welcoming smile every time he entered the CTC Palace in Havana.

lic facilities. Hirigoyen stated that workers in that company were owed four years of vacation pay and presumed that, for much the same reason, *Omnibus Aliados (COA)*, the competing urban transportation *COOP*, would also be nationalized, in spite of the serious reservations of Facundo Pomar Soler, the *COA* labor leader. Mujal limited himself to comment that the government was favoring all around nationalization because of the public service disasters that resulted when Havana Electric Company refused to modernize its 25-years old trolley cars. After 25 minutes on this subject, Foster asked the group what would be their position if Prío was removed from his post before the 1952 elections, to prevent the country to fall in the hands of the *Ortodoxos*, which were much further to the left than the *Auténticos*. A long silence and brief glances from every leader to his associates produced an uncomfortable tension among the participants. Mujal, in a sense speaking for Hirigoyen and Martínez, raised his shoulders and in a nonchalant gesture simply said:

«As long as wage rates are sustained, good service is given to the public and the voice of the workers is listened to, we would favor any government that would prevent the Communists to reclaim the control of the unions.»

That said, the meeting moved to other unimportant issues that were evidently brought up to dilute the impact of the notion of replacing the government of Prío. No mention of Batista or the military was ever made.

The **Palacio de la CTC** in Havana (the building of the Confederation of Cuban Workers, *CTC*). In 1947, Carlos Prío, as *Minister of Labor* in the Grau San Martín government, ordered the Communists to vacate the building, after they had seized control of the CTC with questionable tactics.

Photos, top to bottom, left to right:
A token for one ride in the **tranvías** of the *Havana Electric Company*; **Eusebio Mujal Barniol** in the 1950s; A new bus of *Autobuses Modernos, SA*, popularly known as the **Enfermeras**; a *"servicio especial"* bus from **Ruta 30, Sierra-Parque Central**, running through *Calzada de Columbia, Calle 23, Zapata, Galiano, Zulueta, Monserrate, Neptuno, Calle L, etc.;* **Eusebio Mujal** at a *CTC* convention with guest **Nicolás Castellanos**, Mayor of Havana; the seal of the **Confederación de Trabajadores de Cuba (CTC)**, copied in 1959 by the *Central de Trabajadores Cubanos*, a sham labor organization created by the Communists. The real and democratic **CTC** was created in 1937 and ceased to exist in 1959.

10

The Incorruptible General Quirino Uría
Later in 1951

ON AUGUST 23, 1949, President Carlos Prío, as commander in chief of the Cuban military, fired General and Chief of the Army Genovevo Pérez Dámera. During the same action he promoted colonels Quirino Uría López, Otilio Soca Llánes and Elías Horta Curró to the rank of Generals. Cabrera had been general assistant to Pérez Dámera —in 1949 they were the only two Generals in the Cuban Army. On that August 23rd, the number of Generals increased to four, as Uría was promoted and appointed Chief of *Regimiento Número 6* of the Army (based in Columbia Camp). Eventually he would occupy the positions of Second Chief of the Army, General Inspector of the Cuban Military Force and Chief of the National Police Force, when José M. Caramés was dismissed for undisclosed conflicts with higher authorities.

Photos, left to right:
Generals **Genovevo Pérez Dámera** and **Ruperto Cabrera Rodríguez**,
the two top men in the Cuban military in 1948.

Quirino Uría López (1907- 1984) had been the man who had been responsible for resolving the *Cayo Confites* incident,[29] as well as the officer who sent army tanks to stop the killings in the massacre of *Reparto Orfila* on September 15, 1947. It was said at the time that Army Chief Genovevo Pérez was in Washington on an official visit and President Ramón Grau San Martín was suffering from a strong epileptic seizure which included convulsions, loss of awareness and spasticity.

Once Quirino Uría assumed the position of Chief of the Cuban Police force, on September 22, 1949, he declared war against all gangsters in Havana. During the previous months the mobs had murdered Noel Salazar, Chief of Police of the Ministry of Education (September 1948); had murdered Justo Fuentes Clavel, Vice-President of the FEU (April of 1949); had made an attempt against the life of labor leader Eusebio Mujal (July 8, 1949). Also, a large cache of weapons had been seized in the School of Agronomy at the University of Havana (September 2, 1949). Moreover, Senator Rolando Masferrer —a gangster himself— was attacked and almost killed as he exited his offices in Congress (September 15, 1949) and Gustavo Mejía, a student leader, had been shot dead at the *Balneario Universitario* in Miramar (September 20, 1949).

Immediately after his appointment, Uría began to visit the Police Stations to make known his zero-tolerance principles; his war was against gangsterism, gambling and prostitution. Bare-

---

[29] The *Cayo Confites* incident was a 1947 sordid military action against **Rafael Leónidas Trujillo**, President of the Dominican Republic, organized by José Manuel Alemán, Cuban Education Minister, and Manolo Castro, Cuban Sports Director. It was mostly financed by stolen funds from the Cuban Education Ministry and involved more than 1,200 men recruited among Cuban World War II and Spanish Civil War veterans. They were formally called the **Legión del Caribe**, and were organized in four Battalions (Sandino, Guiteras, Luperón and Máximo Gómez); they had **Cayo Confites** —in the north of Camagüey— and the **Hotel Sevilla**, in Havana, as their bases of military and civil operations. At the request of the US, the invading troops were interned by the Cuban Navy before they could board their ships. Among the participants were **Rolando Masferrer** and **Fidel Castro Ruz**, as well as other members of the *Movimiento Socialista Revolucionario (MSR)*. The weapons, which included 4 ships, 13 aircraft and 1,200 rifles, were returned to their presumed owner, Guatemala President Juan José Arévalo. It was said at the time that President Trujillo paid a sizable sum to Cuban Army and Navy officials to disperse the invasion force. The *Cayo Confites* incident took place the same week (September 20 to 24, 1947) as the *Orfila Massacre*.

ly two months into his campaign he was told by an informer that five notorious gangsters were on a 1948 black Packard sedan traveling west on 7th Street in *el Vedado*, towards the Miramar Bridge.

Uría knew that small groups of gangsters used to spend entire days at *Hotel Comodoro* in the Marianao beach, west of Havana. Getting ready to set up a tight ambush, with the excuse of protecting from *"rateros"* the tony neighborhoods in the vicinity of Marianao's Country Club, [30] Uría had deployed an unusually large number of police cars to the area; they were under orders to patrol the streets and be ready to receive further instructions. On the possibility that his forces could have been infiltrated with *soplones* (snitches), the men in the patrol cars would not know their mission until the operation was under way.

After receiving news of the passengers in the Packard sedan, Uría ordered all available units in the area to block streets leading from 5th Avenue in Miramar towards *Alturas de Miramar* and the area of Kasalta Supermarket in the south, as well as all approaches towards the *Casino Deportivo, Rio Mar* and *La Puntilla* in the north. The elegant 5th avenue was also blocked at the level of a small park between 4th and 6th streets.

The action forced the Packard to turn north on 2nd street; it ended bottled-up halfway on a long block between 1st and 3rd Avenues; by the time the Packard was in the middle of the block, both exits —1st and 3rd Avenue— were covered by 8 *perseguidoras* (police cars) flashing their emergency lights.

There was an initial impasse as the men in the Packard exited from all four doors and took defensive positions around the car. After a few minutes General Quirino Uría stepped on 2nd Street, from the corner at 3rd Avenue. He proceeded to take off

---

[30] On August 16th, 1949, the Country Club home of **Alfredo Fanjul**, the rich sugar baron, had been robbed and vandalized; close to $1.2 million in jewelry had been stolen, including a 12 carat pendant that used to belong to the Russian Imperial family, which Fanjul had purchased at an auction in Paris. Two 35 cm. Sèvres vases had been smashed by the assailants, as a warning of things to come, when they refused to disclose the location of the jewels that Mme. Fanjul kept at home for daily use.

his revolver (a Smith and Wesson .357 Magnum [31]) and conspicuously placed it on the ground; he then advanced — unarmed— towards the Packard.

As he approached the car, he addressed the group:

«I am disarmed. Show up your faces and keep your hands where I can see them. You are surrounded and there is no reason to start a big fight here. I just want to talk to you.»

The men stood up and Uría identified all five of them in a calm but soothing voice: Policarpo Soler (aka *Domingo Herrera*); Orlando León Lemus (aka *el Colorado*); José Fallat (aka *el Turquito*); Jesús González Cartas (aka *el Extraño*) and Eufemio Fernández.[32] They were all *muchachos del gatillo alegre* (trigger-happy boys), on the way to a beach party at the *Hotel Comodoro* at 1st Avenue and 72nd Street, near *Jesús María Church* in *la Playa*. Uría's information was right on the mark.

As he got close to the car, the most outspoken member of the group —Orlando León Lemus— tried to extricate them from their situation.

«General, we were not breaking the law. We are simply on our way to have fun at a Club.»

General Uría responded with a confident and firm voice.

«You are all under arrest. Drop all your weapons and stand in line with your open hands facing me. If you try to fight your way out, I will not see another day but neither will any of you. I have ten times the number of men required to take you back to police headquarters.»

At that point León Lemus stood from his crouching position and asked a request.

«I believe we have the right to make a phone call.»

---

[31] At the time they were the most powerful hand guns in the world, supplying ruggedness, power and sureness of functioning. They were produced by S&W starting in 1935; the first such weapon was sold for $ 60 to FBI Director J. Edgar Hoover on April 8, 1935. This superb revolver would fetch between $2 and $4 thousand in 2013.

[32] It was said that **Eufemio Fernández** had slapped Fidel Castro in the face during the *Cayo Confites* affair in 1947. Castro never forgave him; Eufemio was shot by a firing squad in April of 1961.

The response by General Uría was tough and determined.

«If you wish to make a phone call, remove the car from the middle of the street, park it, turn the keys over to me, and each of you choose one of the police cars and sit down by yourselves. We are all going to the police station at 3rd Avenue and 11th Street.»

After some maneuvering, the men found themselves at the police station, where a phone was made available. León Lemus slowly dialed U-3323, one of the lines at the Presidential Palace. After a brief conversation, he turned the phone to General Uría. The man on the other side was Orlando Puente, 35, former official of the Labor Ministry when Carlos Prío was the Minister under Grau San Martín; he was now Secretary of the Presidency. His sister was married to Angel Cofiño, an anti-Communist leader of the *Confederación de Trabajadores de Cuba (CTC)*. Puente, according to an old report sent by Albert Foster to the US Embassy in Havana was «a little rough, a typical Cuban revolutionary, self-assured, untidy and not particularly able.»

General Uría spoke to him briefly and then, as he motioned the Sergeant in charge to open a large cell, he repeated loudly the last sentence he had spoken with Puente:

«An order like that has to be given to me by the President himself. Please tell the situation to President Prío and ask him if he could come to the phone.»

The situation at the police station became electrifying. After a few tense moments General Uría was back at the phone, this time talking with President Prío. [33]

Uría's words at the end of a long speech by Prío stirred the emotions of all policemen present:

---

[33] Years later, both **Uría** and **Puente** disclosed Prío's alleged words to Uría: «General, we have many commitments to respect in political life. These men were heroes during the fight against Machado. They are now used to an ineffectual and purposeless life of violence. We have to give them the benefit of the doubt and some slack. I wish you would understand that and set them free. I personally will talk to them and will vouch for their future good behavior.»

«Very well Mr. President. I will sign an order to release them, and on the same typewriter I will write you my letter of resignation. Thanks for your trust in me. I hope you will succeed reforming these men. As always, you can count on my respect and devotion to Cuba. Good day.»

The unconditional resignation of General Quirino Uría as Chief of the Cuban National Police Force was reluctantly accepted by President Prío. A few months later, on March 20, 1951, The US Department of the Army issued General Order 16, which read:

«By direction of the President of the US, under an Act of Congress approved 20 July 1942, followed by Executive Order 9280 of 29 October 1942, the **Legion of Merit**, in the Degree of **Commander**, for exceptional meritorious conduct in the performance of outstanding service during September 1949 to February 1951, is awarded to **Brigadier General Quirino Uría y López** of the Cuban Army.»

Photos, left to right, top to bottom:

US General Wade H. Haislip presents the *Legion of Merit* to Cuban **Brigadier General Quirino Uría** at the Pentagon. *From left to right*: General Haislip, Secretary of the Army, Frank Pace, Cuban Major General Cabrera, Cuban Brigadier General Uría and Luis Machado, Cuban Ambassador to the United States.

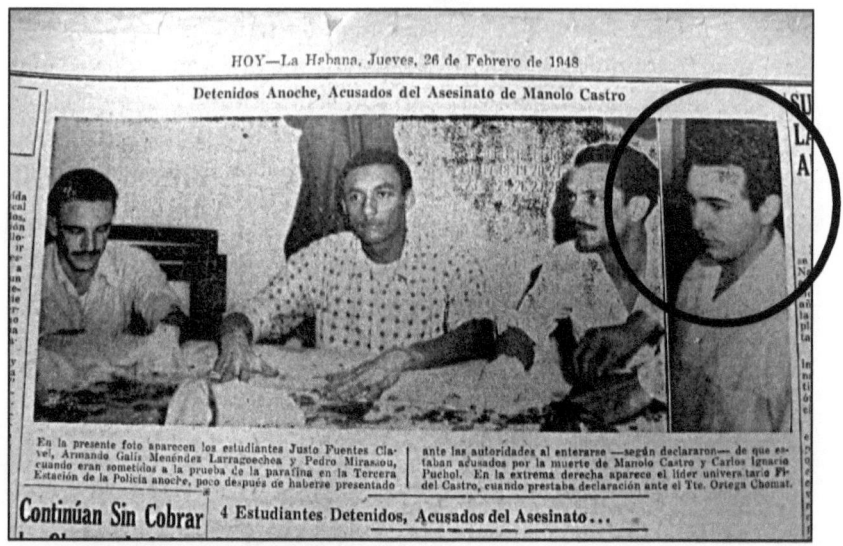

Photos, left to right, top to bottom:

A photo from the days of the "*mucachos del gatillo alegre*" (the happy trigger boys); a page of the Communist newspaper **HOY** dated February 26, 1948, showing a group of students detained and interrogated by the Cuban Police, accused of the murder of Manolo Castro (no kin). On the photo at the extreme right, **Fidel Castro**, member of the *Unión Insurreccional Revolucionaria (UIR)*, a gangster group at the University. Among Fidel Castro's alleged victims, the newspaper mentioned Manolo Castro, Justo Fuentes Leonel Gómez and Oscar Fernández Cabral. His delinquent record started when he was a high school student at *Colegio de Belén*, where Fr. Miguel Larrucea, SJ, confiscated a pistol he was carrying under the shirt of his school uniform.

On the center, lower row, Cuban Brigadier General **Quirino Uría**;

On the left, General Uría at the *University of Havana*, confronting **Fidel Castro** in 1948; on the right, retired General **Quirino Uría** in 1954. By then, he was Manager of *Banco Continental Cubano*; he is shown shaking hands with a police officer that participated in the capture and prosecution of a bank robber.

11

The Store at Neptuno 621
November 1951

SOME OF THE BEST INFORMATION about Cuban politics gathered by Albert Foster in Havana during the early 1950s, was the result of his regular visits to the open *tertulias* at the Tomás Fernández furniture store at 621 Neptuno Street, one of the best located stores in modern Havana. The building was close to 200 feet deep and 40 feet wide. All along its length it was cut by a central hallway flanked on each side by two long lines of rocking chairs. At the deepest end it ended in a workshop where several craftsmen shaped, assembled and finished pieces of furniture in a covered patio.

On any given day, at around 3:00 pm, politicians, sportsmen, actors, painters and retired businessmen converged and sat on both sides of the central hallway. The rules of the house were very clear and duly respected. Since the furniture was all for sale, no one was authorized to displace or move any piece out of position, although they were free to rock and talk at the same time. This resulted in a surrealistic scene, where 10 to 15 grown up men would talk to each other —mostly without interrupting— without looking at each other or even turning their heads. No one coordinated the discussions, everyone was free to express their thoughts and all conversations came to a pause upon the presence of a client at the storefront.

Regulars at some of these daily events were Primo Carnera,

the Italian world boxing champion, a member of *SIOS*, the Italian military Intelligence; Pedro (Perucho) Formental, the powerful slugger of the Havana team in the Cuban league, who had batted for 0.336 in the 1950 baseball session. He was a strong supporter of General Batista; Radio Cremata, Senator of the Republic with a solid reputation; Albert Foster, the CIA man in Havana; Menelao Mora Morales, former member of the *ABC* and the *PRC(A)* parties, an old combatant against Machado and president and lawyer of the *COA*, the *COOP* of buses in Havana; as well as many Cuban politicians that included Aureliano Sánchez Arango (Minister in the Carlos Prío Cabinet) and Santiago Rey Perna, a former member of the 1940 Constitutional Assembly, Senator and unconditional supporter of General Batista.

Less known but not less important were Karl Zimmerman, owner of a store almost across the street from 621 Neptuno, and Mariano Armengol, a sergeant in the Cuban Army, allegedly a good friend, *edecán* and confidant of several members and former members of the Cuban military: Dámaso Sogo Hernández, Martín Díaz Tamayo and Manuel Ugalde Carrillo.

Zimmerman's real name was Alexei Andreyevich Polivanov, son of a man of the same name who had been appointed assistant Minister of War following the disastrous Russian defeat in the 1904-1905 Russo-Japanese War; he had been later dismissed in 1912 for his cooperation with the leftists within the Duma. The real Karl Zimmerman had died at the *Majdanek*, the first Jewish extermination camp discovered near the end of World War II by advancing Soviet troops on July 23, 1944. The young Polivanov was assigned the Zimmerman name before he was smuggled into Cuba in the summer of 1949; his mission was to keep an eye on Cuban Communists and inform Moscow of any ideological or political deviations. He reported directly to Alexander Panyushkin, Soviet Ambassador to the U.S. (1947-1952). Panyushkin was an open sympathizer of General Batista, whom he got to know in 1943 when Batista accompanied a group of Cuban diplomats to a long-winded visit to Moscow. The general had feted him on several occasions at his *Kuquine* country home.

Mariano Armengol was a low level sergeant in the Cuban Army who conspired on behalf of Batista among the Cuban military and retired officers. It was said that he was an illegal but effective "procurer," and his skillfulness as beholder of gifts included fancy government-owned vehicles and exotic hand guns studded with expensive gems. Part of his strategy and the secret of his persuasive zeal were to shower military men with unexpected presents —which included his pimping ravishing young women— at a house owned by the general in the *Reparto Ayestarán*, close to what later became Havana's Civic Center.

Eventually, it was alleged, Armengol delivered to Batista the loyalty and helpful compromise for a *Coup d'État* from Martín Díaz Tamayo, Pilar García, Alberto del Río Chaviano, Luis Robaina Piedra, Manuel Ugalde Carrillo, Fermín Cowley Gallego, Carlos M. Cantillo González, Aquilino Guerra González, Carlos E. J Pascual Pinard, Florentino Evelio Rosell Leiva and Antonio Blanco Rico. All sported jewel-incrusted grips in their weapons and were former visitors to Batista's building in *Reparto Ayestarán*.

As the group was discussing the November 1st US nuclear tests in Nevada, New Mexico, and their impact in international politics —for the first time the atomic explosion had been observed by a large number of US troops and pictures had been published in the papers— a man walked briskly along the sidewalk on the opposite side of Neptuno street, only pausing briefly to look inside the furniture store.

In a matter of seconds Zimmerman stood up and excused himself explaining that he had an appointment with a client. Only Foster knew the real reasons for this unanticipated urgency. The man that had briefly but intently looked for Zimmerman inside Tomás' store was Fabio Grobart. Grobart (known to Cubans as Antonio Blanco, but whose birth name was Abraham Simkovitch) [34] was a founding member of the Cuban Communist Party. He had been sent to Cuba by the *Comintern* in 1922. For decades he had served as the top ideologue —the *éminence grise*— of the Cuban Communists, counting as his disciples Juan Marinello Vidaurreta, Blas Roca Calderío, Julio Antonio Mella McPartland, Rolando Masferrer Rojas and Fidel Castro Ruz. He had chosen "Fabio" as his name in honor of *Fabius Maximus*, the Roman Consul and top tactician of the Roman legions. [35] He was a small and courteous man, with cadaverous eyes always covered by thick glasses, who spoke Spanish with a fake and heavy French accent. He was noted for his bad temper and unforgiving cruelty to his enemies. Lore had it that Grobart was the originator of an important maxim of the Cuban Communist Party:

«*Those who control the past control the future; those who control the present control the past.*»

Fabio Grobart entered Zimmerman's store and eagerly waited for his agent to show up. He had an important and urgent message to transmit to all his men. An hour earlier he had received at the Party's headquarters [36] a radio communication from the Soviet Secret Police (at the time called the *Cheka*, later known as the *KGB*):

«*Do not oppose or support the efforts of General Batista to overthrow Carlos Prío's government. Remain neutral to facilitate the successful completion*

---

[34] **Grobart** many aliases included, among others: Abraham Grovar, Yunger (or Junger) Simkovich, Aaron Sinkovich, Otto Modley or Movely, Abraham Simcowiz, José Micheló and Fabio Michelón. *Grobart*, by the way, means gravedigger or undertaker in Serbian.

[35] Fabio was a common name among Cuban Communists. It was often used as a pseudonym by **Anibal Escalante**, a rabid party member and son of a senior Cuban independence fighter who fought under the command of Calixto Garcia.

[36] On the second floor of a restaurant at 687 Compostela Street, corner of Luz Street in Havana, one of the two party safe-houses; the other one was shared with the Labor Anarchists at 37 Zulueta Street. It was a common practice of the Communists in Cuba to rent apartments near restaurant-bars to hide their presence, using the conspicuous prostitution activities of these places as a cover-up. In the late 1940s, for instance, the "real" headquarters of Cuba's Communist party was on the back of *Lily Bar*, at 269 Avenida de Acosta, near Patrocinio Street, across from a Police Station, in Havana.

of the Coup.» [37]

Zimmerman acknowledged the message and immediately took to the street to notify his contacts. He was intensely afraid of Grobart, knowing as he did that Grobart had personally purged Otto Katz [38] under direct orders of Joseph Stalin a few weeks earlier.

Not three minutes had lapsed after Zimmerman left Tomás' furniture store that Mariano Armengol excused himself, moved behind the business counter on the right hand side of the store and made a phone call. The number dialed was 2-3514. It rang at a house located at 9005 5th Avenue, Marianao. The maid took the message in the absence of the owner, a veteran soldier:

«*The three musketeers have agreed to cooperate with the Cardinal. All is now arranged.*»

The home belonged to Francisco Tabernilla Dolz, former Chief military officer at the *Regimiento de Artillería* based in *La Cabaña* fortress during Batista's control of Cuba starting in 1933. [39] President Grau had forced him to retire from the military in 1944. Aside from informing Batista that three important military men had agreed to join the conspiracy against President Prío, General Tabernilla had the mission of asking a close

---

[37] The Communists had supported Machado before 1933; at his fall they began to organize **agit-prop** actions and set up "**soviets**" in some sugar mills; they opposed Batista on his 4th of September Coup. Later, however, they were admitted by Batista to his Cabinet (Juan Marinello and Carlos Rafael Rodríguez) and controlled the CTC until they were expelled from the labor movement by President Grau San Martín in 1946.

[38] **Otto Katz**, (aka Rudolf Breda, André Simone), a Prague-born veteran of the Spanish Civil War, had been Grobart's boss in Cuba since 1923. He had boasted for many years to have been lover to «*that beautiful sexual-omnivore Marlene Dietrich,*» and that he had fathered a child —María Riva— with her. He was a close friend of **Antonio Guiteras Holmes** and had betrayed his whereabouts to Batista when Guiteras tried to escape from Cuba in 1935 and was murdered at *El Morrillo*, Matanzas. Grobart —an orthodox Stalinist— had also ordered the 1942 assassination in Sancti Spíritus, Cuba, of **Sandalio Junco**, a labor leader and unrepentant Trotskyite heretic.

[39] The Tank and Infantry Regiments of the Cuban Army were based in Columbia Camp, in Marianao, West of Havana. **Tabernilla** (by 1952 best known as "*el viejo Pancho*"), had been a popular Lieutenant at *La Cabaña* Regiment during Batista's 4th of September 1933 *pronunciamiento*. At the time, the only truly charismatic military officers in the 10,000 strong Cuban Army were General Batista and Colonel Eleuterio Pedraza, whose sister was married to Batista's brother in law and whose daughter married one of Batista's sons.

friend, Luis Machado, Cuban Ambassador to the US, to share the news with Rafael de la Colina, the Mexican Ambassador to the US, who had privileged access to US President Harry S. Truman. Batista was hoping to pre-inform some of his unconditional supporters of his intentions to force his way into the Cuban presidency. Truman paid scant attention to the news.

That night, the man less suspected of informing General Batista of the daily happenings at 621 Neptuno Street, made one phone call to the private line of the General. Perucho Formental was one of the few visitors to the tertulias that had little if any personal interest in a political career. Primo Carnera, however, did not make any calls that day. He went back to his hotel on Galiano Street, got drunk and fell asleep.

By the end of 1951, the *Coup d'État* schemed by Batista was old news in Washington, Moscow, Mexico City, Camp *Columbia* or Camp *La Cabaña*. General Quirino Uría, Chief of the 6th Batallion of the Cuban Army in Columbia, had many times — to no avail— sent word to Prío that there was a large conspiracy within the Army.[40] The only Cuban politician not alarmed by Batista's intentions at that point was his ever-trusting adversary: President Carlos Prío Socarrás.

Batista and Prío viewed by their presidential campaigns in 1952

---

[40] As Chief of the Bureau of Investigations, the Cuban Military Intelligence Service and the man in charge of the Presidential Palace security, Uría met with President Prio in Palacio twice a week.

Photos, top to bottom, left to right:

Top left: The store at **621 Neptuno Street** in Havana. In 1956 it was purchased by Roberto Fernández Miranda, brother of Batista's second wife. Fernández Miranda had been promoted to Captain by Batista in 1933 and was forced to retire by President Grau in 1944, together with some 200 military officers loyal to the General. In 1952 Batista reinstated him to the Army with the rank of General. The store was walled-in by Fernández Miranda and, according to neighbors, extensive remodeling of an unknown nature was done inside. In 1960 the Castro regime took over the building without revealing its contents.

Top right: The building purchased by Batista in **Reparto Ayestarán** in 1950. The first and second floors were connected by a circular iron staircase and was used by Mariano Armengol for his "procurement" business. On the third floor Batista stored hundred of documents under the watchful and steadfast eyes of two live-in former military men.

Bottom left: the passport of **Mariano Armengol**, who fell out of grace with Batista after it was discovered he had taken substantial cuts from the money provided to him for recruiting military officials for Batista's conspiracy.

Bottom right: **Tomás Fernández**, the owner of the 621 Neptuno store. He was a Republican exile from the Spanish Civil War with clear anti-Communists ideals.

Some of the good, the bad and the ugly at the 621 Neptuno store:

First Row: **Francisco Tabernilla Dolz**, Batista's closest confidant for many years, who in the end betrayed him in 1958; **Otto Katz**, the man purged by Fabio Grobart in 1949. Katz was murdered in Mexico City, at the corner of *Insurgentes* and *Hamburgo Streets*, in the Zona Rosa, by Grobart himself, who first shot him from a speeding car. Not sure that he had finished his victim, Grobart stepped out of the car, ran to where Katz was lying on the sidewalk and put a bullet to the back of his head; **Luis Machado,** Cuban Ambassador to the US in 1952; **Fabio Grobart,** founder of the Cuban Communist Party.

Second Row: **Sandalio Junco**, Communist labor leader in the *La Flecha de Oro* bus company. At the time, Communists were part of Batista's government. Junco was murdered in 1942 at a meeting honoring Antonio Guiteras in Sancti Spíritus by a man screaming «¡Negro traidor, lacayo del imperialismo!» (Black traitor, lackey of imperialism); **Karl Zimmerman**, the liaison between Moscow and Cuban Communists; **Primo Carnera**, whose manager Lou Soresi stole all the money he had earned as World Heavyweight Champion and left him destitute and at the mercy of underground bosses. Carnera lost his title to Joe Louis in 1937; finally **Aureliano Sánchez Arango**, a life-long fighter for democracy from the ranks of the PRC (*Auténticos*).

Third Row: **Perucho Formental**, the left-handed Cuban Baseball Hall of Famer who ran for the Cuban Congress on Batista's *Partido Acción Unitaria (PAU)* in 1952, the year of the *Coup d'État*; **Eulogio Cantillo Porras**, appointed by Batista as Chief of the Army, although he did not participate in the *Coup*; **Menelao Mora Morales**, a former *ABC* member in the fight against Machado in 1933, author of the 1957 attempt on the life of Batista at the Presidential Palace, and **Radio Cremata**, the leader of the Cuban Congressional group that opposed Batista's illegal destitution of President Miguel Mariano Gómez in December of 1936.

12

Close Encounters of the First Kind
Early in January 1952

OSCAR GANS LOPEZ-MARTINEZ (1903-1965) was Cuba's Prime Minister in early 1952. He had replaced Félix Lancís on October 1st the year before. Prior to that, he had been Ambassador Extraordinary and Plenipotentiary to the US in 1949 and Minister of State and Minister of Justice in Cuba. He had been active in the 1933 downfall of Machado's government but according to his detractors he had been on the wrong side of history. [41] In 1951 Oscar Gans expected to be Cuba's next President. President Prío's personal choice as his successor, however, was Carlos Hevia, one of his Ministers without Portfolio. Hevia was highly regarded among *Auténticos*; Gans was less known and, according to reports from the US Embassy in Havana, *"not simpático,"* which was a prime requirement for Cuban *políticos*.

When Albert Foster first landed in Havana, he had the phone number (3-5685) of Gans, as well as his personal address (53 L Street, Vedado). It was one of the first contacts Foster made in Havana to get the run of the land in Cuban politics. Phone and address were given to him by John P. Glennon, a US

---

[41] On ***August 7, 1933***, a *canard* circulated in Havana that President Machado had resigned and left the country. Hundreds of people started a celebration in front of the Presidential Palace. The guards in the Palace, allegedly led by historian Ramiro Guerra and student leader Oscar Gans, opened machine gun fire upon the crowd, hurting or killing some 40 demonstrators. Years later no one could attest to these rumors. It was hardly credible that Gans and Guerra had participated in this massacre; it had been a complete fabrication by Machado partisans wishing to discredit the forces opposing the dictator.

State Department official who, as a neighbor of Gans in Chevy Chase, Maryland, had befriended him in Washington in the late 1940s.

As a College student at Johns Hopkins' Homewood campus in Baltimore, Foster was a frequent visitor to Washington, DC, where Gans was a professor of political science at Georgetown University. Foster used to meet with Gans in the capital, accompanied by a beautiful girl he was courting, Ruby Alonso, a student at Peabody Conservatory in Baltimore. Ruby was the niece of Juan Francisco Fleitas, a top magistrate of the Provincial Court in Matanzas.

Ruby and Albert had met at the Peabody Bookshop and Café on the basement of a Civil War building on Charles Street, near Baltimore harbor. Their mutual attraction brought them together almost instantly. They spent many hours on Albert's car, parked on secluded places within Sherwood Gardens, near Hopkins, where they got to know each other very well.

The first meeting of Oscar Gans and Albert Foster, took place on January 3rd 1952, at one of Havana's most famous and refined restaurants, *Monseigneur*, at the intersection of 21 and O Streets, facing the *Hotel Nacional de Cuba*. [42] Albert was anxious to know "Who was Who?" in Cuban politics and Gans was happy to comply. As Foster pronounced each name, the opinion of Gans came immediate, straight, and to the point: [43]

Carlos Prío Socarrás, 49.
- Hardworking, intelligent, charming, somewhat vane, too loyal to his friends, too forgiving, slandered to have enriched himself in power.

Antonio (Tony) Varona, 40.
- Slippery, respectable reputation, powerful *politico*, closest man to Prío.

Carlos Hevia Reyes Gavilán, 48.
- US Naval Academy graduate, honest, correct, highly respected, poor administrator, very friendly to the US.

---

[42] The *Monseigneur* was famous for having been the performance home of **Rita Montaner**, the classically-trained singer turned *vedette*, and **Ignacio Villa**, known to Cuban audiences as *Bola de Nieve*.

[43] Gans' opinions at the meeting of January 3, 1952 with Foster, were a corroboration of those expressed in Telexes from the US Embassy in Havana to US Secretary of State William Averell Harriman as far back as 1948.

***Ramón (Mon) Corona García**, 50.*
- Lawyer-newspaperman, affable, pleasant, fair reputation, good political leader in Oriente, former Republican, not an *Auténtico* loyal.

***Rubén de León García**, 41.*
- Pleasant, forceful personality, effective orator, not US friendly, considered a professional revolutionary agitator by many.

***Antonio Prío Socarrás**, 43.*
- Pleasant, affable, not quite trustworthy but friendly to the US Embassy, cooperative but venal. Said to be excessively close to his brother.

***Manuel Febles**, 42.*
- Close friend of Carlos Prío, unknown figure, reportedly honest, hard working and competent.

***Francisco Grau Alsina**, 30.*
- Nephew of President Grau, affable, alert, agreeable, qualified, somewhat suspicious to US officials, idealistic, good reputation. Good man.

***Edgardo Buttari Puig**, 39.*
- US citizen, low grade but astute *politico*, not-so-good reputation, party-changer, nationalistic, undependable, anti US, not very qualified.

***Aureliano Sánchez Arango**, 41.*
- Professorial revolutionary, close friend-advisor to Prío, intelligent, left of center, almost sure to be a socialist, unstable, unreliable to US.

***Alberto Oteiza Setién**, 43.*
- Top *Auténtico* physician, honest, well educated, competent, pleasant, his brother had an uncertain reputation. A good man overall.

***Román Nodal**, 43.*
- A minor *político*, somewhat cooperative with US, narrow-minded, inflexible, short vision, unqualified to govern. Former Republican.

***José Raimundo Andreu Martínez**, 47.*
- Powerful politician in Las Villas, conservative, intelligent, astute, honest, possible presidential ambitions, highly qualified for it. Until recently, a *Republicano*, not an *Auténtico*.

***Virgilio Pérez López**, 42.*
- Close friend of Prío, not interested in politics, will drop out of sight.

***Orlando Puente**, 35.*
- Close to both Grau and Prío, charming but incompetent, somewhat arrogant, very loyal follower but generally unreliable.

***Primitivo Rodríguez**, 42.*
- A tough politician, experienced, too revolutionary for US taste.

***Ramón Vasconcelos Maragliano**, 57.*
- Clever writer, the "old man" of the Cuban 1948 government, unknown ideological fabric, not trusted by many, self-educated, an enigma.

Gans also shared with Foster his opinion that Prío was in denial of his vulnerabilities; a well organized movement to depose him was brewing in the Cuban Army and, in fact, Gans was so sure and so impotent to make the president pay attention that he felt a *Coup d'État* was practically impossible to stop or derail.

Adding to that, Foster shared with Gans, the information that Carlos Márquez Sterling and Pelayo Cuervo Navarro, leaders of the *Ortodoxo* Party, had visited the US Embassy and had a meeting with Ambassador Beaulac, to inform him of a possible Communist-Ortodoxo coalition that would make Roberto Agramonte the presidential candidate of the Communist Party (PSP) and Salvador García Agüero, a life-long Communist, a Senate candidate for the *Ortodoxos*. [44] Gans was also informed that, according to Anibal Escalante, director of *HOY*, the Communist newspaper, the PSP had a secret alliance with the *Auténticos* to secure —through misinformation— the election of Hevia as president in the 1952 elections. [45] In addition, Foster also informed Gans of the possibility of a PAU–Cubanidad–PSP (Batista- Grau-Communists) alliance.

Such was the electoral disorder in Cuba in 1952, and so weak were the political loyalties within all political parties, that Gans reflected at the end of the *Monseigneur* meeting:

«The unjustified strength that the Cuban people gave Grau San Martín when he led the Auténticos in 1944, and the undeserved loyalty of the Cuban military to a man like Batista since 1933, are causing the parties to behave like two confused beasts that will destroy each other and anybody who tries to mediate between them.»

To make the situation even more confusing, **HOY** published on January 4 an article by its Director, Anibal Escalante, under the heading *"Dólares para Pagar Asesinatos,"* accusing the Embassy (specifically Mr. Clark D. Anderson, US Assistant Legal

---

[44] This conversation and the news were eventually reported in Periódico **El Mundo** on January 29, 1952.

[45] It was so disclosed in an editorial of Periódico **HOY** on January 31, 1952.

Attaché, in complicity with the CTC's Eusebio Mujal) of having ordered the assassination of Blas Roca; it alleged that the names of the hired assassins and the amount of money involved were known by the paper: The assassin was to be Jesús González Cartas, *"el Extraño,"* assisted by three of his lieutenants, *"Pistolita, el Italiano* and *Ventrecha."* The amount of money was simply characterized as *"substantial."* The US Embassy did not respond to the editorial in Periódico HOY until March 26, 1952, at which point it simply stated that

«*This case has ceased to be of an immediate interest to the US as a result of developments in Cuba since March 10th.*»

Photos, left to right, top to bottom:
Four key politicians in the 1940s and 1950s: **Aureliano Sánchez Arango, Antonio (Tony) Varona, Carlos Márquez Sterling** and **Pelayo Cuervo Navarro.**

Photos, left to right, top to bottom:

The campaign poster of **Carlos Prío** in 1948; **Carlos Hevia**, President Prío's favorite candidate to succeed him in 1952; **Oscar Gans**, 1952 Prime Minister; the PRC (*Auténtico*) logotype; **Ramón Vasconcelos**, the most experienced man in Prío's government; the campaign propaganda for **Orlando Puente**, the top spokesman for Carlos Prío and the *Auténtico* Party in 1952.

13

The CIA tries to Save the Prío Government
Mid January, 1952

AFTER THE MEETING WITH OSCAR GANS, Foster was alarmed by the youth of the insiders in the Cuban government (a median age of 42), [46] their inexperience and the casualness with which they judged the serious threats posed by the military. From the president down, they were so sure of the hold of democracy in Cuban politics that they were dismissing what was already a well known intention on the part of Batista and his cohorts; they were giving the last touches to a conspiracy that would brush off democracy in Cuba for good.

Albert Foster began to seek contacts within the Cuban military willing to counteract Batista's cronies. One evident opportunity was through his wife's great uncle, Matanzas' Chief Magistrate Juan Francisco Fleitas, a close friend of Colonel Eduardo Martín Elena, Chief Officer of *Regimiento Número 4, Plácido*, based on the Goicuría Barracks in Matanzas.[47]

---

[46] The compositions of Prío's first and Batista's last Cabinets are presented in Appendix I on page 238.

[47] In 1961, **Colonel Martín Elena** was assigned by the *Frente Revolucionario Democrático (FDR)* as the chief training official for the Bay of Pigs Assault Brigade 2506. He resigned his position upon knowing that the members of the invading force would likely be massacred by Castro's forces since President Kennedy was considering withdrawing the promised aviation support. It turned out to be inmaterial since he was passed over as leader of the forces because of his age.

The other, more remote, was Colonel Manuel Alvarez Margolles, [48] Chief Officer of *Regimiento Número 1, Antonio Maceo* at the Moncada Barracks in Santiago de Cuba, the largest military force in Cuba except for Columbia Camp in Havana.

Foster decided to make a connection with Colonel Martín Elena and asked Judge Fleitas for help. The meeting was arranged at the old *Hotel Velasco* in Contreras Street near the *Parque de la Libertad*, in the center of the city of Matanzas. Judge Fleitas advised Colonel Martín Elena that Foster was the top CIA in Cuba, a circumstance that was evidently not cumbersome for Martín Elena. To Foster's surprise, Martín Elena showed up in full uniform and with his accustomed escorts, in full view of the visitors to the Municipal building on the other side of the street.

Foster began to express concerns about the ambitions of the military in Havana [49] and the rumors of a *Coup* by officers that had been retired during Grau San Martín's clean-up of Batista's followers within the troops; Martín Elena looked intrigued but not surprised. When his turn came to speak, he anticipated to Foster what the turn of events would be during a Batista Coup:

«Batista will try to control the Presidential Palace, Columbia Camp and *La Cabaña* Barracks. That would be more than enough to control the Army and the Navy. Most of Prío's Cabinet would be placed under house arrest, as well as the top military loyal to the Republic. US Ambassador Beaulac would be contacted early and reassured of the cooperation of the new government with the US and the fulfillment of

---

[48] On the day of Batista's Coup, **Colonel Alvarez Margolles**, Oriente's military chief, attempted to resist with a large crowd of students and citizens that had come running up Aguilera Street towards the Moncada Barracks. They were intercepted at Marte Square by Captain Juan Antonio Delfín, Alvarez Margolles' secretary, who had joined the *Coup*. From Columbia, Batista announced a pay raise for the soldiers and trucks full of soldiers began shouting "*¡Viva Batista!*" Colonel Alvarez Margolles knew that it was the end of his resistance; within minutes, Captain Alberto del Río Chaviano took over command of the Moncada Barracks.

[49] **Juan Francisco Fleitas** had originally identified Foster as an Assistant to the US military Attaché in Havana; nothing was said initially about his intelligence duties. Foster quickly gained the sympathy of Martín Elena, who had studied at the School of the Americas in Fort Benning, Georgia, a US training facility founded in 1946 for cadets and officers of Latin American nations; Martín Elena was very friendly to the US.

all of Cuba's international obligations. Batista's men will control all radio stations, telephone and telegram services and newspapers. There will be very little traffic in the streets of Havana. Batista will justify his *Coup* by accusing the Prío government of having promoted an alliance between the gangsters and the politicians. These are clearly the right moves and techniques for a perfect military Coup in Cuba,» added Martín Elena. «Batista has always been a superb strategist.»

Foster asked Martín Elena if in his opinion the *Coup* could be blocked.

«The only possible approach would be to make a strong stand in Santiago de Cuba,» was Martín Elena's answer.

«Is that possible?» was Foster's inquiry.

«At the Moncada Barracks in Santiago, the man in charge is Colonel Alvarez Margolles. I talked to him about Batista's evident intentions last December 15th, during the *Día del Soldado* celebration. [50] He told me he would support the Republic and its Constitution if Batista tries to take the government by force, but that he saw very little chance that Batista could be stopped. He also told me that, should the military in Havana made any moves to bring about a *Coup*, he was ready to arrest General Ignacio Galíndez, a former aide to Batista, and Captain Alberto del Rio Chaviano, brother-in-law of Tabernilla and Chief of the Guardia Rural squadron in Palma Soriano, near Santiago de Cuba.»

«Are these two the men that would try to control the military in Santiago?» asked Foster.

«Absolutely,» was the answer by Martín Elena.

«What do you think the people of Cuba would do if Batista tries to take control of the government?» asked Foster.

---

[50] Originally, September 4th had been designated by Batista as *Día del Soldado*. Grau San Martín moved the celebration to December 15th, in honor of the **Battle of Mal Tiempo** (Bad Weather); at this battle, in 1895, Generals Máximo Gómez, Antonio Maceo, Serafín Sánchez and Brigadier Luis de Feria, during 3 hours, defeated with relentless *machete* charges the Spanish 42 Batallion from the Canary Islands and entered the territory of Cienfuegos. The battle ended the myth of the invulnerability of the Spanish Army and opened the path to the West for the Cuban Invading Army.

«Well... believe it or not Batista has a lot of following in Cuba,» was his answer. «The *Auténticos* have squandered their idealistic appeal. Corruption and gangsterism have characterized their two governing periods. The young revolutionaries of the 1930s have proved to be very inept to govern. Right now the main anti-American slogans come from the Communists and the *Auténticos*; that is not what the people were hoping for. Businessmen, housewives, students, government employees, sugar workers, sugar barons... everyone wants peace and stability and Prío has failed to provide it. I am afraid the population will not be ready to fight for the *Auténticos* and the Constitution. Batista knows it; he is ready to strike and be back in power. He has the means and he will use them.»

As the conversation was coming to an end, Foster gave Martín Elena his private phone and offered to ask the Department of State in Washington and particularly Mr. Foster Dulles, their ideas about any strategies with which the Prío government could help to preserve democratic government in Cuba. The general feeling was that it was too late; that the dice was cast and Batista had a free path to resuming power in Cuba. It was a depressing thought that Foster took back to his apartment at 525 Escobar Street. From all his news sources he knew that Rolando Masferrer's Radical Union Party [51] was ready to support Batista. So was Eusebio Mujal, [52] Secretary General of the Cuban *Confederation of Labor (CTC)*, the man who had seized control of the labor movement from the Communists but was now likely to withdraw his support for Prío. There was no chance that he would call a general strike if Batista staged a *Coup* (in the end, he initially did but failed to follow-up). Batis-

---

[51] **Masferrer**, in fact, was a staunch supporter of Fulgencio Batista. He had fought alongside the Communists in the 1936-1939 Spanish Civil War, where he was reported to be an enforcer for the International Brigades. It was said he was feared for the thumping of his wounded leg as he approached his victims. By the 1950s he was a devoted anti-Communist. In 1957 he set up a guerrilla (*Los Tigres de Masferrer*) to protect Batista from his enemies.

[52] **Eusebio Mujal** enjoyed Prío's support to seize control of the CTC from the Communists in the late 1940s but was ready to support Batista in order to keep his leadership position. He made sure no general workers' strike succeeded in Cuba after 1952.

ta could also count on many former military officials purged by Grau San Martín in his quest to rid the Army from Batistianos.

Of all the men Foster was afraid would be part of the government of Batista, the most cynical and distrusted was Francisco Tabernilla Dolz.[53] He was the head of a clan than included his oldest son Francisco Tabernilla Palmero (Grau had retired him in 1944 as Lieutenant) and Carlos Tabernilla Palmero (also retired as Lieutenant in 1946). At the time, Carlos had a secret yearning to lead the Cuban Air Force. Also part of the clan was Tabernilla's brother-in-law, Alberto del Rio Chaviano. An equally potential loyalist to Batista was Brigadier General Rafael Salas Cañizares and his three brothers, all with ambitions

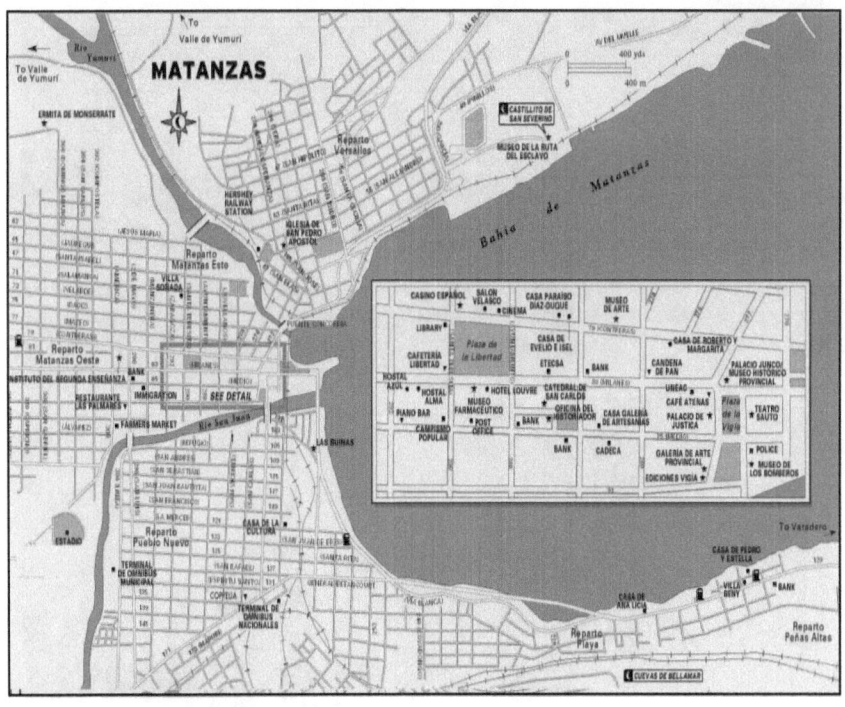

---

[53] In the pre-dawn hours of January 1st, 1959, **Tabernilla** would steal the *Guáimaro*, Batista's aircraft, from Columbia Air Field (his sons Wincy and Tony were both pilots) in order to escape to the Dominican Republic. This forced Batista to make do with a smaller and less comfortable aircraft for his family. At the tarmac, Tabernilla pretended to kiss his grandchildren good-by and walked to the terminal while the family went aboard. After joining his followers at the terminal, he touched his pockets simulating he had forgotten something in the *Guáimaro* and ran to the aircraft. Once he entered, the door closed and the *Guáimaro* took off immediately, leaving his friends on the ground astonished that the General had resorted to such a dirty trick.

to control and be part of the hierarchy of Cuba's National Police. After the conversation with Colonel Martín Elena, Foster never tried to contact him again. He was filled with pessimism and had lost his interest in talking with Colonel Alvarez Margolles.

Photos, top to bottom:

Generals Batista and **Tabernilla** at a celebration, with **General Cantillo** in the background; the **Goicuría Barracks** (headquarters of Regimiento Número 4, *Plácido*, in Matanzas); the **Moncada Barracks** (headquarters of Regimiento Número 1, *Antonio Maceo*, in Santiago de Cuba); a photo of Tabernilla's brother-in-law, **Colonel Alberto del Rio Chaviano**.

14
Prío's Good Works were not Good Enough
Late January 1952

TRYING TO START A DIFFERENT CONNECTION with the government of Carlos Prío, Foster began to be a regular visitor to the day-time *tertulias* at Tomás Fernandez' furniture store. There he had met Herminio Portell Vilá during one of the occasional visits of the man who had become Cuba's foremost historian from his position as professor at the University of Havana. Their relationship of trust had been increased and reinforced by the friendship of María Teresa, Portell Vila's wife, with her bridge partner Ruby Alonso, both members of the St. Paul's Lutheran Church in Havana, and the Havana Woman's Club.

On February 7 of 1952, Foster finally met Portell Vilá at one of the *tertulias* and concerted a meeting for the following Friday at Alberto Alvarez-Cabrera's old office at the University of Havana. Alvarez had been a member of the *Directorio Estudiantil* during the fight against Machado, was elected Senator in 1950 and had presided the United Nations Security Council in March of 1949 as Representative from Cuba. [54] Foster agreed

---

[54] **Alberto Inocente Alvarez** was a close friend of President Carlos Prío, and served as Minister of Commerce in his Cabinet in 1951. That year he became the spokesman for a group of Cuban investors that had the support of President Truman for a small participation in the capitalization and operation of the **Nicaro Nickel Plant** in Oriente Province. The plant had been rehabilitated by the US government to meet defense needs for this critical metal. By the end of World War II, the US had invested close to $1 Billion in *Nicaro* and the Cuban capital participation was part of a *quid pro quo* that would guarantee granting Cuban customs exemptions and port privileges, Cuban admission of foreign technicians and Cuban labor organizations help in the resolution of labor disputes. See page 37. Over >>>

with Portell Vilá that Varnum Lansing Collins Jr., Second Secretary of the US Embassy in Havana, would accompany him to the meeting.

Portell Vilá and Albert Foster began their conversation before Alvarez-Cabrera arrived at his office.

«Dr. Portell Vilá,» Foster started, «How do you see the forthcoming elections and the chances that a *Coup d'État* by Batista would interrupt the slow democratization progress in Cuba?»

«Well,» Portell replied,

«In 1944 the new *Auténtico* administration under Grau San Martín purged Cuba's armed forces of those that had controlled army positions thanks to their personal relationship with Batista. Over 200 officers were retired, including many at the highest ranks. More were to be discharged in 1945, as well as the entire top command of the National Police. We tried to substitute them with professional, academy-trained junior officers. [55] Unfortunately, those well-formed new officials were dismayed by the widespread corruption of the Grau and Prío administrations. How can we possibly now blame them for supporting a change?... How can we ask for their loyalty when all they could see during Prío's and Grau's terms of office was graft, nepotism, gangsterism?...»

Foster was about to interrupt when Portell Vilá continued:

«I do not believe that any regiment of the Cuban Army, Air Force or Navy would take up arms today to defend the corrupt constitutional order of the *Auténticos*...»

By 1951 Nicaro was producing 27.5 million pounds of nickel oxide per year, mostly for stockpiling. On a communiqué from **Thomas C. Mann**, Deputy Assistant Secretary of State for Inter-American Affairs, to **John Moors Cabot**, Assistant Secretary of State for Inter-American Affairs, Alberto Inocente Alvarez was criticized for his *«alleged private immorality and venality in public office,»* even though he was not even a shareholder of the Cuban corporation investing in *Nicaro Nickel*.

[55] **Dr. Portell Vilá**, together with **Roberto Agramonte**, **Salvador Massip** and **Rafael García Bárcena**, taught at the *Escuela Superior de Guerra* (War College), located at the *Castillo de Atarés*, Havana, whose founder and Deputy Director was **Major Ramón Barquín.** They were all either *Ortodoxos* or attracted to *Ortodoxo* politics. It was said after March 10, 1952, that Batista's *Coup d'État* had been "*conceived and cooked*" at the *Escuela Superior de Guerra*, whose alumni included Jorge García Tuñón, Juan Rojas, Luis Robaina and Dámaso Sogo, some of the most important players in the *Coup* of March 10, 1952.

He continued, uninterrupted.

«Prío has condoned gangsterism; it is not farfetched to believe —like Batista will argue— that Prío is seeking to perpetuate himself in power; that Prío will even make a pact with the Communists if he needs to; that Prío has shamelessly enriched himself and allowed others to profit from the existing graft.»

«Are there any redeeming values to the Prío presidency?,» Foster finally asked.

«Oh yes,» was Portell Vilá's answer. «Prío has probably been Cuba's best President since Tomás Estrada Palma. It is a long story, but worth remembering.»

«Go ahead, Dr. Portell, I am eager to know.»

«Truth be known, Cuba is not one of these countries that receive substantial foreign aid from the US. We are not indebted to foreigners and our economy has developed remarkably enough; this has allowed corrupt government officials to enrich themselves without bringing excessive poverty to the citizenry. The US power over Cuba —and its military presence— has been relatively modest since the abrogation of the Platt Amendment; so has the level of US investments in Cuba. But the corruption of the *políticos* and their compromises with proper staffing of public positions is beyond belief.» [56]

Portell Vilá continued:

«Unfortunately, political corruption is world-wide these days. All administrations in this and previous Cuban governments have been corrupted; hence, it is unfair to accuse Prío for simply following the tradition. I have heard Prío, on occasion, defending his government saying «everybody does it so it must be all right.» [57]

---

[56] At the request of **Francisco Tabernilla Dolz**, for instance, Batista appointed the Tabernilla's family cook as police lieutenant in 1952. In 1962, Tabernilla openly acknowledged receiving from Batista a cut from the mafia's regular contribution to Batista's personal checking account.

[57] According to US former Assistant Secretary of State **Spruille Braden**, Ambassador to Cuba in 1942... *«Of course, there has always been corruption... even in Manhattan island, not to say the rest of New York City... these criminal situations are common place.»*

So had said Batista. [58]

«Listen,» added Portell Vilá,

«Between 1946 and 1950, Price-Waterhouse, a very reputable international accounting firm, determined that the Cuban government receipts exceeded expenditures by $59 million; yet a deficit of $10.6 millions was shown in the books. How could that be possible? The only explanation is that there were $70 million of extra budgetary accounts that had no supervision and zero accountability. Where are those millions? In the personal investment accounts of Carlos Príoo, his ministers and his cronies!»[59]

Privately, Foster believed that although Portell Vilá had been regarded as a friend to the US, he was frequently very critical of the *Americanos* and had written many articles with a definitive anti-American bias. He had given credibility to numerous gratuitous innuendos by Latin-American leftists against the US, probably more because his need to be recognized as a "super Cuban intellectual" than because of actual animosity against the US. [60] Portell Vilá was also known to be inconsistent in his love-hate relationship with the US. He disliked and severely criticized Teddy Roosevelt, while excessively loved FDR. [61] Foster knew that Portell Vilá, head of the Cuban-American Cultural Institute, was no longer a helpful influence in the development of Cuban-American cultural relations.

---

[58] **Batista's** words in 1952: «*We do not deny that dishonest acts have been committed; they could be identified, it occurs everywhere. Large sums of money are always needed to buttress every political regime.*»

[59] During the following years, **Batista** concocted the notion that he and his son Rubén had to be "business associates" of every company needing government permits or legislation to secure their business success. Rafael Leónidas Trujillo was contriving the same scheme in the Dominican Republic.

[60] In December 4th, 1951, for instance, on a speech at CMQ Radio, he accused the US —and Secretary **Dean Acheson** in particular— as instrumental in the establishment of a policy «*to maintain in power many Latin American dictators for the exclusive benefit of US businessmen.*»

[61] To Portell Vilá, **Teddy Roosevelt** was «*a big toothed man with a falsetto voice; a pitiful convinced expansionist,*» while **FDR** was the «*defender of Americas' way of life, and the only hope of the world against Communist aggression and domination.*»

Point blank, Foster asked Portell Vilá if there was anything in Prío's government that he would consider a positive contribution to the democratic development of Cuba.

Portell Vilá's answer was, to a certain extent unexpected:

«Carlos Prío is the culmination of a new period in Cuba's history; our 1940 Constitution was the end of one age and the onset of another. Prío represents our liberal democracy, our social justice and our economic freedom: the triumph of Cuba seeking a place among the modern constitutional democracies in the world. He is the living confirmation of three successive national victories over political disorder, tyranny and ignominy; the evidence that we are an advanced nation that prizes the rule of law as a condition of civilization and modernity. With Prío, we have established forever a permanent climate of freedom and a solid ambition to be a great nation.»

«Isn't this too generous to Prío?,» asked Foster.

«Not at all,» answered Portell Vilá.

«Prío had numerous accomplishments; they included respect for human rights, freedom of the press, a democratic climate and a relatively open and transparent government. The reformist zeal evident during the presidency of Grau San Martín, however, was gone or highly diminished. Cubans expected the same type of reforms implemented during Grau's administration when Guiteras was part of the government; Prío's agenda was not as decisive. »

After a pause, Portell Vilá continued.

«It can be said in his favor that gangsterism has diminished within the University of Havana. Yet history shows, in today's Cuba, that once a citizen becomes a politician, he enters into an elite group that makes him impervious to the dreams of other citizens. His or her allegiance to the electorate disappears and an endless appetite for power and fortune takes over. Prío has tried to do away with gangsters, for instance, using the *Grupo de Represión de Actividades Subversivas (GRAS)*.» [62]

---

[62] Prío's enemies falsely accused him of creating the **GRAS** to «*repress political opponents and labor unions.*»

«It has never worked, though,» he concluded his words. [63]

At that point Foster interrupted to suggest that Portell Vilá would probably be interested to know the opinions of the US government towards the situation in Cuba, in which case «it would be worthwhile to listen for a few minutes to Varnum Lansing Collins as a voice from inside the US Department of State.» Portell Vilá unreservedly agreed.

Lansing Collins began his brief analysis.

«There is no doubt that during recent months the government of President Prío has deteriorated; there is a great deal of instability and uncertainty. Public trust has soured due to high-level corruption, rapacity, gangsterism and general dishonesty. This has affected the young academy-trained officers of the Army in ways that nobody in government understands. Frequent and unstoppable assassinations and defamations have discredited the government; junior commanders are disillusioned. [64] The histrionics and weekly denunciations of malfeasance by Eduardo Chibás have completely demoralized the population and undermined the trust in the national leaders. We know that there are conspiracies to overthrow Prío, moved by dissident officers that have reached a broad base of support among civilian political and economic sectors.»

Nothing that Lansing Collins described was new to Portell Vilá. He thanked him for the time and interest he had taken and for his championing of the cause of democratic Cuba within the US government. He left the meeting more anguished and pessimistic than when he arrived. In silence, he cursed the day

---

[63] Prío's presidency was as violent as Grau's. After the creation of **GRAS**, a bomb exploded in **María Luisa Gómez Mena's** home; the yacht of Senator **Diego Vicente Tejera** was set on fire; **Alejo Cossio del Pino**, owner-director of *Radio Cadena Habana* was murdered; and a bomb exploded at the law offices of Orthodox Senator **Pelayo Cuervo Navarro**, who had denounced the unrelenting government corruption in his articles in newspapers *El Mundo* and *Alerta*. On January 27, 1949, these articles became the basis for the famous **Causa 82** for «*embezzlement, fraud, prevarication, defiance, delinquency and disobedience*» against the top ranks of the *Auténtico* Party. In the long run, Cuervo Navarro paid for his denunciations with his own life.

[64] With the hope of getting word to President Prío —if he did not know it already, which was unlikely— Portell Vilá, during this meeting, was given specific names of officers whose military units were drawing pay for 84 members when, in fact, they had only 52 enlisted soldiers. He was also provided the name of a **Chief of Staff** who had embezzled several million dollars from the Armed Forces Retirement Fund before he himself retired and went back to Las Villas province as a civilian.

he had met Chibás and had become an *Ortodoxo*. [65] As a historian he knew it was too late to reverse the course of inevitable events.

The next time Portell Vilá coincided with Albert Foster at the 621 furniture store *tertulia*, he made a point of going home at the same time as Foster. As they began to walk towards Belascoaín Street, Portell suggested dropping by the *Siglo XX* café for a cup of coffee. Once inside the establishment Portell Vilá shared with Foster the feeling that he had probably been too negative in his judgment of the Prío presidency.

«I failed to recognize that, just like Prío showed some weaknesses when dealing with his former student friends of 1933, he also made an effort to surround himself with good men during his government.»

After a long pause he continued:

«Look at Pepín Bosch and José Alvarez Díaz, both ministers under Carlos Prío. So were Felipe Pazos, National Bank President and Justo Carrillo, president of the Agricultural and Industrial Development Bank, both appointed by Prío during his administration. I can also think of Manuel Antonio de Varona and Felix Lancís, Prime Ministers of his government; Carlos Hevia, Aureliano Sánchez Arango, Lomberto Diaz, Luis Casero Guillén, Luis Pérez Espinós, Alberto Cruz, José Antonio Rubio Padilla, Oscar Gans, Pepe San Martín, Segundo Curti and many more I could mention. Some were formally appointed to positions in his government; other were advisors that remained very close to Prío after the end of the Grau presidential term.»

After a second, longer pause, he continued.

«Gosh, I cannot think of any other man in Cuba that could have brought to his side so much honest and patriotic talent. It is a pity he

---

[65] The *Partido del Pueblo Cubano (Ortodoxo)* had been founded as an offshoot of the *Auténticos*, at a July 14, 1946 meeting in Holguín, Oriente Province, where **Eduardo Chibás** was elected its President. At the time they had three reasons for splitting with Grau and Prío: the realization that Grau was corrupt; the belief that Carlos Prío, Grau's protégée, would be his successor and would cover-up Grau's dishonesty; a zeal for rural rehabilitation (rural schools, cement floors, sanitary latrines and available well water in every *bohío*), which was not particularly shared by Grau or Prío.

was so anxious to be liked that he did not cut all of the thieves and common burglars that plagued his presidency at their feet.»

Foster listened in silence. He knew many of these men and was in agreement with Portell Vilá.

«Cubans are either too sentimental or too venal,» were the final words of Portell Vilá, «and some of them are both; people like Prío would excuse any major fault if it comes from a friend; on the other hand he is considered and accused in vane by his enemies as eminently bribable; God knows what lurks in the moral soul of a man. After all, the devil rides on the dollar bills. Again… there has been no better president in Cuba than Carlos Prío Socarrás. Period!»

Photos above, left to right:
Two contrasting photos, on the left, some members of the Cabinet of President Carlos Prío in 1948; average age, 42. On the right, some of the members of the Cabinet of Fulgencio Batista in 1952; average age, 61.

Photos, left to right, top to bottom:
Two photos of the **Castillo de Santo Domingo de Atarés** in Havana, location of the War College of the Cuban Military in the 1950s; **Herminio Portell Vilá**, Cuba's foremost historian, member of the 1940 Constitutional Assembly; The Ignacio Agramonte Law School of the University of Havana. Shown in a circle, the office of **Alberto Inocente Alvarez**, Prío's Minister of Commerce in 1951; **Eduardo Chibás** (in a circle) and other Orthodox leaders on the day when the *Partido del Pueblo Cubano (PPC)* was founded; the logo of the PPC; finally **Varnum Lansing Collins Jr**, photographed in 1963, after his retirement, in his Princeton home.

15
Was Eduardo Chibás Prío's Rasputin?
Mid 1951

IT HAS BEEN ARGUED THAT Grigori Yefimovich Rasputín (1869 –1916), aka the "Mad Monk", helped to discredit the Russian Tsarist government to the point that it lead to the fall of the Romanov dynasty in 1917. [66] Historians have argued that a similar role was played by Eduardo R. Chibás (1907-1951) during the Prío government in Cuba. The analogy is not as farfetched as it seems. On August 2nd, 1951, Earl T. Crain, First Secretary of the US Embassy in Havana, dedicated a full confidential report to the US State Department as a follow-up to a previous report by Dunaway G. Clark, an Embassy senior political analyst and *Chargé d'Affaires*, on June 18, 1951.

The D.G. Clark report referred to a luncheon given by the manager of the Cuban Esso Company, attended by prominent members of Havana's American business community, in which Senator Chibás was invited to outline his personal views and policies. He was absolutely convinced he would succeed Prío as President of Cuba and was «*on his best behavior, impressing his listeners with his sincerity,*» according to Crain. At the meeting, he stressed his long proclaimed isolationist policy of not seek-

---

[66] Contemporary opinions saw **Rasputin,** a peasant in the village of Pokrovskoye in Siberia, either as a saintly mystic, visionary, healer and prophet or, on the contrary, as a debauched religious charlatan. When he heard reports of Tsarevich Alexei's illness (Haemophilia, a widespread disease among European royalty descendent from the British Queen Victoria, Alexei's great-grandmother), he offered his services to his mother, the Tsarina Alexandra in 1905. His intrigues began the downfall of the House of the Romanovs.

ing or accepting any alliance with any other political group, much less the Communists. To him it was a matter of «*not contaminating the party with those he constantly berates.*» In the opinion of Clark, however, Chibás had lost much of his early charisma and was losing electoral ground to Batista and Hevia.[67]

Carlos Hevia, in the opinion of Chibás, was an easy opponent to defeat, even though he was a man of undisputed prestige and solid reputation. In fact, Chibás believed he had been instrumental in having the *Auténticos* recruit high caliber men such as Hevia to key positions.[68] Clark thought otherwise; his report indicated that Chibás would not have an easy sailing to the presidency since he was splitting the opposition votes with Batista against a unified *Auténtico* Party.

The official position of the US Embassy was ambivalent with respect to Chibás. Nevertheless, the reports of Crain and Clark to the US Secretary of State in Washington stressed the following points in the *Ortodoxo* platform, according to Chibás:

1. Chibás most important economic-political policy position was to "cubanize" all economic activity.
2. He favored distribution or heavy taxation of all idle arable land, financing of government sponsored irrigation projects, technification of crops with mechanization and the creation of "*cooperativas campesinas.*"
3. Nationalization of all public utilities and free trade with strict control of production and exports.
4. Full cooperation with all international bodies and collaboration with higher forms of world organizations (ONU, FAO, UNESCO).

---

[67] He was paying a price for his relentless accusations against **Aureliano Sánchez Arango**, Prío's Minister of Education. After indicating he had proofs of Aureliano's investments in Guatemalan real estate with stolen funds from the Ministry, he was forced to admit he could not prove his charges.

[68] As a curmudgeon, Eduardo Chibás was one of the men most responsible for bringing to the PRC (*Auténticos*) functionaries of the caliber of **José M. (Pepín) Bosch** (to be Secretary of Hacienda and future President of Bacardí, Ltd.), **Ernesto Dihigo López-Trigo** (a prestigious lawyer and soon to be Foreign Minister) and **Luis Casero Guillén** (a wealthy shipbuilder, Mayor of Santiago de Cuba and future Minister of Public Works).

5. Defense of the interamerican regional system, free access in equality terms to world trade; opposition to all tyrants, from Stalin to Trujillo and from Franco to Perón.
6. Normal, sufficient and stable economic relations with the US and alliances and democratic and enthusiastic participation with the US in the event of a 3rd World War.

Crain and Clark also pointed out the penetration of Communist militants into the leadership of the Ortodoxos, eventhough Chibás was obstinately opposed to it; an example was the presence of Congressman José Pardo Llada, a man, according to the US, uncomfortably close to the Communists.

In the event of Chibás' election to the Presidency of Cuba, in the opinion of the US Embassy,

«There was a certain probability that he would be assassinated, considering the large number of persons that have been assured of imprisonment or loss of property; a course to which Chibás was fully committed.»

Everything considered, the fact was that Eduardo Chibás became the *Rasputin* of Cuban politics. He had regular access on Sundays to a prime time slot on CMQ, the strongest radio station in Cuba. At many of his programs he sounded like a madman or a hysterical and mentally deranged lunatic, yet he was — at the same time— a man of undisputed integrity, Cuba's most popular radio political commentator, its best shaper of public opinion and its most effective self-promoter. In the 1940s, for instance, he never asked Batista for subventions, which Batista granted under a maxim popularized by General Genovevo Pérez: «*A la prensa se le paga o se le pega.*» [69]

In the early 1950s the middle class was disgusted with gangsterism from the "trigger-happy" boys; the *Auténticos* had crushed the hopes of campesinos; city dwellers had given up on any improvements in roads, schools, water and hospitals. The voice of Chibás never failed to rally the best of Cuban causes and heroic traditions. He descended from a family of

---

[69] A play on words "When it comes to the press, abuse it or subsidize it."

patricians [70] and made promises that could be carried out if those in government simply stopped stealing from the national treasury. The relentless attacks of Chibás, however, weakened the entire political system, particularly when he saw the need to exaggerate, imply, overstate, hyperbolize and even fabricate accusations. All this was throwing the country into chaos. It got so bad that Cubans did not know if Chibás was the protector of probity in government or an empty sloganeer.

As it happened with *Rasputin*, Eduardo Chibás did not live to see the fall of the *régime* that he had so forcefully denounced. On August 5, 1951, he had promised to furnish evidence of Aureliano Sanchez Arango's malfeasance; instead, he digressed, warning that Batista might attempt a military coup. At the end of his radio hour he made a farewell statement [71] and shot himself. The effect he was trying to achieve went unknown to the radio listeners since an ad for *"Café Pilón"* interrupted him before he pulled out his weapon. The entire country grieved wide and long for Chibás. He was buried and was incomprehensibly forgotten by most Cubans within a few months.

Photo on the right:
Eduardo Chibás, holding his empty briefcase, on the day he could not present the "evidence" of Aureliano Sánchez Arango wrongdoings, August 5, 1951, a few hours before his suicide during his Sunday night program at CMQ radio.

---

[70] Chibás father, **Eduardo Chibás Guerra**, was the map-maker of Roosevelt's Rough Riders in the Cuban Independence War of 1898; his mother, **Gloria Ribas Agramonte**, was a niece of Eduardo Agramonte Piña, a Colonel in the same war, cousin of Major General Ignacio Agramonte, the 1868 Cuban War hero.

[71] He called it «*su último aldabonazo,*» a term that had to be explained to many Cubans. (his last "toll of the bell").

Photos, top to bottom:

Grigori Yefimovich Rasputin, the man who most contributed to alienate the Russian people from the Imperial family; **Eduardo René Chibás Ribas**, the furiously anti-Communist scion of a well-off family, a flamboyant, fanatic and charismatic Senator who dominated Cuba's political discourse and most contributed to estrange the Cuban people from their elected officials; *bottom right*, the enormous funeral procession that accompanied Chibás to his last resting place.

16

Comments and Arguments from Kuquine
Early 1952

KUQUINE WAS THE NAME that Fulgencio Batista gave his one *caballería* estate [72] and official residence in the southern area of Havana province when he returned to Cuba in 1948. (See map on page 105.) The main house, sitting next to a small but superbly landscaped pool, had all the frills and conveniences of a rich-man's home: air conditioning everywhere, seven huge bedrooms with large closets paneled with precious Cuban woods, a four-car garage, beautiful custom-made furniture all over by *Orbay y Cerrato*, phones in every room, including —in the library— a gold plated modern square apparatus, a gift from *ITT* (today's *AT&T*). The most conspicuous sculpture in the house was a solid gold crane in the living room, the symbol of his *Partido Acción Unitaria (PAU)*, The most luxurious and large room was the library, built in an elongated area where originally the architect —not quite knowing Batista's favorite pastime— had built a bowling alley. On one corner of the 7,000 volume library was a large exquisite 12-seat conference table where Batista liked to meet with his associates.

It was around that table that Batista had a brief encounter with Fidel Castro in 1951. Castro had been invited to *Kuquine* with his brother-in-law Rafael Díaz Balart. Castro was impressed with the library and had only one comment:

—«Aquí falta un libro.» (There is a book missing here.)

---

[72] A Cuban ***caballería*** is slightly larger than 33 acres or 1.44 million sq.ft.

—«¿Cuál?,» preguntó Batista. (Which one?)
—«*La Técnica del Golpe de Estado,* by Curzio Malaparte,» respondió Castro. (Technique for a *Coup d'État*)

For Batista, libraries were always essential in his quest to be an educated man. Once he had been promoted to Colonel, in 1933, he spent hours at home, always in his library, talking and taking lessons from Juan J. Remos, Yoyo García Montes, Jorge Mañach, Carlos Saladrigas and Amadeo López Castro. This was remarkable since, in contrast with other Latin-American nations, the Cuban families never considered the military as a good career path for their children and never sent them to military schools; as a consequence, the Cuban Army was always populated with *guajiros* or men without much education. An additional difference was that Cuban members of the military got their advanced education in the US while in other countries of the Americas their officers were mostly going to military schools in France, the UK or Spain.

In Batista's library at *Kuquine*, most of the volumes dealt with Cuba's political history; the souvenirs consisted of documentation that vouched for his successful career as a military man in Cuba. There were condecorations that he had earned as Sergeant on the Cuban Army, the stars obtained when he was promoted to Colonel, as well as all sorts of pictures and trophies from his military days. He was the type of reader that wrote and made notes and comments on the books he read, hence it was easy to find out which books he had read. When his birthdays came up, his friends and family knew that all he wanted were books; no ties, handkerchiefs or colognes.

It was also in that library at *Kuquine* that Batista received many friends and influential news people; he hoped they would recount in the future the reason he was determined to produce a *Coup d'État* in Cuba. On March 3, 1952, for instance, he received six important guests: Edmund A. Chester, a former CBS newsman and director of the Associated Press in Havana. He came with Guillermo Alonso Pujol, Cuba's VP and presi dent of the Cuban National Party. Also visiting was Dr. Andrés Domingo y Morales del Castillo, his friend and ally of many battles, Rafael Esténger, biographer of Maceo, Heredia and Luz y Caballero and a frequent journalist in the pages of *Bohemia*, *Avance* and *Alerta*; Anselmo Alliegro y Milá, former Prime Minister, and Colonel Arístides Sosa de Quesada, more of a poet than a military man. They were all alarmed at the prospect of Batista breaking with constitutional order.

The papers in Havana were full of rumors. One rumor had it that several military officers had had a meeting with General Ruperto Cabrera, Prío's Army Chief of Staff, and tried to persuade him to prevent the holding of national elections. Other rumors were that Prío was not pleased with Hevia's lack of charisma and had decided to postpone the elections. Moreover, word circulated that the *Ortodoxos* had resolved to render the institutions inoperative if their candidate Roberto Agramonte was robbed of the election. Anselmo Alliegro was rumored to have made a pact with Prío in *La Chata*, Prío's country home, after reading some tapped telephone transcripts signaling a probable attempt to steal the presidential elections.

During the meeting, Dr. Juan J. Remos called Batista to let him know and confirm that Prío was very distressed and was ready to carry out his own *Coup d'État*. Batista asked Remos to carry a message to Prío that «a violation of the constitutional order would result in a civil war in Cuba.» Two days later Remos sent a message to Batista: «*Prío has not changed his mind.*»

During the March 3rd meeting, Batista made a brief aside with Edmund A. Chester and told him that his home at *Kuquine* would be attacked or, most probably, he would be assassinated as he attended a meeting of young women and labor leaders in Guanabacoa; a meeting from which «*he would not be returning home.*» The rally proceeded without incidents, however, as was a second gathering in Matanzas, where a crowd of 30,000 assembled to praise and support Batista.

Edmund A. Chester was a good friend of Batista [73] but he was also a top notch journalist and during the aside at the meeting, he asked Batista pointblank:

«General, is true that you have been meeting since early this year with former officers of Cuba's military forces, seeking their support for a violent access to the presidency in violation of the Constitution and ignoring the opportunity to gain this position through a democratic election?»

Batista was caught off guard. After a few seconds he responded, giving him full details.

«Some of my old comrades had asked me to meet with them. It was on Saturday, January 26, at the offices of the *Partido Acción Unitaria (PAU)*, our headquarters at 306 17th Street in El Vedado. They were Generals Tabernilla, Manuel Larubia, Ugalde Carrillo, Cruz Vidal and Pilar García.»

«What was the purpose of the meeting, if I could ask?»

«We discussed how difficult the political landscape was for my presidential aspirations, given the strength acquired by the political supporters of Hevia; as you know, he is now counting with the support of Mayor Castellanos. They added that, for the good of the republic, I had to come to power violently if need be. I was assured that there would be an overwhelming support from the Armed Forces. I was also told that Prío was preparing his own *pronunciamiento* to prevent the Ortodoxos to gain control of the country.»

Edmund Chester was about to interrupt when Batista continued.

«I met with the same group on February 7 here in *Kuquine*. It was the day after Grau made amends with Prío and the *Partido de la Cubanidad*

---

[73] In 1964, **Edmund A. Chester** wrote *Un Sargento Llamado Batista* for Henry Holt and Company of New York. It was a very biased and sympathetic homage to his good friend General Batista, calling him «one of the most interesting public figures Latin America has ever produced.»

promised to support Hevia for the presidency. [74] None of us liked the *Partido Acción Unitaria* to be left alone without any alliances? [75]

Before Batista got back to the meeting, Guillermo Alonso Pujol commented

«Batista has indeed a great deal of support. Many of his former cronies in the military had been retired or passed over for promotion by Grau and Prío: it is my opinion that many of these officers would be going ahead with the takeover by themselves if they cannot convince Batista to go along with it.»

When Batista re-joined the meeting he said some words that confirmed for his guests that the General had already made up his mind to interrupt Cuba's constitutional life.

«The "*Auténticos*" are no longer a power house in Cuba. They have never achieved maturity as a party. They have wasted their political muscle and clout. They have never been able to convince the masses that they are a viable alternative to dictatorship; with their collapse goes the last opportunity of the 1933 generation to establish a democratic regime without the help of the military. I am the real alternative to dictatorship. But to be free you have to be disciplined first.»

No one disputed the General's words. That night Rafael Esténger y Neuling went home in a severe state of depression. As he gathered Esperanza, his wife of 20 years, and his children Otto y Miriam, he ventured to make a prediction that would come to pass in a few years:

«We are looking at a new period of uncertainty and misery in Cuba. This time we will have to leave and will probably never return.»

---

[74] At the time **Carlos Hevia** was Minister of Agriculture; the coalition supporting him had been expanded to include the *PRC (A)*, the *Republican Party*, the *Liberal* and the *Democratic Party*, as well as Grau's *Partido de la Cubanidad*.

[75] Unconfessed by Batista was the fact that on February 7, the retired army conspirators that supported him had agreed to compel **PAU's** youth groups to incur in all kinds of public altercations, creating a sense of alarm among the population that would make more palatable the capture of the government by illegal and unconstitutional means.

After they left Cuba, Rafael Esténger and Esperanza Valiente died in exile in 1982 and 1995. Their children never returned to live in their country.

Photos, left to right:

The entrance to Batista's **Kuquine** home; **Edmund A. Chester**, a good friend of the General, author of the book *A Sergeant named Batista*.

General Arístides Sosa de Quesada, **Rafael Esténger Neuling** and **Anselmo Alliegro Milá.** All three were honest and loyal followers of General Batista and in 1959 took the road to exile.

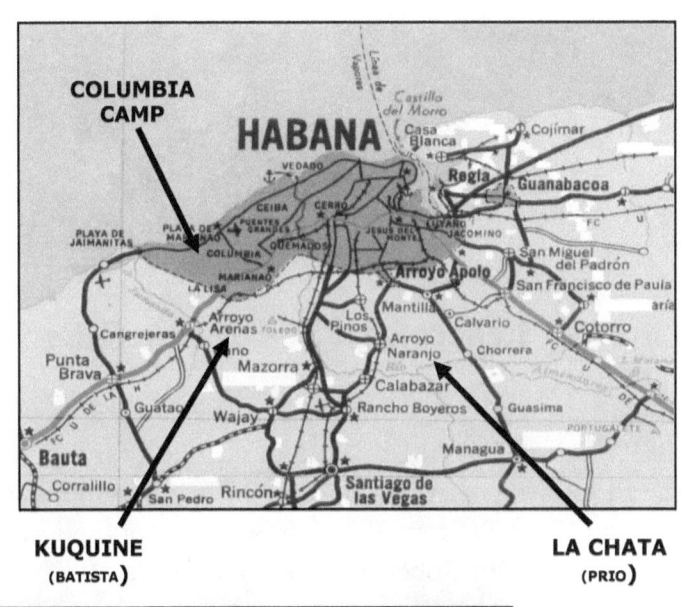

Photos, top to bottom, left to right:

The locations of **Kuquine** and **La Chata**; the pages of **Bohemia** magazine after the events of March 10, 1952; Batista's favorite **portrait** by César Betrán; the family at **Kuquine's** front lawn.

17

The Last CIA Report from Democratic Cuba
March 1952

ALBERT FOSTER WALKED into the US Embassy on March 7, 1952, not knowing that it would be the last time he reported his findings to Earl T. Crain, the First Secretary of the Embassy. He had just met with Roberto Agramonte at his offices in the Ignacio Agramonte building of the Law School of the University of Havana, and had visited Emilio (Millo) Ochoa at his residence in *Calle 10 número 107* in Marianao.

Millo Ochoa y Ochoa was an old 1940 *Auténtico* Senator from Oriente province, who had abandoned the party in 1948 and with Eduardo Chibás formed the *Ortodoxo* party. In 1944 he had been elected Senator with a plurality of 100,000 votes. In 1948, loyal to the *Ortodoxo* Party, he ran for Governor of Oriente and lost the election. It had been a big sweep by Prío, who obtained almost 1 million votes to Ricardo Nuñez Portuondo's 600,000, Eddy Chibás' 300,000 and Juan Marinello's 200,000. As things stood in 1950, Ochoa had been elected Representative from his base in Holguín and became a logical *Ortodoxo* candidate to run with Roberto Agramonte for the Vice-Presidency. He proved to be a loyal follower of his fellow *Holguinense* General Calixto García Iñiguez.

The first questions from Crain had to do with the opinions in Cuba about the elections in Puerto Rico and the announcement of the new US budget for defense ($7.9 Billion). Foster's opinions were definitive:

«Nothing in these two events has developed any interest in Cuba. What dominates the press now are Cuba's forthcoming elections: the *Ortodoxos* nominating the Agramonte-Ochoa ticket and Batista's *PAU* reaching at the bottom of the pail and nominating *políticos* that had been by-passed for nomination by their own parties.»

«Any chances of Batista's party winning the election?» asked Crain.

«None,» answered Foster.

«They are in the same situation as the *Republicanos*, who had many overtures to the *Ortodoxos* with no results so far. Batista will form an alliance with whoever takes him in. The same thing that Grau's *Cubanidad* party will try; they are both non-entities.»

«What's happening with all these resignations from Prío's Cabinet?»

«Carlos Hevia as Minister without Portfolio, Ramón Zaidín as Minister of Commerce and Luis Casero as Minister of Public Works, they have all resigned to run for office. Casero is the probable VP nominee and, of course, Carlos Hevia the presidential candidate. Prío has convinced Grau to support Hevia. The fever of the elections has not yet run its course. The *Auténticos* believe that if they lose, it would be because the untimely recent outbursts of violence.» [76]

«What's your opinion?» asked Crain.

«Not by a mile, the *Ortodoxos* will win the elections, more so since the death of Eduardo Chibás has done away with the strongest anti-Communist from the party. Moreover, the Communists are not joining Batista this time because the General —unlike the Communists— has said he would back the US in a War against the USSR. I believe Batista will support the *Ortodoxos* with or without a pact. The accusations are flying in all directions. Batista is accusing Prío for the stealthy disappearance of some $47 million that were supposed to be burned; he is attacking Agramonte for having shielded *UIR* and *MSR*

---

[76] Some of the most egregious acts were: The vengeful revenge against **Segundo Prendes**, an alleged cutthroat, member of the Secret Police during the Machado administration. Prendes was slain by three unknown assailants on December 14, 1951; UIR's murder of **Alejo Cossío del Pino** on 15 February 1952, to avenge the death of Emilio Tró during the massacre of *Orfila* in 1947; a petard explosion at Senator **Pelayo Cuervo Navarro** on March 5 1952, with three injured bystanders.

mobsters [77] in the Mexican embassy. Agramonte is attacking Hevia for his complicity with the gangsters that have sapped and exhausted the national treasure. Batista is attacking Prío for promising Castellanos seven senatorships and the government of Havana as payment for his support. Deep down, something that we do all the time in the US. Prío, for instance, has announced that his government has already sold a record 5.9 million tons of sugar from the 1952 harvest. That announcement is not true, and coming just prior to a general election has total and absolute political intentions.»

«Any truth to the rumors that Prío will stage a *Coup d'État*?»

«I spoke last month with Juan J. Remos, a prestigious author and journalist, who was Minister of Education, Secretary of State and Ambassador to Spain during Batista's government between 1936 and 1940. [78] He warned Batista of a Prío conspiracy to stay in power. Batista sent a message to Prío warning him of the consequences of such an act. A second warning went to Prío through Anselmo Alliegro, who told me of a conversation he had with Prío about a civil war ensuing if the *Auténticos* forced the result of the 1952 elections.»

«Any other news besides those relating to the elections?»

«Juan José Arévalo, former Guatemala president, is attacking the US from its refuge in Mexico *City*. *HOY*, the Communist newspaper, is printing his articles on page one. *HOY* is also headlining a report that the US is using germs to seek an advantage in the Korean War, describing the horrible sequel of suffering by the "brave and heroic people" of North Korea. On the economic front, the Cuban Sugar Stabilization Institute is shipping 75 million gallons of sugar cane molasses to the US, adding to the 18 million gallons sent and stored there last year. They are pricing the molasses at 20 cents a gallon, and nothing less. Prío is announcing that everything is fine in the sugar industry but foreign buyers are refusing to meet Cuba's prices and, not having enough storage space in Cuba, there are predictions of re-

---

[77] After the 1952 *Coup*, **Roberto Agramonte** sought asylum in the Mexican Embassy in Havana, where he had very good contacts.

[78] **Dr. Remos** was with **Ramiro Guerra**, one of the authors and director for publication of the 10-Volume *Historia de la Nación Cubana*, a monumental work that was started in late 1940s and finally attained publication in 1952.

trenchment for the industry as all this sugar will be difficult to move into consumption for quite a while.»

After presenting his report, Foster gave a closed envelope to Crain containing a "for your eyes only" list of radio and TV stations that the CIA agents in Cuba «*have found would be taken over by Police Lieutenant Rafael Salas Cañizares during the first hours of a Coup d'État:* »

The list included:

- **CMBF**, Canal 4, San Miguel and Mazón Streets.
- **CMCB**, Radio Reloj, Radiocentro, 23 and L Streets, Vedado.
- **CMW** Radio and TV, Radiocentro, 23 and L Streets, Vedado.
- **CMCO**, Radio Caribe, 111 Prado Avenue, Havana.
- **COCO**, Avenida de la Independencia and Arrollo Street.
- **TV Canal 2**, Telemundo, Ambar Motors, 23 and P, Havana.
- **Unión Radio**, 78 22nd Street, Havana.
- **Radio Cadena Habana**, 104 San José Street, Centro Gallego.
- **Radio García Serra**, 260 Prado Avenue, Havana.
- **Radio Progreso**, Menocal Avenue and 25 Street, Vedado.
- **Radio Salas**, 108 San Rafael Street, Havana.
- **Radio 1010,** Mil Diez, 314 Reina Street.
- **Radio Aeropuerto Internacional**, RAI, 1111 25 Street, Havana.

The report also contained the last known information about the *cuartelazo* (Coup) that Batista was planning before the 1952 elections. It was prefaced by a statement from Foster to the effect that President Prío, Prime Minister Gans and VP Alonso Pujol [79] had been informed of these plans and had found them lacking credibility and importance, mostly by President Prío. Foster added:

---

[79] **Guillermo Alonso Pujol** had had a conversation with Batista at *Kuquine* during which Batista complained of the terrible situation of security in Cuba. The General mentioned that the citizens did not sense outrage against the gangsters because the victims were always low class hoodlums themselves. He lamented that nothing like the assassination of Calvo Sotelo in Spain had occurred in Cuba, which was what was needed to hurt public sensibilities. For a moment, Alonso Pujol though Batista was insinuating that it would be convenient if the gangsters would kill someone of relevance, to produce in Cuba an uprising, like the death of Calvo Sotelo had resulted in the revolt led by Sanjurjo, Franco and Mola in 1936 Spain, which started the Civil War.

«As of this date there are rumors, with a certain level of credibility, that competing with Batista there are a group of military officials led by Captain Jorge García Tuñón planning to topple the Prío government. It would not be difficult for Batista to ally himself with these disaffected troops.»

After a long pause, Foster continued,

«The best odds to overturn the government are Batista's; we have concentrated on him, following his steps and those of his people.»

«The Aviation Camp would be taken over by Commandant *Manuel Larrubia Paneque*, Colonels *Roberto Fernández Miranda* and *Carlos Cantillo González*; *La Punta* Garrison (seat of the Cuban Navy Command) would be taken over by Rear Admiral *José Rodríguez Calderón*; the control of the National Police would be assumed by First Lieutenant *Rafael Salas Cañizares*.»

«The second line conspirators were one commandant, 14 captains and 11 first Lieutenants; they would all be promoted to the next rank on the day of the *Coup*. We have found that the first decrees of the new government would be:

1) Elimination of the right to strike;
2) Abolishment of the 1940 Constitution and establishment of a series of *Estatutos Constitucionales* in its place;
3) Wiping out the *escalafón militar* (existing military promotion ladder);
4) Invalidation of the documents that under Grau and Prío ordered the retirement of the officers that supported Batista in the past. These officers would need only to return the retirement funds received and would be reinstated in the Army.

«A total of 77 officers would be retired, among them Mayor General *Ruperto Cabrera Rodríguez*, General de Brigada *Quirino Uría López* and Colonels *Eduardo Martín Elena*, *Urbano Matos Rodríguez* and *Epifanio Hernández Gil*. That decision would dismiss from the Army those officers with the most military experience and knowledge, which goes against the proclaimed intention of Batista to develop a modern, well equipped and educated army.»

«Exactly my thoughts,» expressed US Ambassador Willard Beaulac when he read the report the following day. «Batista will likely return the Cuban army to the days of nepotism, militarism and submission to the *políticos*, in opposition to the lessons of the well accredited professors of the War School. [80]

Photos top to bottom, left to right:
Presidents Prío and Grau with Army Chief of Staff **Genovevo Pérez Dámera** at the presidential Palace in 1947; nobody could deny that Batista was a skillful politician: on one hand, a poster and a cartoon accusing him of "soft on Communism," while on the other hand, a photo of his speech at the US House of Representatives in 1942.

---

[80] See General **Tabernilla's** comments on page 177. Batista, in effect, would appoint loyal rather than capable officers in 1952. It was the same strategy he had followed in 1933. After 1952, the Armed Forces of Cuba were full of military men, policemen and navy men with last names Tabernilla, Salas Cañizares, García Báez, Casillas Lumpuy, Ugalde Carillo and Fernández Miranda. Many of these officers received new medals and honors such as the *Gran Cruz de las Fuerzas Armadas*, the *Cruz de Honor Maceo* and the *Orden del Mérito Militar*. On March 10 1952, Batista also increased the payroll of the Armed Forces by 12%. See page 191.

Photos, top to bottom, left to right:

Dr. Emilio (Millo) Ochoa, **Dr. Juan J. Remos** and Police Lieutenant **Rafael Salas Cañizares**; Fulgencio Batista addressing the press on March 10, 1952. On his side **Alberto Salas Amaro** (with dark glasses). Alberto Salas Amaro is shown on the bottom right as he was detained after January 1, 1959.

II The Consummation

«On Saturday January 26, 1951, at the offices of the PAU, Calle 17 No 306, Vedado, former President Fulgencio Batista met with a group of retired military officers. Among them were Francisco Tabernilla, Manuel de Larrubia, Ugalde Carrillo Cruz Vidal, Pilar García and others. They discussed the need to assume power even if it had to be violently. The retired officers said they had plenty of support in the Armed Forces and agreed to keep their contacts alive, to further explore the environment, and to prepare to act when necessary.»

CAPITAN **SALVADOR DÍAZ VERSÓN**, MEMBER OF THE SERVICIO DE INTELIGENCIA MILITAR (SIM): CONFIDENTIAL REPORT TO CUBA'S PRESIDENT PRÍO AND TO THE JEFATURA DE LAS FUERZAS ARMADAS, MARCH 1951.

«I have accepted the pressing mandate after being informed... of the imminence of a Coup d'État hatched by President Carlos Prío Socarrás for next April 15, with the objective of sidestepping the electoral decision scheduled for the first of June.»

GENERAL FULGENCIO BATISTA ZALDÍVAR, AT COLUMBIA CAMP, MARCH 10, 1952.

« There was a momentary paralization of urban transport in Havana but soon troops were used to run the Havana buses. There were also strikes in two petroleum refineries, various railroad delegations and one or another labor center. There was partial abstention in the Ariguanabo Textile Firm and some other enterprises, but the rest of the workers in other economic activities either did not hear about or ignored the calls of the CTC.»

EFREN CORDOBA, CLASE TRABAJADORA Y MOVIMIENTO SINDICAL EN CUBA, EDICIONES UNIVERSAL, COLECCIÓN CUBA Y SUS JUECES, 1995.

A Telex to Secretary of State Dean Acheson

```
E.T. Long - ARA - 9/20/78            UNCLASSIFIED        ACTION COPY
FOI 920723 Rabasa
```

```
                        TELEGRAPH BRANCH
25-M    F780011-0276  RESTRICTED SECURITY INFORMATION
Action                                   Control: 4146
AR4                                      Rec'd: March 10, 1952
                                                 4:31 p.m.
Info    FROM: Habana
SS
G       TO: Secretary of State          DEPARTMENT
PR                                       BUREAU
L       NO: 599, March 10, 1 p.m         INTER-AMERICAN
E
DCL     NIACT.
SAM
PSB     PASS ARMY, NAVY, AIR.
P
IIA     Fol mil movement which apparently began about 4 this morning
R       Gen Batista has taken over Habana practically without opposition.
OLI
CIA     Batista is at Camp Columbia and is acting as army chief staff
DS      while Col Cantillo, former head Air Force, has agreed serve as
DCR     adjutant gen. Col Cantillo states all mil forces in country
DCRM    behind Batista. However, at least one radio station Camaguey
        broadcasting in favor Prio an hour ago.

        Small mil force in fifth district Habana under Col Perez Alonso
        reported early this morning be still loyal to govt but nothing
        heard recently and apparently no fighting in Habana so presumably
        it also has joined revolt.

        Two persons reported killed at Pres Palace early this morning.
        About eight this morning Palace press secy gave me copy declara-
        tion which he said Prio had drawn up in Pres Palace claiming mil
        in provinces loyal to govt and exhorting people resist. However
        Batista forces in charge radio stations and declaration not to
        broadcast. It has just been published by press however.

        Pres Prio left Palace 8:30. His present whereabouts unknown.

        The four generals of Cuban Army under arrest in Batista's finca
        near Habana. Col Cantillo accepted post adjutant gen after
        consulting former chief of staff, Caberera, who is one of those
        under arrest.

        Consulate Santiago and consular agent at Camaguey report all
        quiet. One station Santiago broadcast Commie charge US insti-
        gated revolt to get troops for Korea. Station now off air.

        CTC gen strike in favor Prio forecast.
                                                    MUJAL
        Airport and dockworkers reported ordered out on strike. Jmujal*
        reported in custody.

                                              Coastguard
                    RESTRICTED SECURITY INFORMATION
PERMANENT
RETAIN COPY   • This copy must be returned to DC/R central files with notation of action taken •   REPRODUCTION OF THIS
                                                                                                   MESSAGE IS PROHIBITED
```

18

Columbia, where Cuba began to Break Apart
Years before March 1952

IN 1898, AFTER THE US occupation of Cuba, U.S. governor, General Fitzhugh Lee, established his military headquarters in Marianao and called it *Campamento de Columbia* (Camp Columbia). Once Cuba gained its independence in 1902, Columbia became headquarters for the Cuban Army; it was from there that Sergeant Batista gained power on September 4, 1933 as leader of the Sergeants' Revolt. In 1952, he reemerged there with his March 10th *Coup d'État*.

To commemorate his 1933 victory, Batista had a tower erected in 1944 at the center of the traffic circle facing the main entrance to the camp at Avenida 31 and Avenida 100. The tower doubled up as a beacon for the military airfield. It became known as the *Obelisco de Columbia* (or the 4th of September Obelisk.) In 1952 he insisted on going by the obelisk as he entered the garrison, even though there were easier means of access.

Photos, left to right:
Fitzburgh Lee exploring the territory in Marianao where he decided to establish his "Camp Columbia" in 1898; **General Fitzhugh Lee.**

Photos, top to bottom, left to right:

Fitzburgh Lee's map presenting the territory in Marianao where he decided to establish his "Camp Columbia" in 1898 (circle in the Photo); in the map, the location of Columbia is designated as "Armas;" below, the first **US troops** lining up at Camp Columbia in 1899.

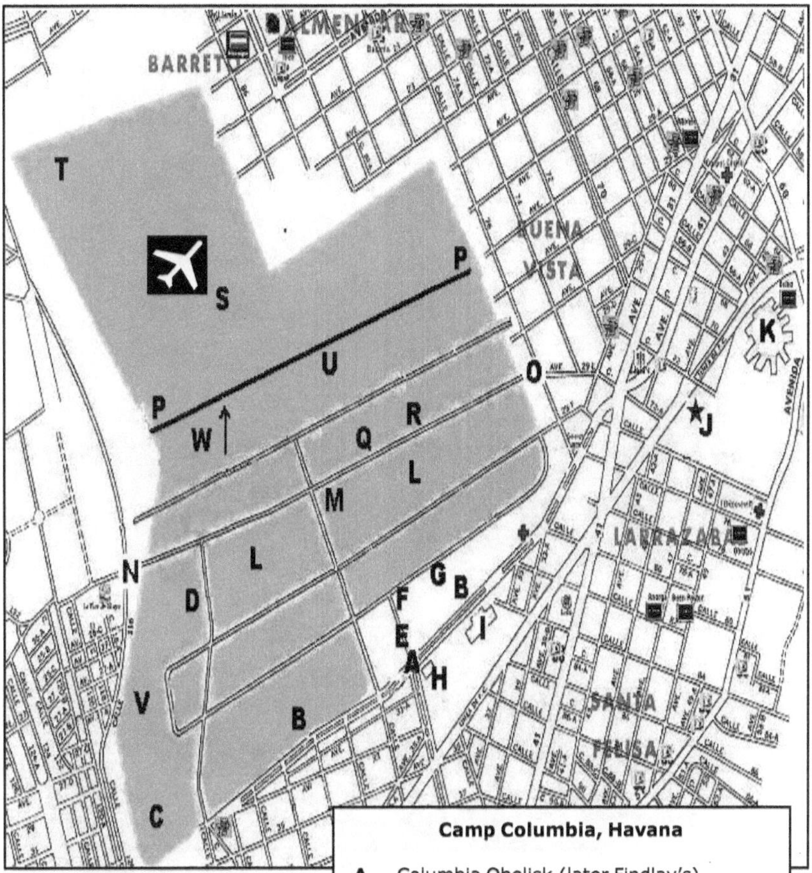

Camp Columbia, Havana

A   Columbia Obelisk (later Findlay's)
B   Barracks
C   Military Hospital
D   Cuban Army Headquarters
E   Number 4 Post
F   Number 6 Regiment Headquarters (Alejandro Rodriguez Regiment)
G   Movie and Auditorium Theater
H   Homemakers School (Escuela del Hagar)
I   Workers Maternity Hospital
J   *Tropicana* Nightclub
K   *Belén* School
L   Polygon Parade and Exercise field
M   Glorieta and Ceremonial Podium
N   Number 10 Post
O   Number 6 Post
P   The "Trench"
Q   Chief of the Army's House
R   Officers Club
S   Military Aviation fields
T   Aerovías Q Headquarters
U   Old lighthouse ruins
V   Horse Stables, Tank Squadrons
W   Slope toward the "Trench"

Columbia Obelisk, *Calzada de Columbia* (31st Avenue) and *Avenida de Columbia* (100th Street).

Photos above, top to bottom:
The **Number 4 Post**, (main entrance to *Camp Columbia* in the 1950s); the **Movie Theater** (**G** in the map on page 119); the **Officers Club** (**R** in the same map).

Photos above, top to bottom:
The **4th of September Obelisk**, (at the rotonda in the intersection of 31st Avenue and 100th Street, **A** in the map on page 119. It later became the **Findlay Obelisk**); the **Glorieta** from where Batista addressed the troops in 1952, (**M** in the map on page 119); the **Aerovías Q airfield** (**T** in the same map).

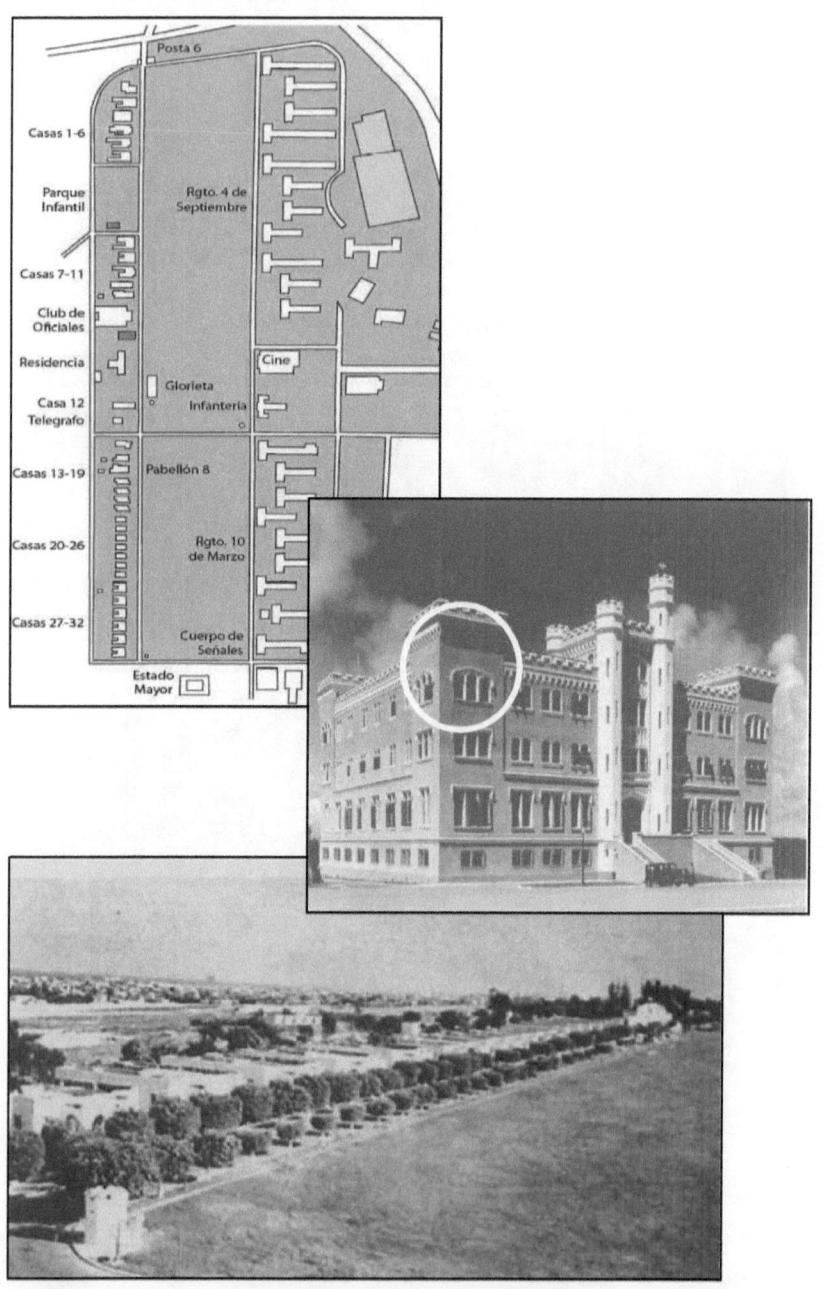

Photos above, top to bottom:
A detailed sketch of the area known as the **Polígono**, where the troops were formed for inspection and military parades. *On the center*, an old picture of the **Estado Mayor**. The offices of the Chief of the Army are circled.
On the bottom, the view of the **Polígono** from the **Estado Mayor**.

19

The Wolf comes out of its Lair
Early March 1952

SINCE 1933, CUBA'S ARMY HAD seven regiments, each 1,300 men strong. Two of those regiments where at the *Cabaña* and *Columbia* garrisons. Five others were one in each of the other provinces, Pinar del Río, Matanzas, Las Villas, Camagüey and Oriente. Due to the distance of Oriente province to the capital —on the other extreme of the island— military strategists had long concluded that whoever controlled the two regiments in Havana would control the other five, one at a time. In addition, the regiments at Havana counted with aviation, the bulk of the army tanks and heavy weapons, plus small detachments at places like *Quinta de los Molinos* and *la Fuerza*. The regiments at the *Cabaña* and *Columbia* garrisons were very much in the mind of General Fulgencio Batista in the early days of March of 1952.

March 7, 1952, was a special day at *Kuquine*. A substantial detachment of current and former military men entered the country estate of General Batista, out of uniform, in small groups and inside common ordinary cars. The intersection of the highway leading from Marianao to Punta Brava with the private road entering *Kuquine* was festooned with balloons, banners and streamers to conceal and camouflage the large traffic of entering cars as if there was a festivity or birthday celebration inside the property.

The country road to the *Kuquine* property was surrounded

on both sides by tall and mature *palmas reales*, (royal palm trees, *Roystonea regia*). Secluded behind the trees near the entrance to the unpaved road were two bunkers with heavy armed guards that could barely be seen from the property access way. As the road approached the main house an electrically operated gate could be turned into an impregnable obstacle for those attempting to rush the property. Solid stone fences made it impossible to bypass this defensive line. Inside the home, General Batista had several Smith and Wesson M1917, M1 Garand rifles, automatic Caliber .45 pistols and Winchester 12-gauge pump-action riot-version shotguns placed at strategic places, fully loaded and ready to defend himself and his family.

The men entering *Kuquine* on that day were Alberto del Río Chaviano, Arístides Sosa de Quesada, Carlos Tabernilla Palmero, Dámaso Sogo Hernández, Fermín Cowley Gallego, Francisco Tabernilla Dolz, Pilar García García, and Roberto Fernández Miranda. Excluding these military men, the only other invitees were two civilians, Rafael Guás Inclán and Alberto Salas Amaro. The men began to arrive at 2:00 PM and all the expected guests were inside the property by 5:30 PM. The mood was sober and austere, in spite of generous available offerings of Scotch whiskeys and rums. [81]

At 6:00 PM, the group gathered together for business in the Library. Marta Fernández, the General's wife, and their children left for the pool side of the house. General Batista opened the meeting:

«Gentlemen, this is our last meeting before the action starts. Let's review our schedule and the mission of each group.»

A discreet silence invaded the room.

«Those going with me to *Columbia* will meet here not earlier than 1:30 AM, to depart in two vehicles at 2:00 AM. Each of you bring your best hand weapon; only one. We do not want any rifles or carabins. If you get early in the area, you can wait in the parking area of *Tropi-*

---

[81] The General favorite drink was the silky rich and fruity 12-year old Johnny Walker Black Label.

cana; by the way, stay inside the car. Dámaso [82] and his group should be near Posta Número 4 inside Columbia by the time we get there at 2:30, and should have the sentries under control. The group going with Pancho —only one car— will be at the parking lot of the *Esso Belot refinery* at 1:45 AM, to proceed to *la Cabaña* at 2:00 AM sharp. Again, only one hand weapon each. Rodríguez Calderón and his people will wait until 1:45 AM at Prado Avenue and Refugio Street, and will enter *Castillo de la Punta* at the same hour than all others. Finally, Salas Cañizares will capture the *Police Motorized Section* and control the *microonda* transmissions. Everyone has to be on the designated unit by 2:30 AM. The time for everyone will be according to the *Radio Reloj* station.»

The meeting continued with many other organizational issues. Batista, as a former General-President was forceful, decisive and treated his co-conspirators as children in need of counsel, support and —if need be— discipline.

At the end of the meeting he disclosed to his comrades some of the points he had confidentially made to Willard Beaulac, the American Ambassador, at his first meeting with him.

«One of the reasons we have to proceed with this take-over of the government in Cuba, is to set things straight and not present the weak, informal and inconsistent image that we have in the eyes of the Americans. For the US, Cuba is a spoiled child among Latin American nations. They believe that only some sort of special treatment works with Cubans, unlike the way they relate to other nations in the hemisphere. Our tantrums, they say, are not very pretty spectacles in the eyes of the rest of the continent. Most Latin governments feel that Cuba should exhibit a certain amount of conformity with the processes other nations find satisfactory in their relations with the US and among themselves.»

Batista continued with the points he had presented to Beaulac:

---

[82] Captain **Dámaso Sogo Hernández** was the day's officer in command of Columbia on March 10. His participation at the meeting of March 7 confirmed his support in the most critical step of the conspiracy: to open (without violence) the gates at *Posta Número 4* in Columbia, situated at 31st Avenue and 100th Street, Marianao, across from the Obelisk.

«I am afraid that should the situation arise that Cuba becomes politically or economically destitute, we would not have the sympathy of other American republics. Should we fall into deep economic or social crises as a consequence of our own failing to meet obligations or fall short of entering into undertakings that all our sister republics regard as right and proper, our friends will consider that the symptoms of our disgrace would be our own fault, only curable if and when we see the light and act properly.[83] Our friendly neighbors would have to be convinced that we are not exercising special pressures for egregious purposes. They have instances in their own histories in which they have engaged in severe situations and they have had to extricate from them by themselves.»

It is fair to say that most of those present at *Kuquine*, with the possible exception of Arístides Sosa de Quesada, did not quite grasp the meaning of Batista's words. Sosa de Quesada had discussed the very same issues with José Ignacio Rivero, Gastón Baquero, Senator José Manuel Casanova and Eugenio Sosa Chabau, director of *Diario de la Marina* in the 1940s and a classmate of John F. Kennedy at the all-boys prep school *Choate* in Wallingford, Connecticut.[84] They had all understood.

Fulgencio Batista
the racketball player, at his court in *Kuquine,* aided by a junior army officer.

---

[83] In retrospect, those words of General Batista became prophetic when Cuba was taken over by the Communists in 1959.

[84] After 1959, **Eugenio Sosa Chabau** (See page 127) spent 21 years in Cuban jails as a political prisoner. Upon arriving in exile in 1980 he denounced suffering 14 sessions of electroshocks at Mazorra, in Havana. He was tortured for having informed President Kennedy that the Russians had placed missiles with atomic warheads in Cuba. To this day, few Cubans are aware of the heroic sacrifice of this man, scion of one of the oldest Cuban families. He completed his sentence and reached Miami as an exile in 1980.

Gracias te doy Señor por tus bondades;
porque trabajo y gano mi sustento;
porque puedo vivir entre los libres;
porque puedo expresar mi pensamiento.

Más te olvidas Señor, de los que andan
sumidos entre sombras y tormentos;
de los que gimen en silencio, y callan;
de los que ríen sin estar contentos.

¡Ah, los que tienen que aplaudir por fuerza!
los que se hielan bajo un sol de fuego;
los que les cortan, al nacer, las alas;
los que viven sin Dios, sin fe, sin sueños.

Por ellos es mi ruego; que yo tengo
bastante con mi taza y mi librero,
una bufanda que me cubre el pecho,
y un ventanal para mirar el cielo

ARÍSTIDES SOSA DE QUESADA

Photos above, top to bottom, left to right:
Batista with Captain **Dámaso Sogo**; **Eugenio de Sosa Chabau**, director of *Diario de la Marina*; a poem by **Arístides Sosa de Quesada**, the poet-general; Batista campaigning in 1952, both among the military and among civilians.

20

The Last Carnival in a Free Cuba
Sunday, March 9, 1952, first of the **Three Days in March**.

LIKE EVERY SPRING SINCE colonial times, Havana was celebrating its carnival on Sunday, March 9, 1952. It was a tradition that had started in the 1870s, when slaves recreated the songs and dances of their remote African regions to the delight of their accommodating masters. Once the feasts were over, it was back to work, sweat and mistreatment.

During the first years of the republic, most of the *jolgorio* (revelry) in Havana took place along the waterfront. Dozens of *carrozas* (floats) would loop around *Belascoain* Street, the *Paseo de Malecón* and *el Prado* Avenue. Around the floats there would be groups of dancers, disguised to the point where they would not even be recognized by their friends, in case they exceeded the mores of the times in their gyrations and sensual innuendoes.

On Saturdays, formal *comparsas* (dance groups) delighted viewers with their rythmic choreographic whirling and splendid uniforms. They were traditionally called *Las Bolleras, Los Marqueses, Las Jardineras, Los Dandies* and other festive and folkloric designations; membership was strictly controlled and exclusive for descendants of the original founding dancers.

On Sundays, however, it was a free for all. Anyone could dress anyway they wanted, climb inside a decorated truck or a convertible car and be merry. All would pause briefly and applaud deliriously at the sight of the *Reina del Carnaval* and the *Rey Momo* in their float, usually the highlight of the celebrations, as they went in rhythmic euphoria through the streets of Havana, in an atmosphere of total exhilaration. All along, there would be *rumba* percussion ensembles, spectacularly attired dancers, food and beer stalls in front of some stores, and thousands of streamers in the air and the pavement. It was always an explosion of color, contagious drum rhythms, conga lines, fancy outfits, fireworks, *faroleros* (men holding rotating colorful pickets resembling streetlights), and frenetic dances.

Not everywhere people were dancing and in a festive mood.

At *Kuquine* the last touches were made for the *Coup d'État* agreed by General Batista and his men. Phone calls were being made to loyal followers of the ex-President to ascertain the possible reactions of the commandants of the *regimientos* outside Havana. Batista, Rio Chaviano, Fermín Cowley and Tabernilla were contemplating strategic issues and making choices. A decision was made to grant an immediate raise in salary to all soldiers, as well as commissioned and non-commissioned officers. It would be announced through the P.A. systems at Columbia and la Cabaña in the first hours of the *Coup*.

The group agreed —at the suggestion of Batista— that no one would be hurt, no officers would be incarcerated, all commanders, adjutants, aides and soldiers whose loyalties were not clearly established would be "invited" to congregate in comfortable locations to await vetting and to determine their futures. The most important leaders and chiefs of the troops would be given the choice of being taken to the home of María Marta Miranda, Batista's mother-in-law's home at 5th Avenue and 86th Street in Miramar, or to be restricted inside their own homes. It was also decided that Batista and the leaders of the movement would not dress in uniforms since the *Coup* was driven by "concerned civilians" and was not a typical military *golpe*.

After all decisions were made, Batista and Tabernilla stayed at *Kuquine* while the others were dismissed and went home. Batista was worried about the possibility of an infiltration amongst the conspirators by agents of Prío; or some of the plotters getting cold feet and denouncing the imminent take-over. Together they decided to change some of the agreed plans at the last minute, once the action was already in motion, to fluster any counteraction or ambush. Having planned these defensive maneuvers in every detail, Batista wrapped his arms around *el Viejo Pancho* and sent him home. They had been together in dozens of adventures and this was probably the most significant one. It could cost them their life in front of a firing squad if things went wrong.

As these events were happening at *Kuquine*, Aristides Sosa de Quesada was receiving Gastón Baquero at his office in 468 Cuba Street, near the *Convento de Santa Clara* in old Havana. Far from the noisy sounds of Havana's Carnival, the streets were calm and deserted, and that was what they needed for discretion and peace of mind.

Sosa de Quesada had had many conversations with Baquero, the agronomist that José Lezama Lima had invited to join *Orígenes* and who soon after became a poet, a journalist and a political analyst.[85] This time the conversation was centered on the words Sosa heard about the Cuban character and Cuban politics.

After Arístides Sosa reviewed Batista's words, Baquero began to give his opinions.

«There are certain facets of the Cuban personality that have had a pronounced effect on our relations with the US,» were his first words. «I completely coincide with Portell Vilá's conclusions about the Impossible Neutrality.[86] After passionately attacking the Platt Amendment as a *vicio de coacción miserable* (miserable coercive vice), Portell postulated that Cuba should never be neutral with respect to the US

---

[85] By the early 1950s, **Baquero** had already become the most influential poet for new generations of writers in Cuba. **Sosa de Quesada** was a military man in his early 40s when he began his friendship with Baquero, who was eight years his junior.

[86] In many of his writings, Baquero defined that even under the permanent and undesirable interference of the US in Cuban affairs, there was no escaping the need to work with the Americans to secure prosperity and freedom for Cuba.

because it was not in its best interests, given that Cuba was a few miles from US coasts. Whether you want to call it *determinismo geográfico* or something else, the truth of the matter is that it would be silly not to form a close alliance with such a powerful country which is almost within eyesight of Cuba's coasts.»

Raising his voice for emphasis, Baquero concluded,

«An alliance Cuba-USA is without doubt good for Cuba. It was, it is and it will be forever!»

«How do you see our character having an effect in our relations with the US?» asked Arístides Sosa.

«To begin with,» responded Baquero…

«Cubans have a bipolar and at times morbid reaction to US influence on our affairs. Sometimes we completely surrender to this influence, in our tastes, our way of life, the desire for freedom and our lust to live as well as they do; other times, because a *rescoldo* (remains of a now extinguished fire) of *hispanismo*, because the persistent *requiebros* (wooing) of the Communists and our own *recelo* (misgiving) nacionalista, we repudiate anything coming from the Yankees. Right now we are at a time of *rescoldo, requiebros* and *recelo,* and not at a time to welcome their influence in our lives. Today, we even prefer Franco and Perón, for the simple reason that they have become our best defenders and have promised to help us economically. They are both anti-Americans in their perspectives. I have to see the day!»

Before Arístides Sosa had time to process these thoughts or interrupt, Baquero continued.

«Cuba, without a doubt, has been opportunistic in its relations with the US, particularly after the War. The *Americanos* have patiently tolerated postponement of trials, delayed claims, expropriations, non-compliance with treaties, withdrawal of reciprocal rights for merchant vessels and many other irregularities. We always cry foul when there is a reaction to this behavior. As a price, we have to bear the jealousy of our sister republics for Cuba's favorite position. If Batista believes that, I fully agree with him.»

«What is then your assessment of what Cuba has to do after reaching the maturity of 11 years of constitutional life,» asked Sosa.

«Very simple,» responded Baquero,

«We have to recognize our community of interests with the US and cast aside *hispanismo*, Communism and reckless nationalism; we need to throw away our peculiarities and live by the same code of conduct *vis a vis* the US that other Latin American countries have; we need to make sure that our democratic progress continues. If it breaks down, from Mexico to Patagonia no country will help us after our years of arrogance and ungratefulness.»

«You don't see much of a chance for that to happen, do you?,» asked Sosa.

«No. By the way, thanks for the Brandy. The take-over by Batista, from what you tell me, is imminent. It goes against everything he is predicating. The history of Cuba is reversing its course. Soon we will regret we did away with the *Plattistas*.»

Photos, top to bottom:
The great tradition of the **Havana Carnival**. *On top*, in the 17th Century; *On the bottom*, during the times of the March 10, 1952 *Coup d'État* by Batista.

Photos, left to right, top to bottom:
Pool side at **Kuquine**; the Havana Carnival **poster** for 1952; a **Comparsa** with **Faroleros** in 1935; journalist **Gastón Baquero** in 1952; the 1952 Havana Carnival as it passed through the **Malecón**.

21
Batista seeks the Advice of his Grand Paê (1)
Earlier, January 3, 1951, 3:00 PM

IN JANUARY OF 1951, Batista had received in his home at *Kuquine* a very special guest; a man that brought him so much spiritual peace and energy that he had been invited several times to Daytona Beach for consultation and conversation. His real name was **Omo Ti Iansa**, but in Cuban society he called himself Gabriel García. He practiced the *Candomble de Ketú* religion; had been initiated in the *Line of Nagó*, had completed all his *Axes* and gained for himself the entire pantheon of espiritism: from *Bará Lodé* to *Oxala*, the Axes of Oromilaia (with 32 Bucios), the Casicado of Caboclo from *Paês* Ogum Sechi Espadas and Adrián de Bará, the Axes of Kimbanda from the hand of *Paê* Omolú and *Maê* Karina de Oxum and many other merits from *Paê* Sechi Poeras. Batista never memorized or understood those awards and honors bestowed on his guest, but he felt very comfortable in the presence of Gabriel García and always asked him to visit his home in times of big decisions.

As Gabriel entered the living room of Kuquine, Batista received him with a head inclination and the classical words «*Mo Júbà.*» (My deepest respects). He knew Gabriel pretty well. On several occasions he had asked him to perform *batukes*, *kimbandas*, white *umbandas*, as well as throw *natales*, try predictions and discuss the Tarot of the Orixas, numerology and the fate of cabalistic angels. The man had 32 years of experience in the religion and 15 children (followers) crowned with *Axe de Ifa*.

«It is good to see you again, Gabriel,» declared Batista. «I am anxious to talk to you about religion and to ask you for a vision and a blessing.»

«It is difficult to conceptualize the term "religion,"» riposted Gabriel.

«Since the beginning of time, man had the need of offering something to a superior being, and so when Christ and his group ceased to exist, they left us a mute testimony in their altars. Cicero once said "No animals, except man, has knowledge of a supreme being," and among men there is no nation so fierce and wild, that will ignore what God should be and would disregard the necessity to have one. The belief system is an intrinsic human need, it is a universal fact. No matter how disparate human groups are and how different their belief systems, we find that there are ancestral similarities; most important, it is written in our genes that there is a creator, a supreme being to whom —I believe— we owe respect and without which we would be mere orphans adrift.»

«Certainly,» Batista answered.

«As Plutarch said, you can find cities without borders, without homes, without garrisons, without laws, without money, and without lyrics, but a people without God and no prayers, no one has ever seen.»

«Well said,» was Gabriel's reply.

«Well said by me or by Plutarch?» asked Batista.

«By both, my General,» was the answer. «Tell me, what brings me here today?.»

Batista thought for a moment and then spoke.

«I have two concerns. The first is, what would be the reception Cubans would give me now that my political enemies have been slandering me with repeated accusations that I am not a white man but an inglorious mixture of races? The second is, how successful would be my decision to once again assume political power in Cuba?»

«My son, the discrepancies in the skin tone in Cuba are profound and not just white to black, although it is the most common. They are also from black to white and black to mulatto. And what is worse, there is discrimination of black to the blacks. The black race is captive to its color. It gets shrapnel from all fronts.»

After a pause he continued.

«A sort of subliminal racism has always existed in Cuba. At times it apparently subsides. But it's like a dormant volcano.»

Gabriel took a sip of the Bacardi White Label that Batista had served him and continued his elocution.

«Traditional racism from white to black has always been there. It rejects me not only for my color, but because whites assume I have lower intellectual gifts. Even after we excel and have had the opportunity for education, racism is dormant; a blind hatred for the color of the skin that will always persist among whites. They will always consider us —you and I—unfit.»

«I agree. It extends even to cross-breeds like me,» acknowledged Batista. According to a popular saying, mestizos are the concern of whites and the envy of blacks.»

«You are quite right, my son. People who are of mixed races are not well liked by whites or blacks. In the case of blacks, they do not want to *atrasarse* by marrying a darker black (retrocess in their whiteness).»

«It is amazing,» Batista commented,

«regardless of my skills and power, I am sometimes treated like if I were one of these unfortunate people that live in the worst neighborhoods of Havana like Colón, San Leopoldo, Cayo Hueso, Los Sitios, Chamizo, Jesús María or Belén.»

«In those neighborhoods, my son, black santeros hold sessions for lily-white powerful and rich people. They charge $500 for an *Iyabó* (a saint or "deliverance" ceremony). The whites enjoy everything, down to the golden crowns in the smiling teeth of the *santeros* (saint ceremony priests). The *Paês* (master santeros) take their money and go away to have fun at carnivals and in public places like the *Salón Rosado* of *La Tropical* Gardens; there, they are feted by the best bands of the moment. The aggressive *tumbadoras* (a sort of self-standing *conga* drum) make their bodies gyrate as only black men can do. Among infamous lap dances and cheap beers and rum, they spend their well-earned illusion-making dollars and have more fun than any white man can imagine.»

«Racism in Cuba is not explicit,» added Batista, «In the family atmosphere of many white families, it is common to hear jokes about blacks, comments about children with "bad hair," and even hints that one has to be careful with the *prietecitos* (dark skinned kids). It is a phenomenon inherited from parents and grandparents.»

Batista, as usual, was enraptured by Gabriel's deportment. He was as black as an old Bakelite telephone and spoke with the same French accent he had noticed during their first encounter 20 years ago. He was from a royal Senegalese family, yet he had cut sugar cane like a slave. His hands were huge, thick skinned and callused from his days as a laborer at the Portugalete, Soledad, Río Cauto and Cacocún sugar mills. In his youth he had been a Communist, like many blacks. After all, the *Partido Socialista Popular (PSP)* had a Black President (Blas Roca), and attracted black leaders like Jesús Menéndez (assassinated in 1948), Aracelio Iglesias, chief of the *estibadores* (longshoremen, also assassinated in 1948), Lázaro Peña (Secretary General of the CTC in 1939), as well as many black intellectuals like Senator Salvador García Agüero and poet Nicolás Guillén.

«My dear Gabriel,» Batista said,

«This country of ours, stained and mongrel, unruly and soiled as it is, is a land where blacks, mestizos and whites walk past each other in silence, ride the same buses, go to the same baseball parks and occasionally talk to each other. We all know there are barriers. Formally we are not a racist country, but two worlds coexist and we know different: one is white, the other black. Black men rob to live their lives better. White men steal to have even more and enrich themselves. Both can speak freely, though, protected from day one by Article 25 of our 1901 Constitution.»[87]

«General,» —after so many years Gabriel didn't quite know how to address Batista—

---

[87] **Article 25**: Every person may freely, without prior censorship, express a thought, in word or in writing, through the press or by any other means, without prejudice or the liability imposed by the laws when, by any of those means, the honor of the people, the social order or the public peace are attacked.

«We live in a white-man's world. Since the world began, the white man has been on top of the blacks. They are more capable and intelligent. If not, how do you account for the fact that blacks came first in Africa when Europe was empty, and yet the whites have prevailed in the civilized world? I do not doubt it, they are better.»

«It only happened,» riposted Batista,

«because when America was discovered, Africa was replaced as a route to the wealth of the Asian markets. Later, with the *Tratado de Tordesillas*, [88] Africa became the source of slaves: Congo, Nigeria, Ghana, Senegal, Gambia; not far from the Black empires from the XII century, Sudán, Benin, Mali. We hope to continue having in Cuba governments that will not lie to the people and pretend there is no racism or segregation black-white. So far we have not succeeded. From José Miguel Gómez on, going on Menocal, Zayas, Machado, Mendieta, Grau and Prío; all our republican governments have lied to the people and profess that blacks and whites are the same.»

«But now, General, «What specifically do you want from me after having consumed this splendid Bacardi fermented and distilled spirit that I have so selfishly and conceitedly usurped from your bar?» [89]

«I was pleased to offer it, master,» was Batista's answer.

---

[88] Dated 1494. The **Treaty of Tordesillas**, established that Spain and Portugal would share the new world: America would belong to Spain and Portugal would own Brazil and the continent of Africa.

[89] The story of Batista's passion for *espiritismo* is well documented. His **Babalawo**, by the time he left Cuba in 1959, was *Albino Macongó* (aka, Elpidio Rivera) a man of «remarkable powers.» In late 1958 Albino suggested an invocation for Batista since, «the sign of divinity in the smoke is negative, tragic, hopeless.» His recommendation was «Sacrifice six steers, six pigs, twelve chickens and bury them in *Kuquine*.» Batista did not quite like this *encomienda*, but promised Albino to consider it. «I will beg the Saint several times and he will indulge» was Batista's promise to Albino.

«*¡No, no y no!,*» Albino riposted. «The saint is angry... the roads are closed and he is approaching a sea of red. The saint cannot hide his anger against your disobedience... he has decided to leave you... » Batista became alarmed and decided to take the advice seriously. He placed an order with his butcher and decided to leave government.

«I guess I do not have any other choice. Prolonging my stay in Cuba could have a tragic outcome... through my veins, however, does not run the blood of martyrs.» On the night of December 30th, 1958, at eleven fifty, Batista came to his residence in Columbia, woke his son Jorge Luis,16, and told him: «Prepare your books, do not share this with anyone, we will be leaving Cuba tomorrow...»

«It makes me good natured and contented but shallow minded,» was Omo Ti Iansa's reply.

Photos, left to right, top to bottom:

Jesús Menéndez, **Blas Roca** and **Aracelio Iglesias,** three black Communist leaders from the 1940s. Menéndez and Iglesias were murdered in 1948.

Gabriel García, aka **Omo Ti Iansa**. For years he claimed to have been Batista's Grand Paê (spiritual counselor);

The **Seven Top African Powers of Santería**. The Yoruba theogony has a pantheon of *Orishas* that include *Babalú Ayé, Orula, Yemayá, Obatalá, Obà, Eleguá, Ochún, Olofi, Changó*, and many others.

22

Batista seeks the Advice of his Grand Paê (2)
Earlier, January 3, 1951, 4:30 PM

«BEFORE WE GET TO BUSINESS, my dear Gabriel.» Batista intoned looking deeply into his *Paê's* eyes, I have always been curious about your devotion to *Ochún*. I would like to share your veneration and hope you can talk me into it.»

«My dear General. *Ochún* is one of the deities that are part of the *Yoruba* pantheon; she is the *Orisha* (goddess) of love and all sweet things, including voluptuousness. *Ochún* pours honey. It is the most highly regarded and admired deity in Cuba; one that inspires respect from everyone. It has been syncretized with Our Lady of Charity, our patron saint, just like Yemayá was syncretized as the Virgen de Regla; this has contributed decisively to both being highly revered and loved by all *santeros*, Cubans in general, particularly the *babalawos*.»

«What is the history of *Ochún*,» asked Batista.

«The story is told that *Orula*, the greatest of *babalawos*, when he was old, had nothing to eat, and had many other health problems that afflicted him. *Ochún*, who was his wife, dared to hold sessions in their house against all tradition and custom. One day, when *Orula* returned home, he saw fish, eggs and vegetables on the table and asked: "Where did you get all this? Either you've got a man who has paid for all these things, or... She interrupted and said: "There was a gentleman, and I decided to make a session..." *Orula* looked thoughtful and asked "What letter did you guessed for him?... what letter did let him leave satisfied with your answers?" To which *Ochún* answered: *"Oche*, the five" And *Orula* said: "Well, from now that number will be yours. You are five."

Batista looked puzzled. «*Omo Ti Iansa*, please continue,» expressed Batista not knowing why he had now called Gabriel by his spiritual name.

«*Ochún* is terribly important to *babalawos*. However, not all *Ochunes* who came to earth, in their various avatars or roads, were the same. Some were very serious and others, perhaps a little more cheerful.»

« Is it true,» Batista asked, «that the daughters of *Ochún* are the best *apetebbís* (companions and ritual helpers of the *babalawos*)?»

«Decidedly,» was the answer of Gabriel. «The best *apetebbís* are the followers of *Ochún*, although some say they are the daughters of *Yemayá*, who was also an *apetebbí* for *Orula*. So it is a matter of judgment. I've always believed that the true and best *apetebbí* for *Orula* was *Ochún*. Why? Because *Ochún* is fearless. However, *Yemayá Achabbá*, if I remember correctly, was once *Orula's apetebbí*, and also helped him.»

Batista gave up trying to understand Gabriel and decided to get to the second point:

«When is it propitious and opportune for me to take *el mando* (power) in Cuba, and will my move be successful?»

Before moving to that point, Gabriel thought it would be best to clarify a point for Batista.

«Remember that *Yemayá* is a mother, *Ochún* is not. *Yemayá* looks on humans with better eyes. *Ochún* is very energetic and drastic, an *Orisha* hard to face if you make a mistake. She does not like to be commanded but would rather do the commanding herself. I do not think you can talk directly with either of them, however. They will only pay attention to you if you talk through the *caracoles* (conches), the *cocos* (coconut) and the white rum, always with great respect and care. With respect to me, I always thought that my santo would be *Changó*,[90] but when I was initiated the *Orisha* that showed up was *Ochún*»

---

[90] ***Changó*** is the *Santeria* manifestation of *Santa Bárbara* in the Catholic tradition.

Batista decided to be more specific in his request for dates, predictions and blessings. Gabriel, however, anticipated him and asked a question.

«Do you ever get rum and honey for *Santa Bárbara*?»

«No, but I had always placed *elegguas* [91] behind the doors in Columbia, in Daytona, in rooms in the hotels in New York, Paris and Madrid, and now in *Kuquine*.»

Batista, somewhat tired of waiting for specific advice from Gabriel on abstract issues like luck, predictions and probabilities of success, began to anxiously insist that Gabriel concentrate in giving him a good date for his assault on Columbia. In the succulent *ajiaco* of Cuban culture,[92] he thought, he would rather get a date and hour than all the mumbo jumbo about African deities and myths.

Gabriel finally got to the point.

«Nothing will impede your success on the third month of the year. But you must get rid of the shadow of *arallé* [93] to prevent treason from some of your friends. According to *Ifá*, you must make a lotion and spread it on your head: 12 sticks of *Albahaca de Anís* (Anis basil), 12 *Pétalos de Rosa* (Rose petals), 10 drops of *Anisado* (French Pastis), 30 drops of *Oñi* (honey blessed by *Ochún*); the *Oñí*, I can supply to you.»

«And the date,» Batista insisted.

Gabriel began a series of chants and prayers and threw 16 *caracoles* over a small mat in front of General Batista, placing them in two rows, half of the *caracoles* facing up, alternating with the other half facing down. He closed his eyes and re-

---

[91] **Elegguá** is one of the most well-known deities of the *Yorùbá* religion, a protector of travelers, deity of roads, particularly the crossroads in all human decisions.

[92] Batista had read one of **Lydia Cabrera's** treatises on *Orishas* and numerology. Cabrera was the foremost Cuban ethnologist in the XX century. The quotation remembered by Batista was: «For the Orichas the elements, places, things, beliefs, animals, dignities, professions, trades and moods of men, could all be translated into numbers.» Batista's interests were obviously month, day and hour of his best opportunity to produce a *Coup d'État* in Cuba.

[93] In the Orisha tradition, *Arallé* was married to *Ogundá*. She was killed by her husband for faithlessness. *Ogundá* had been the protector of *Shangó* but he was cursed by *Oshún* because he never respected *Arallé*. Batista could not care less about this, but he made the lotion and, for a full week, used it in lieu of shampoo.

mained quiet for a long time, to the exasperation of Batista, who felt his *Paê* had gone to sleep. While Gabriel remained motionless with his eyes closed, according to explanations he gave Batista later on, the *caracoles* had turned into *odduns*. He touched one from each row without opening his eyes. He then opened his eyes and spoke to Batista.

«*No hay ningún Icú* (sign of death), therefore you will be safe and successful. I touched two *odduns* representing numbers. When a number appears twice in the same *ebbo* it is called *Ocana Melli*. In your case they were both times the number 5. That means the best day to take your chances is the 10th of the month.»

Batista was about to make a comment when Gabriel interrupted him.

«The deities have expressed their designs with the help of an adivinatory sign —*Oggún, Ochosi* and *Obatalá* through *Oggunda*. Your fate is now associated with a number in extrinsic form, although the actual association depends on multiple factors. All these traditions and experience-specific religious considerations are very complex; if I were to explain them, it would make my visit too extensive.»

Batista was glad the session was over and he had his date blessed by the entire universe of *Obatalá, Ochún* and *Changó*. He noticed that eight pieces of coconut and two turtle shells he had been asked to bring to the session were not utilized, but he was far from asking why. The 10th of March was OK with him, and that was all that mattered. He had a date certain for his *Coup d'État*.

Photo at right:

Albino Macongó (aka, Elpidio Rivera), Fulgencio Batista's **Babalawo**, at the time he left Cuba in 1959. According to Batista, «Albino was a man of great experience in *ifa* and had remarkable powers.» Albino was born in Bijarú, near Banes, in Oriente. After 1959, he relocated to *Palmas de Gran Canaria*, where he continued to practice **osodegán**: consultations with people interested in divinations, foretelling of luck in upgrading and gratifying their libido, as well as all issues having to do with the rigors of *Santería* and *ifa*.

Photos, left to right, top to bottom:

Top left, **Yemayá**. Her name is a contraction of the *Yoruba* words: *"Yeye omo ejá"* that means "Mother whose children are like fish." A main *Orisha* (deity) of *Santería*, her image has evolved from being the *Virgen de Regla*, to a voluptuous sexual fantasy;

Top right and bottom left, **Elegguá**, an *Orisha,* one of the most well-known deities of the Yorùbá religion. He is the protector of travelers, a deity of the roads, and the *Orisha* with the most power over fortune and misfortune. He is a spirit of chaos and trickery; her motto is "Bringing strife is my greatest joy." *Eleggua* is syncretically the Spanish *Niño de Atocha*. It needs to be placed behind the entrance door to protect those living in a house;

The practice of divination is one of the pillars of Cuban *Santería*; it is practiced by means of **caracoles** (snail shells), as well as the so called *Biague* (4 pieces of coconut); it is handled exclusively by *Babalawos*. Snails are literally the "voices of the Orishas".

23

The Start of the Madrugonazo
Monday, March 10, 1952, 2:45 AM, second of the ***Three Days in March***.

THE FIRST STEP IN BATISTA'S well conceived plan was to take control of the communications network of the Police, which was independent —and as good if not better— that the one used by the military. Salas Cañizares placed his brother José María Salas Cañizares at the *Planta de Radio Telegrafía* in the Police Headquarters Building in Chacón and Cuba Streets, and agent Sotero Delgado Méndez [94] to cover the *Sección Radio Motorizada* of the National Police in Sarabia and Cerro Streets. The Department of Communications of the Bureau of Investigations at 23rd and 32nd Streets was covered by Orlando Piedra Negueruela, who had been a policeman since 1941 and had ambitions to be Inspector General of the Bureau. Based on the loyalty of his old friends in the Police Department, Salas Cañizares established his communications headquarters at the 4th Police Station in Dragones and Lealtad Streets; by sheer coincidence it was less than a block from Albert Foster's apartment in Escobar Street.

By 1:45 AM, the control of all police communications in Havana was in the hands of Salas Cañizares. In the meantime, taking advantage of the carnival atmosphere, a group of 5 members of the police department assigned to the Presidential Pal-

---

[94] **Sotero Delgado Méndez** with **Orlando Piedra Negueruela** were accused but never convicted in 1957 —Folder 321-57, Marianao Courts— for the assassination of **Dr. Pelayo Cuervo Navarro**, hours after the failed attempt by the *Auténticos* and students from the University of Havana to take the life of Batista in an attack to the Presidential Palace in Havana.

ace were having drinks and a good time at a well known and popular *Posada* at 12 *Pajarito* Street, near Carlos III and Infanta Avenues, a love hotel with an art deco façade, imposing columns and stylish architectural details, where rooms were rented by sex-starved macho-men on an hourly basis. That left the Palace relatively understaffed at precisely the time they were most needed. The guards at *Kuquine*, however, were in full alert. Batista had cancelled all furloughs on the pretense that former President of Costa Rica, José Figueres, was to visit imminently. [95]

Batista's property looked like an impenetrable fortress. The gate at the main road was discretely manned by machine-gun toting men. The bunkers were fully staffed, as well as the house. Inside the house a nervous Batista was pacing in the library while his wife and children slept peacefully after watching *Quo Vadis*, the popular movie starring Robert Taylor and Deborah Kerr. [96]

In these last moments before the *golpe de estado* was to take place, Batista placed a large manila envelope at the top of the conference table in the library. It was addressed to his wife and children. Inside, it contained letters bidding them a fond farewell, a political testament unburdening himself of any guilt feelings for trying violently to save democracy in Cuba and some legal documents: the property deeds for the residencies in Daytona Beach and *Kuquine*, the certificate of property for a debt-free building at 5th Avenue and 42nd Street in New York, across from the New York Public Library, and his checkbook for the account at the First National City Bank in New York.

At the parking lot of *Tropicana*, two black Buicks were waiting for the right time to arrive at *Kuquine*. Inside the property, a

---

[95] At the time, however, **José Figueres** was an implacable enemy of Batista and other dictators like Perón, Trujillo, Duvalier, Rojas Pinillas, Somoza and Pérez-Jiménez.

[96] According to a reportage by Germinal Barral López (aka **Don Galaor**) the social journalist from magazine *Gente* and the newspaper *Prensa Libre*, Batista's wife, **Marta Fernández Miranda**, a consummate film buff, had correctly spotted *Sophia Loren* as an extra among a group of slaves and *Elizabeth Taylor* playing the role of a Christian prisoner, both Cameos uncredited by the producers.

third car, driven by Captain Luis Robaina, was already in position. [97] At Columbia Camp, Mayor General Ruperto Cabrera and Brigadier General Quirino Uría were in bed by 11:00 PM and Captain Dámaso Sogo had already placed his men at Posta Número 4, the main Columbia entrance.

One of the cars at the *Tropicana* parking lot began to make its way to Kuquine at 1:45 AM. It was driven by Lieutenant Angel Soto. On the back seat were Andrés Domingo y Morales del Castillo, and Justo Luis del Pozo y del Puerto. As this car arrived at the road leading to the *Kuquine* property, the car that had been inside the property was emerging into the Highway. Inside was Batista, dressed as civilian, with a beige leather jacket over grey trousers and with a black leather belt holding the holster of a .38 caliber pistol. Two other military men were in this car: Martín Díaz Tamayo, Roberto Fernández Miranda and Francisco (Silito) Tabernilla Palmero. [98] The car driven by Soto got in line after the car driven by Robaina and both waited a few seconds for the third car, which speedily joined the procession. The three Buicks began to move towards Columbia at less than 30 miles an hour. They had not yet travelled a mile when Batista asked Robaina to pull on the side of the road.

«Anything wrong, General?» asked the driver.

«No, nothing wrong, but we are changing cars here,» replied Batista, pointing to a light blue 180-D Diesel Mercedes at a gas station on the right side of the road.

«But General, they are waiting for us on this car.»

«That's precisely why we are changing cars, in case the wrong people are waiting for a black Buick!,» answered Batista.

---

[97] In late February, Batista had bought three black Buicks at **Vaillant Motors** on 25th and Hospital Streets, in Havana, to facilitate easy recognition by the men waiting for him inside the gate at Columbia Camp.

[98] **Silito Tabernilla** accompanied Batista during his *Coup* of March 10, 1952. He remained a *Batistiano* until December 31, 1958, when both he and his father fled the country. For the rest of his life, *Silito*, as well as his father General Francisco Tabernilla Dolz, have believed that Batista made a mistake on March 10th and did succumb to Castro because either he sub-estimated the rebel leader or because, deep down, he wanted to protect him.

Once they had changed cars, the convoy continued in the direction of Columbia. They travelled without incident through *La Lisa* and in front of the *La Salle de Marianao*. As they were approaching 100th Street to take 31st Avenue North, Batista ordered Robaina to go north on 100th Street.

Nervously, Robaina addressed Batista. «General, I thought we were going towards *Posta Número 6*, and it is easier to take 41st Avenue.»

«No, we are entering through *Posta Número 4*, that's where Sogo has his people. Go straight after the Rotunda with the obelisk.» It was 2:45 AM on March 10, 1952.

Few men in Columbia knew that during the quiet hours of the early morning, a small group of conspirators had made arrangements to facilitate an easy control of the camp. First Lieutenant Rodríguez Avila, for instance, had quietly moved the tanks in combat position, pointing their weapons towards the *Estado Mayor* building, the Electrical Plant, the *Escuela Superior de Guerra*, the Avenue of the Generals and the Officers Club.

At precisely the same time as Batista was entering through *Posta Número 4*, former Commandant Manuel Larrubia Paneque, who had been given access to Columbia by Dámaso Sogo, was knocking at the door of Mayor General Ruperto Cabrera. Larrubia was carrying an M42 .30 caliber submachine gun. Cabrera's wife, Arminda Burnes, was told that the General was under arrest and would be taken to Batista's mother-in-law's home. The men accompanying Larrubia ripped off all phones in Cabrera's home but did not see the unit in the master bathroom. As soon as they left, Arminda dialed 6-8996 in the Presidential Palace, warning Lieutenant Vicente León, the officer of the day, that Batista was in the midst of a *Coup d'État*.

As Arminda was spreading the word that the republic was in mortal peril, Captain Hernando Hernández and Lieutenant Victorino Díaz were placing Field Generals Quirino Uría, Otalio Sosa Llanes and Elías Orta under arrest. Batista was hoping that Uría would join the rebellion; he was taken to the second floor of Columbia's *Estado Mayor*, the building facing the *Polígono*, the main field for marches, celebrations, practices and maneuvers. The other Generals were placed under house arrest. Without consulting Uría, the outdoors PA system of the Pentágono began to repeat incessantly:

«*Batista Jefe del Gobierno, Uría Jefe del Ejercito... Batista Jefe del Gobierno, Uría Jefe del Ejercito...*»

Most military men cheered upon hearing the news. Those who had served under Uría and were acquainted with him, knew that it was a fabrication and a perverse deception.

At 8:00 AM, Miguelito Uría, the 15-year-old General's son, took a weapon from his collection, got on his bicycle and began to frantically look for his father all over Columbia. Upon arriving at the *Estado Mayor* he passed between two soldiers armed with .30 caliber submachine guns and rushed upstairs, entering the office of the Chief of Staff with the gun on his hand. Batista was on the phone and immediately jumped to his side to calm him down. «**Miguelito, your Dad is safe and doing OK,**» were his words.

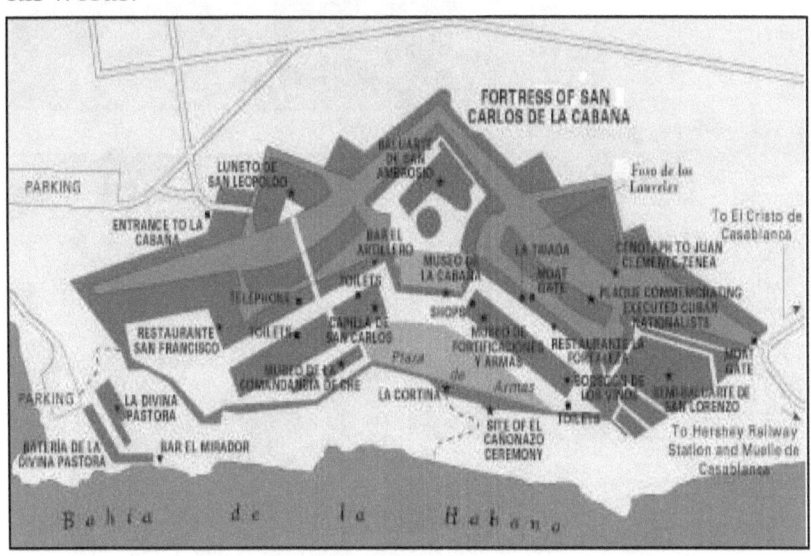

Photos, top to bottom:
Details of the *Fortress of La Cabaña*, assigned to **General Tabernilla** for take-over;
A caricature of **Genovevo** telling **Grau San Martín**: «If he had not fired me, this would not have happened,» referring to Prío's decision to retire him.

THREE DAYS IN MARCH - 149

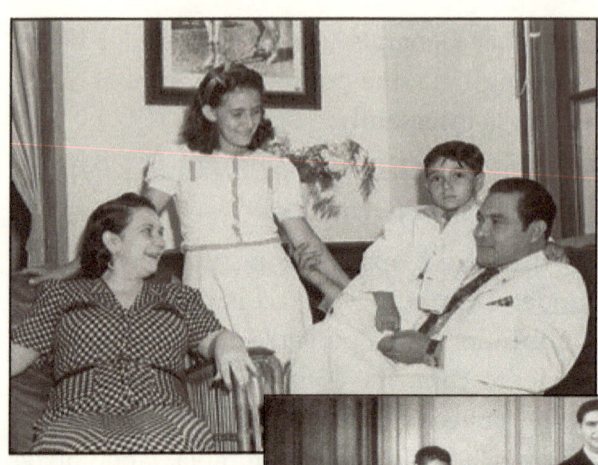

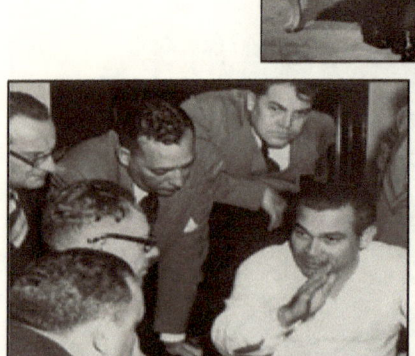

Photos, left to right, top to bottom:

Top two photos: Batista's **first family**, wife Elisa Godínez, daughter Mirta, son Rubén (Papo) with the General in 1940. They were divorced in 1944;

Batista's **second family**: standing, sons Roberto and Jorge, sitting, the General, sons Carlos, Fulgencio Jr., baby Marta María and wife Marta Fernández Miranda in 1953;

Bottom two photos: Batista in 1952 with **Justo Luis del Pozo**, future Mayor of Havana, (with thick glasses) and **Pablo Carrera Jústiz** (leaning on a chair in the back);

Batista in 1952 with **Richard Nixon** and **Andrés Domingo y Morales del Castillo**, future Secretary of the Presidency. Justo Luis del Pozo and Morales del Castillo were in the car with Batista when he entered *Columbia Camp* on March 10, 1952.

HOW REVOLUTIONS OCCUR IN CUBA: A *COUP D'ÉTAT*—AND BUSINESS AS USUAL.

BEFORE THE COUP D'ÉTAT BY WHICH HE WAS DEPOSED: DR. CARLOS PRIO SOCARRAS (LEFT), ELECTED CUBAN PRESIDENT IN 1948, IN THE PALACE WITH UNIVERSITY STUDENTS.

SURROUNDED BY SUPPORTERS: DR. CARLOS PRIO SOCARRAS (CENTRE, FACING CAMERA) BEFORE HE FLED FROM THE PRESIDENTIAL PALACE.

AT A RALLY OF HIS SUPPORTERS NEAR CAMP COLUMBIA: GENERAL FULGENCIO BATISTÁ (SEATED AT THE TABLE, CENTRE, BETWEEN TWO WOMEN), THE EX-PRESIDENT WHO SEIZED POWER ON MARCH 10.

CUBA'S EX-DICTATOR, WHO SEIZED POWER BY A SUCCESSFUL COUP D'ÉTAT AT THE REQUEST OF A MILITARY JUNTA: GENERAL FULGENCIO BATISTA WITH A GROUP OF CUBAN SOLDIERS.

THE REVOLUTION IN PROGRESS ON MARCH 10: A TANK AND A LORRY WHICH CONTAINED ARMED TROOPS, OUTSIDE THE PRESIDENTIAL PALACE, HAVANA.

RELEASED AFTER ARREST DURING THE REVOLT: DR. RAMON GRAU SAN MARTIN, PRESIDENT FROM SEPT. 1933 TO JAN. 1934; AND FROM OCT. 1944 TO JUNE 1948.

The revolution in Cuba by which General Fulgencio Batistá, a former dictator, and President from 1940 to 1944, seized power on March 10, was carried out at lightning speed, with the loss of only two lives; and is reported only to have interrupted business in the island for one day. General Batistá, supported by the Army, seized command at Camp Columbia, Army Headquarters, early on March 10, and broadcast to the nation. One of his supporters took over Police H.Q., and tanks and lorry-loads of armed troops converged on the Presidential Palace, in Havana. Dr. Prio Socarras, President since 1948, took refuge in the Mexican Embassy, and on March 13 flew to Mexico. On arrival there he stated that he has not resigned, but has left Cuba "under pressure." On March 10, General Batistá selected the members of his new Cabinet and they were sworn in on March 11. No provisional President was appointed and General Batistá is directing the Government as Prime Minister. He states that his Government is to remain in power "so long as was necessary to establish normal conditions and to arrange for honest general elections." The reason for the revolt is stated to have been "because people could not put up with the existing state of affairs."

The *Illustrated London News*, March 22, 1952

24

March 10 outside Columbia Camp
Monday, March 10, 1952, 5:30 AM, second of the *Three Days in March*.

NOT KNOWING TO WHAT EXTENT the military outside Havana were loyal to him, Batista ordered his men to close and disconnect the Communications facilities on Pavilion 14 at Columbia Camp. From 2:30 AM on, all incoming and outgoing messages were to be transmitted through the Radio-Telegraphy facilities of the National Police, already under the command of Rafael Salas Cañizares.

The first such message was directed to *Regimiento Número 7, Máximo Gómez,* at *La Cabaña* fortress. It was answered by Tabernilla's men.

«All is fine here. We have assumed complete control of *La Cabaña* under cheers and full support of the entire garrison. There was absolutely no resistance.»

Other calls went to *Regimiento Número 1, Antonio Maceo,* at the Moncada Barracks in Santiago de Cuba; *Regimiento Número 2, Ignacio Agramonte,* in Camagüey; *Regimiento Número 3, Leoncio Vidal,* in Las Villas; *Regimiento Número 4, Domingo Goicuría,* in Matanzas; *Regimiento Número 5, Juan Rius Rivera* in Pinar del Rio and *Regimiento Número 8, Calixto García,* based in Holguín, in the Northern part of Oriente. Only in Matanzas and Santiago de Cuba [99] the troops were proclaiming their loyalty to the con-

---

[99] At the Antonio Maceo Regiment in Oriente its leader, **Colonel Manuel Alvarez Margolles**, was loyal to President Prío until he was made prisoner by a lowly First Lieutenant, **Fermín Cowley Gallegos**, years later known as the *Chacal de Holguín*.

stitutional government of Carlos Prío.

Everywhere else was Batista's territory. The largest and most important unit of land-based troops in the Cuban Army, with modern weaponry and great mobility, was the Infantry Division *Alejandro Rodríguez*, based at Columbia; it was followed by Artillery Regiment Número 7, *Máximo Gómez*, at *La Cabaña* and Tank Regiment Número 9, *Adolfo del Castillo* based at the Managua Military Camp. They were all loyal to Batista.

Without any doubts, the *cuartelazo* of March 10, 1952, was proof of an impeccable organizational craftsmanship. Key military installations in Havana fell easily and bloodlessly in the hands of the conspirators. After the military control of the capital was assured, the rest of the provinces fell one by one. Garrison commanders were preventably arrested until their loyalty was assured; troops were stirred up and prod into action after being assembled to listen to the promises and flag-waving messages of Batista, "the man". His 8-point strategy had been:

1. Secure the loyalty of soldiers, police, naval units, *guardia rurales* and politicians in the provinces by presenting the *Columbia* take over in Havana as a *fait accompli*.
2. Absolutely refuse entrance to anyone at Columbia, *La Cabaña* and *La Punta*, (headquarters of the naval forces).
3. Bring all naval units to their normal bases, and give them the control of custom houses and ports.
4. Get all available police cars to patrol the cities in silence and all military equipment to remain inside their *cuarteles*.
5. Temporarily transfer all public services (banks, public transportation, phone and telegraph, water), into the hands of the military, including Havana's Electrical Plant at *Tallapiedra*.
6. Decree a total black-out of news and have the radio and TV stations continue their broadcasts with regular, normal schedules.
7. Occupy Havana's *Central Telefónica* (Aguila and Dragones Streets); monitor all telephone conversations, particularly those emanating from potential supporters of President Prío.

(Holguín's Jackal). When the call came from Columbia, Cowley personally answered it saying «This Regiment will unconditionally follow the orders of General Batista.»

8. Occupy the headquarters and detain the leaders of the Worker's Union (*CTC*); surround the University of Havana (without making any detentions) to prevent excessive congregation of students; occupy the offices of the *PSP* (Communist Party).

It could not have been better conceived by Curzio Malaparte in his 1930 *Tecnica del colpo di* Stato (Coup d'État: the technique of revolution). [100]

The only unsolved issue at 4:00 AM on March 10, 1952, was what to do with Matanzas.

At 4:30 AM, Prío arrived at the Presidential Palace with his wife and his brothers Paco and Antonio, his aide Rafael Izquierdo, Segundo Curti and Félix Lancís, his Ministers of the Interior and Education. Not knowing the level of loyalty of the heads of the *regimientos*, he made a call to Colonel Eduardo Martín Elena, the man he thought would be most likely to be loyal to him.

«Eduardo,» asked the President. «What's your position with regard to the happenings of this morning in Columbia?»

Without vacillation Elena responded,

«I will remain in this post for as long as I can fulfill my obligations and protect the Constitution and the laws of the Republic. I will not follow any orders coming from anywhere except from you as President of Cuba.» [101]

Following this call, Martín Elena assembled all officers in his Regimiento and asked them if they should formulate a plan to resist the *Coup d'État* with their arms. He had already assembled the troops to discuss the possibility of a siege of the Regiment by Batista forces. The troops responded with patriotic and effusive rallying cries. At the officers' assembly, however,

---

[100] For **Malaparte**, the essential differences between the concept of **Coup d'État** with those of civil war or revolution were the use of surprise and a low relative duration of operations, limiting any armed confrontation to minimum size and intensity.

[101] Half an hour earlier **Martín Elena** had answered a call from Columbia and had spoken personally with Batista. He gave the General the same answer he gave Prío. Batista was furious and exploded with anger: «We are the law. Follow my orders or resign your position!»

only one of them responded positively; the others sat in a non-committed silence. Elena decided to call Columbia to express his opposition to the *Coup*. Not having the regular military communications system, he dialed 20-7091 on the phone, the direct line of the Chief of Staff. Colonel Eulogio Cantillo came to the phone:

> «I would have never suspected that you were part of this conspiracy,» were the words of Martín Elena.
> Cantillo answered: «My thinking was similar to yours but they have persuaded me to be a part of this.»
> «I am sorry you were so easily converted to treason.»
> «Look... *Columbia* and *La Cabaña* are on Batista's side. If you do not join you will be very lonely.»
> «I'll never be lonely with dignity on my side.»
> «Help yourself,» were Cantillo's last words. To which Martín Elena responded «Take a chance with history.» [102]

For a few hours Colonel Martín Elena held the Goicuría barracks loyal to the Prío government. Word quickly spread out in the city. Some families came out of their houses and wept inconsolably in their doorways. Others began to converge at *Parque de la Libertad* from all directions. Others went inside the Cathedral of *San Carlos Borromeo*, the *Casino Español* or the *Café del Louvre*. At the regimental headquarters led by Martín Elena, many youngsters, workers, clerks, professionals, students, *Auténticos* and *Ortodoxos*, were asking for weapons to defend the Prío government and the 1940 Constitution. Many were proposing a general strike.

Despite their numbers and their willingness to fight, Batista was evidently succeeding in seizing the government. People were asking where was Prío, where were Felipe Pazos, Justo Carrillo, Portell Vilá, Salvador Massip and other of the so called

---

[102] **Martín Elena** resigned his position in the Cuban Army and went into exile. His prestige remained forever untainted on the side of the Republic. Two years after the collapse of the republic in 1959, he would be appointed by Tony Varona, from the Frente Revolucionario Democrático (FRD), as military chief for the Bay of Pigs invasion; he was objected because of his age by Manuel Artime's followers, who wanted a much younger leader and had already chosen 31-year old José Pérez San Román, a former Batista loyalist who was also in exile. Martín Elena never betrayed his loyalty to Cuba.

generación de los puros (young idealistic cadets) that opposed corruption, gangsterism, deal-making and even politicking? The soldiers from Goicuría could not resign themselves to be under Batista. He was, after all, the man who had ordered the assassination of Antonio Guiteras, the 1933 revolutionary, founder and leader of *Joven Cuba*, as well as a member of one of the most distinguished families of Matanzas. The only concrete things the youngsters loyal to Prío could accomplish were to strike four textile factories: *La Rayonera*, in Matanzas, Textilera *Ariguanabo*, near Bauta, west of the city of Havana, *Cuban Cordage*, in Guanajay, Pinar del Rio and the *Matanzas Jarcia*, in Matanzas. Close to 30,000 workers went on strike. There were numerous arrests. Following its anticipated plan, the textile factories were placed in the hands of the military. The strongest massive support for the 1940 Constitution and the government of Carlos Prío was demolished in less than a week.

Photos, top to bottom,
left to right:
The precautions taken by Batista before his March 10 *Coup d'État*:

All **telphones**intervened; Havana's **electrical plant** at *Talla Piedra* militarized; all **Communist leaders** detained; all **military fortresses** under lock and key.

Photos, left to right, top to bottom:

Segundo Curti, Minister of the Interior with Grau and Minister of Defense for Prío, went into exile in 1951 and returned to Cuba in 1959, where he died in 2000;

Félix Lancís, known as *El Chino*, Prime Minister in the Grau government. He stayed in Cuba after the revolution of 1959;

Two views of Matanzas, the only hope Of Carlos Prío to resist: the **Casino Español** and the **Parque de la Libertad**;

Ffinally, the book that Batista could have written and would have exceeded the fame and fortune of its author, **Curzio Malaparte**.

25

The Whereabouts of Prío during the Coup d'État
Monday, March 10, 1952, 8:00 AM, second of the **Three Days in March**.

CARLOS PRIO SOCARRAS NEVER liked spending the entire day at the Presidential Palace in Havana.

«The day is full of *políticos* asking for favors, *guatacas* (sycophants) hoping to be my favorite bootlickers, long meetings with government executives jockeying for their points of view and seeking from me a favorable decision, *bona-fide* organizations seeking the proceeds of one lottery drawing [103] and trusted party loyals seeking a *botella* (sinecure),»

Prío had declared to the newspaper *Prensa Libre* on one occasion that he would rather be at *La Chata*, his country property in Arroyo Naranjo, South of Havana than in *Palacio*; it was at *La Chata* where he spent most weekends.

Prío knew of several efforts to undo his government since 1950, but felt unexplainably secure in his elected position. He dismissed rumors that a group of young officers from the *Escuela Superior de Guerra* (War College), all under prodding by their teachers Roberto Agramonte, Herminio Portell Vilá and Rafael García Bárcena, had asked Eduardo Chibás to lead a *Coup d'État*. At the time, Chibás was profoundly depressed for his defeat in the 1948 elections; he did not take the offer seriously but he didn't rebuff it. He later called Prío and de-

---

[103] Saturday's **lottery drawings** were sinister sources of corruption in Cuba. What Had started as a good public policy idea —bringing a one-time substantial funding to an organization of merit— developed into an easy way to steal from a non-budgeted income stream easy to keep outside the books.

nounced Jorge García Tuñón as the leader of the incipient revolt. Prío took no action. He was sure the high command of the armed forces would not support such violation of the 1940 Constitution.

Without been asked by the president, the *Servicio de Inteligencia Militar (SIM)* began to track Batista's movements and intercepted his telephone communications. They knew every movement of Batista and recommended to Prío that the Chiefs of Regiments 5, 6 and 7 make a critical effort to protect access to the areas under their command, barring entry to retired military officers and all civilians. Prío thought it was an exaggerated precaution that could offend some of his followers and did not consider the recommendations.

Commandant Jorge Agostini, Chief of the Secret Service Police force at the Presidential Palace, approached Carlos Prío on February 21 and brought him a formal written report about the imminent possibility of a *Coup d'État*. Agostini included in his report the names of civilians his men had been following: Colacho Pérez, Ramón Hermida and Pablo Carrera Jústiz, and assured the president they were involved in the conspiracy. The president dismissed him saying «You are very nervous, Jorge. Go and try some shooting practice to calm yourself.»

On January 9, Mario Kuchilán, [104] in his column *Babel* in the newspaper *Prensa Libre* and in his *Canal 2* TV daily program, presented "proofs" that a conspiracy within the army was about to explode:

«We have just received a report verified through a second channel, that a conspiracy is brewing between army officers and former military men in plain clothes, and that the date to act would be May 1st.»

---

[104] **Mario Kuchilán** (1910-1983) was a very popular columnist in the 1950s, considered as Cuba's Walter Winchell. He started his TV program saying «Good morning my friends and those of you who are not.» and ended them with «Until next time, God willing and if the devil does not interfere.» *Babel*, his *Prensa Libre* column, used *Terencio's* motto «Nothing human is foreign to me.» After March 10, 1952, he was kidnapped and beaten by Batista's henchmen wanting to know Aureliano Sánchez Arango's location. After 1959 he joined the revolution and wrote for *Verde Olivo*. He died an active supporter of the Communist regime in Cuba.

Prío dismissed the news as unfounded. [105]

At 4:00 AM on March 10, however, Prío had to pay attention. Vicente León, military chief of Palacio in 1952, had called him at *La Chata*, his country home.

According to his recollection after the *golpe*, León told Prío:

«The young officers that were obsessed with the idea of "saving the republic," have continued their conspirational meetings and found a leader, Fulgencio Batista; he is already inside Columbia.»

«Why Batista?,» asked Prío. [106]

Very harshly, León responded:

«Batista is popular inside the armed forces; he claims he seeks glory and not money; he has good relations with the US and will likely be easily recognized by the American government; as a military man, *Auténticos* and *Ortodoxos* know he can control the gangs.»

The day before, March 9, 1952, Prío enjoyed the carnivals at the *Paseo del Malecón* in Havana from a borrowed white Oldsmobile Convertible, property of Ambar Motors, the GM dealer at 23rd Street and Infanta Avenue. His wife Mary and her two small girls were with him. His brother Antonio and Prío's best friend and frequent companion Segundo Curti, with their wives, were following on an identical car.

Prío retired to *La Chata* at 8:00 PM, while Antonio decided to have some fun at *Sans Souci* night club (Km 15 of the Arroyo

---

[105] Years later, in 1955, **Kuchilán** was asked why Prío had ignored so many signals that Batista was ready to produce a *Coup d'État*. His answer was: «After the defeat of his brother Antonio Prío as a candidate for Havana's mayor, Prío came to the conclusion that the *Auténticos* were going to lose the elections in 1952. The *Ortodoxos* had publicly made a commitment to take Prío to court and confiscate his presumably embezzled properties. Under those conditions Prío was willing to allow Batista to take over. Since Batista did not have the votes to win an election, Prío reached the conclusion that the only way to prevent Roberto Agramonte, the *Ortodoxo* candidate, to be president was to allow Batista to overthrow the *Auténtico* government.»

Regardless of Kuchilán's speculations, Prío was apparently fed up with government by 1952. His friends were saying that the insults, the attacks, the disorder, the unemployment, the stagnant economy and his inability to control the mobsters —several of which were *Auténtico* candidates for the 1952 election— had done him in.

[106] At the time, other unconfirmed and deceitful rumors had it that Prío and Batista had made a secret pact to get **Carlos Hevia**, the *Auténtico* candidate, elected and thus prevent the *Ortodoxos* (tilded as radical leftists) to win the presidency. Batista was to receive a serious amount of money for his support. Neither Prío nor Batista ever commented —one way or another— on this rumor, which was decidedly untrue.

Arenas road) and Segundo Curti went for dinner at *Rancho Luna* restaurant in Wajay, also in Havana. Curti was looking forward to Prío's announcement of his new Cabinet —where Curti was to be Prime Minister— on Monday, March 10th. Mary Tarrero, Prío's wife, was also looking forward to the March 10 concert of the XXVII season of the *Orquesta Filarmónica de la Habana* —she was honorary President— at the Auditorium Theater. The program included Rachmaninoff's Concerto No. 3 and Strauss' Don Quixote. Some of the best names of Havana's intelligentsia were expected to attend: the Le Riverends, the Miró Cardonas, the Inkláns, the Sicres, the Chediaks, the Agostinis, the Kourís, the Suárez de Bustamante and the Colls. As we know, none of that came to pass.

At 3:45 AM, Arminda Burnes had called Lieutenant Colonel Vicente León in Palacio. At 4:00 AM Prío was awakened with the news that Ruperto Cabrera, Quirino Uría and Otilio Soca Llanes were under custody and he probably was no longer President of Cuba. The whereabouts of Eulogio Cantillo were not known because Captain Pilar García, in charge of arresting Cantillo, was so clumsy that had let him escape though a window of his house; Cantillo, commandant of the Aviation force, took refuge at his own Headquarters in Columbia. As we already know (see page 155) he would join the conspiracy a few hours later.

Once Prío learned of the situation in Columbia, he gave orders to Vicente León and his men in Palacio to shoot at any group of military men trying to enter. The only group attempting to enter and detained by León was one led by the President's dentist, Dr. Juan Mendive, who, having never been a conspirator, showed up at 4:20 AM with half a dozen drunk sailors he had picked up at the end of the show at *Palermo Club* in Amistad and San Miguel Streets. [107]

---

[107] An unconfirmed rumor had it that another visitor to *Palacio* in those wee hours of the morning was a man who years later would be a spokesman for Batista, every day at noon time, hosting a program called "Por Cuba" at CMQ TV: **Otto Meruelo**, a member of a distinguished Cienfuegos family and a fierce Batista supporter. See page 171.

At 4:30 AM Prío arrived at Palacio. The first thing he heard was gunfire from a *perseguidora* (police car) attempting to enter the building through the Monserrate Street entrance. Two men from the president's escort fought the men in the car with gunfire from a Thompson; two assailants were killed, Lieutenant Julián Negret and patrolman Guillermo Escanaverino; an escort resulted killed from ricochet fire, Sergeant Rosendo Hernández while Sergeant Sócrates Alvarez was wounded. What was later proclaimed as a bloodless *Coup* had already claimed the first casualties. Once the gunfight ended, Alvaro Barba, Danilo Baeza and two dozen members of *Federación Estudiantil Universitaria (FEU)* arrived, asking for weapons with which to make a stand at the University of Havana. A picture was taken as they surrounded Prío. A promise was made to retrieve arms from the *Cuartel de San Ambrosio* and transport them to the Law School building on the *Colina Universitaria*. As the students waited to receive orders and strategies to resist the military, word came that *Cuartel San Ambrosio* was already in the hands of Tabernilla's men who had extended their territory from *La Cabaña* to the Railroad Terminal, the Esso refinery and the *Cuartel San Ambrosio*; they had joined forces with troops at Atarés Castle and had total control of the Southern and Eastern sides of Havana harbor. Prío decided to leave Palacio but he did not know where to go.

Photos, left to right:
Pablo Carrera Jústiz with **Francisco Tabernilla Dolz**; **Colacho Pérez**, one of the March 10 conspirators; **Alvaro Barba**, FEU's president in 1952.

(NY8-Mar.10)SCENE OF CUBAN REVOLUTIONARY VIOLENCE-The slaying of two guards today in front of Havana's Presidential Palace, heralded the outbreak of a Cuban revolution. Cuba's oldtime strong man Fulgencio Batista,launched the revolt with support of the army. President Socarras left the palace this morning amid rumors that he was under arrest after calling upon all Cubans to resist. (APWirephoto)(See Wire Story)(jdc21110fls) 1952

Photos, top to bottom:

Havana's Presidential Palace, early in the morning, surrounded with troops loyal to Batista on March 10, 1952, as reported by the *Associated Press*;

Students from The University of Havana meeting with President Prío at the Presidential Palace on the morning of March 10, 1952. They had come to request weapons with which to fight for the republic. Unfortunately, all weapon depots in Havana were already taken by Batista's forces.

26

Prío Could not get Support from his Followers
Monday, March 10, 1952, 8:45 AM, second of the *Three Days in March*.

A TWO-TONE BLUE 1950 BUICK was running at high speed along the *Carretera Central*, the highway that connected Havana with the city of Matanzas along a route that would take it through *el Cotorro*, San José de las Lajas, Catalina de Güines Madruga and Ceiba Mocha. Three men were inside the car: Dieguito Vicente Tejera y Rescalvo, 40, who had replaced Luis Pérez Espinós as Minister of Education in 1945 (he was the oldest son of a distinguished jurist of the same name); Sergio Mejías Pérez, 43, *matancero* like Tejera, who had presided the *Cámara de Representantes* as an *Auténtico* member (see page 230), and a third man, dressed in a sports outfit and half-covering his face with a large *sombrero guajiro*: Dr. Carlos Prío Socarrás, 49, President of Cuba in the process of being deposed. [108]

Just before the students visited President Prío at the Presidential Palace, the president had made two phone calls. The first went to *La Cabaña*, asking for General Eugenio Velázquez,

---

[108] Minutes before, on the inside patio of the Presidential Palace, Prío had improvised a note to Cuba's national media. The note was written leaning on the fender of his own car, on a pad of blue lined paper. In the note he said:

«The army general staff has been taken over by former military officers following instructions from General Batista. Army commanders in the provinces are maintaining their loyalty to the legitimate constitutional government. People should not overlook what it means to the republic to break the constitutional order at a time when all parties are preparing for an electoral consultation. I trust people will keep their oath of allegiance to the republic. At this time, I ask workers, students, farmers, industrialists, in a word, all Cubans, to withstand this treacherous attack. I trust all of you.»

the chief of the garrison.[109] Prío told him that he was on his way there and to wait for him. Velázquez reply was «Look Mr. Prío, do not come now. I will let you know the right time.» Minutes later, Velázquez's wife called and told the president that Velázquez was under custody and Tabernilla had seized control of the garrison. Prío hung up the phone visibly upset.

The second call went to Colonel Manuel Alvarez Margolles, head of the Regimiento Maceo in Oriente province. Prío was very tense and agitated but this time his face showed a ray of hope.

Alvarez Margolles answer to Prío's request for news was:

«We are not supporting this movement by Batista. We are loyal to the constitutional government. Come here, we have many patriotic men and abundant mountains where we could resist.»

Prío was pleased. The troops in Palacio had taken several military men prisoners; these renegades had attempted to take over the President's house. Even though he knew he had no means to get to Santiago de Cuba, Prío was now full of optimism after the words by Alvarez Margolles. It was then that Prío received Alvaro Barba and the FEU delegation. He became emotional, feeling the same sensations he had felt in 1933 when he had led the FEU students to topple Machado.

After the news about Tabernilla's control of *Cuartel San Ambrosio* was made known, Prío advised the students that *Palacio* was no longer safe and that he was going to search for a place where he could make a stand against the *Coup*. He got on his car as the students moved to the protected territory of the University of Havana. [110] In spite of Colonel Velázquez words, he decided to go to Matanzas. By noon time, Batista's forces had gained control of the Presidential Palace.

---

[109] **Velázquez** was a Sergeant in 1933 and had joined Batista during the September 4 upheaval. He was, nevertheless, an officer faithful to constitutional life and remained loyal to Prío in 1952. His son, a Lieutenant in the 1958 army, was shot by a Castro firing squad in 1959 at *La Cabaña*, the same garrison his father had commanded.

[110] The **autonomy** of the University of Havana was endorsed in Article 53 of the 1940 Constitution, which stated: "The University of Havana is autonomous (outside the jurisdiction of the armed forces of Cuba) and shall be governed in accordance with its own Statutes and Laws."

Prío had decided to appoint Martín Elena as Chief of the Armed Forces; he felt it was important to have him at his side. As his Buick sped towards Matanzas, it had to get off the road on several occasions due to the presence of military patrols. The tension in the car could be felt. Diego Tejera advised Prío to shave his moustache, which was a telltale sign of his identity. He had done that in 1933 but now he refused on the grounds that it was undignified and would keep him from connecting emotionally with the Matanzas troops.

Albert Foster had asked his wife Ruby Alonso to stay home and not report for work at the Presidential Palace. He tried unsuccessfully to get Prío on the phone during the entire morning. He finally gave up and rushed to the US Embassy to bring the Ambassador up to date.

That morning, most stores in Havana failed to open their doors because the uncertainty created by the heavy and fast moving traffic of military vehicles in almost every neighborhood. Schools sent the students home. School buses did not attempt to leave their garages. Students from the *Institutos* (Secondary Schools) began to concentrate at the University by 10:00 AM. The mood was pessimistic and with tones of outrage and hopelessness. The store at 621 Neptuno Street remained open but empty in the morning. None of the people normally attending the *tertulias* showed up in the afternoon. The Zimmerman store never opened and no one knew his whereabouts. Other store owners in the area met informally in Neptuno street trying to get news from each other. Otto Meruelo found his way inside Columbia. The streets were deserted, as if everybody had died that day.

Carlos Prío, on his way to Matanzas, asked Sergeant Alvaro Suárez, his chauffeur, to stop at the town of Jamaica, near the quarries of the same name and a cement factory, just before San José de las Lajas, to make a phone call. He had agreed to wait there for Tony Varona, who was on his way to Las Villas to try to appeal to the troops. Prío had been in the town of Jamaica many times and had always purchased two dozen of the famous *panqués* to take to Mary and the girls, as well as to all his close employees and visiting politicians in Palacio. [111] This time he was paying no attention to the delicious pastry and, without leaving the car, asked Sergio Mejías to make a phone call.

The call went through to the *Cuartel Goicuría* in Matanzas. Someone answered the phone shouting «Viva la revolución del 33! Viva Batista!» Mejías hung up the phone with tears in his eyes. He walked slowly to the waiting car and gave the bad news to President Prío. «Goicuría has fallen to Batista. Leopoldo Pérez Coujil has taken over from Martín Elena.» [112]

Tony Varona showed up a few minutes later in front of José María Cruz' bakery. He spoke very briefly with the president, not wishing to call attention to his car; he then continued his journey to *Las Villas*.

A second phone call was made by Mejías at the request of Prío. This time the call went to Herminio Portell Villá, to his private home at 9th Street in *el Vedado*. Portell was receiving calls from his military students across the entire island and was probably better informed of the situation than any radio station or even the police radio network under Salas Cañizares control. He had sour and disappointing news for Carlos Prío.

«Batista has completed the encirclement of all military bases in the island,» were Portell's words to Mejías.

---

[111] The genuine and lawfully begotten **Panqués de Jamaica** were easily identified by the words "*José María Cruz, Panqué Legítimo, Jamaica*"; they sported a proud rooster on the greasy flat paper upon which they rested. They were as famous and desirable as Proust's Madeleines but heavier, bulkier and more serious and buttery. They could not be confused with earthly mundane muffins; the smooth dome with which they were topped was not intended to be removed in one piece and eaten first; they were designed to be osculated-at (in a kiss-like fashion) all around its perimeter until the top of the dome would be isolated and could be removed with a swift and sweet bite. Years later they would be available in Miami, four at a time, moist, fresh and as delicious. One of many good cultural exports of a dying country.

[112] There was no attempt to resist in Matanzas after Martín Elena found out the news from other military installations. He turned over the garrison to Batista followers after his troops were seduced by promises of promotions and benefits. No organized civilian group was ready to confront the *Coup* with violence although there were strikes and public denunciations. Students from the *Instituto de Matanzas*, for instance, used the public address system of the school to denounce the *Coup* for most of the day on March 10th. The army in Matanzas, now loyal to Batista, encircled the *Parque de la Libertad* at noon time and dispersed the protesting students.

«Every *regimiento* is in his hands, every radio station, telephone and telegraphic communications, the police stations, the Presidential Palace and the *Capitolio*. The only way to stop him now would cause a blood bath in Cuba. I advise the president to seek refuge at a foreign embassy. I spoke an hour ago with people in Mary's escort and they will seek refuge in the Mexican embassy. I understand the president and the first lady had agreed on that decision before they parted company this morning.»

At that time, two soldiers approached Prío's car and asked why they had been there for so long. Dieguito reacted very fast:

«*Es que traigo al viejo enfermo y lo llevo para Matanzas a ver un médico.*» (My old man is sick and I am taking him to see a doctor in Matanzas).

Prío was covering his mouth with his handkerchief and rocking slightly up and down. As one of the soldiers looked like he was about to ask: Why Matanzas if Havana is closer and has more hospitals?, Dieguito jumped:

«*Es que el Viejo es de Matanzas!*» The soldiers left.

The urgency now was to try to intercept Tony Varona on his trip to Las Villas. After running frantically a few kilometers past Catalina de Güines, [113] they decided that it was too late to reach Varona; the Buick turned around and went back in the direction of Havana. They stopped at the home of Armando García Sifredo in *Guanabo* Beach. From there he tried to call the Mexican embassy to talk to Mary, his wife, and to inquire about his two daughters. Inside the embassy, Rubén de León, Segundo Curti, Ricardo Artigas and Aureliano Sánchez Arango had already found refuge. All the phones in the embassy were busy with their calls to their families and political supporters. Not knowing if Mary and the girls were already there, Prío gave his last orders to the chauffeur: to move to the Mexican embassy at 307 Kholy Avenue in *El Vedado*. No one in the car spoke a word until they got to the embassy.

---

[113] One other place had been considered for the Prío-Varona rendezvous, the *Cafetería El Congo*, in *Catalina de Güines*, an eatery famous for preparing the best *butifarras* (sausages) in Cuba. At the last minute *El Congo* was discarded because the exposure of its parking area and the uncertainty of its being open that early in the day.

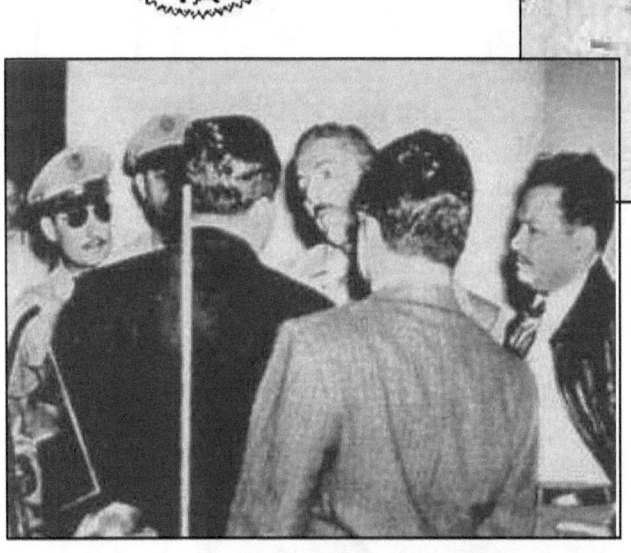

Photos, top to bottom, left to right:
Carlos Prío's family a few days before the March 10, 1952 Coup: Marian, President Prío, Maria Elena and Mary Tarrero de Prío; the logo of the **Panqués de Jamaica**; **Leopoldo Pérez Coujil**, the man who on March 10th replaced Martín Elena as the commandant of the Matanzas barracks; a photo of **President Prío** conferring with his followers in Palacio before leaving for Matanzas.

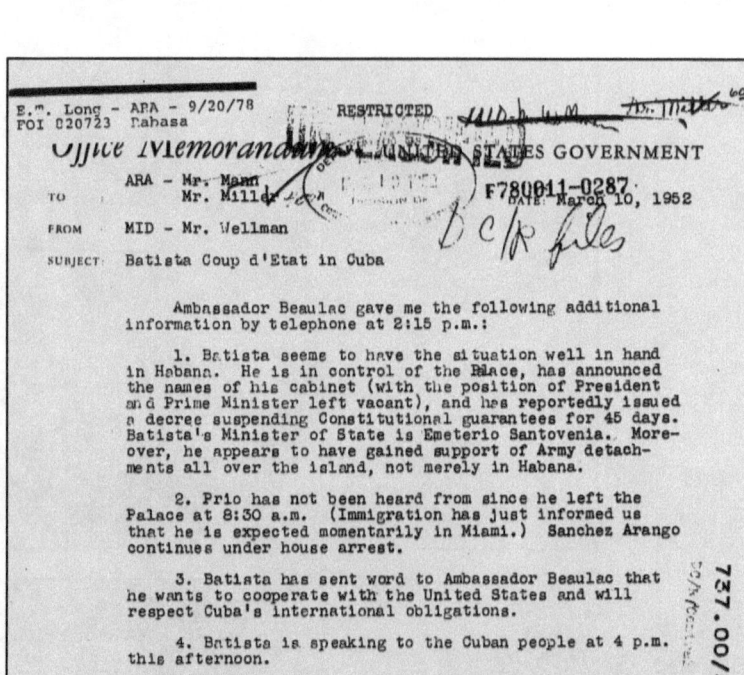

Photos, left to right:
Generals Ruperto Cabrera and **Quirino Uría.** In 1952 the CIA and the US Embassy in Havana speculated that had Uría been Chief of the Cuban Army in 1952, Batista's *Coup d'État* would have been very unlikely to succeed.

Photos, top to bottom, left to right:

March 11, 1952: **Carlos Prío** sitting glumly alone in the Mexican Embassy in Havana, where he sought refuge when Batista forces won control of Cuba;

Armando García Sifredo, loyal anti-Communist *Auténtico*, youngest Senator during Grau's government. In exile in Miami in 1959, with Alberto Rodríguez and Ernesto Montaner, he founded the newspaper **Patria**;

Otto Meruelo, loyal anti-Communist *Batistiano*. He was sentenced to 30 years in 1959;

Aureliano Sánchez Arango, served as Minister of Education and Foreign Minister in the Prío government. He died of a heart attack in Miami in 1976.

27

All Resistance to the Coup d'État Collapses
Monday, March 10, 1952, 5:45 PM, second of the ***Three Days in March***.

KNOWING THAT PRÍO WAS at García Sifredo's house in Guanabo, Fulgencio Batista personally dialed 90-1179 and called the house from the office of the Chief of the Army at the second floor of the Estado Mayor building at Columbia Camp. García Sifredo's wife Hilda answered the phone and Batista told her he wanted to talk to García Sifredo.

«Do you still have President Prío at your house?» asked the General.

«You know very well that I do,» was García Sifredo's answer.

«Tell Prío that he will have all sorts of freedom and security in Cuba. He will not be harassed, he will not be exposed to any hostility, I will personally vouch for his family security and his own; he should not harbor any fears.»

«I am sure the President will be grateful for your call,» was García Sifredo's polite answer. [114]

Batista then asked, «On a personal level, do you understand why we had to take the government to prevent a continuation of this *Auténtico* era of corruption, mobster control and Communist threats?»

García Sifredo remained in silence for a few seconds and furiously hung up the phone without bidding Batista goodbye.

---

[114] Years later, enemies of Prío created the improbable tale that Prío had asked Batista to return to him a large manila envelope that was inadvertently left behind on his desk. In the story, Batista went personally to Prío's desk after he reached the Presidential Palace on March 11th and looked for the envelope. He found it. It was not sealed. Batista presumably opened it and found inside 400 US $1000 dollar bills. The story ends saying that Batista sealed the envelope and sent it to Prío, who by now was in Mexico City.

He transmitted the General's message to Prío, however, knowing what Prío's reaction would be.

«I am the Constitutional President of Cuba and will not accept any deals from the hand of a man that has violated the law in such blatant and shameless way.»

Dieguito Vicente Tejera and Sergio Mejías stayed at García Sifredo's house while Alvaro Suárez, Prío's chauffeur, took the deposed president through the streets of Havana towards the Mexican embassy. Once more, now by himself, Prío remained silent and meditative.

At the Mexican embassy, Ambassador Benito Coquet received Prío at the gate to the embassy. The deposed president was tired, unshaven, wearing the same shirt, trousers and jacket he had in the early morning when he arrived at the Presidential Palace. His characteristic nervous twitch was exacerbated by the tensions of the moment. He briefly talked to the ambassador about the events of the day and was shown to the elegant reception room of the embassy. Mary and the girls were already at the embassy, resting inside a guest suite on the second floor. Prío was anxious to see them but lacked the essential energy; he collapsed on a chair, in front of one of several Sèvres bases adorning the room. He closed his eyes briefly and then stared into the vacuum. Not since 1933 he had felt so lonely or had people seen in him such a prolonged, self-absorbed mood. He knew he had to contain his tears and not show his despondency in front of Mary or the girls.

In silence, he began to utter untruths to himself:

«I am pleased with the Cuban Army. The *Coup* was an action by low level officers, below the rank of *Capitán*, who joined Batista unreservedly. The *Coup* was executed with very few men. I had Batista watched flawlessly by men of my absolute confidence. I never wanted to use regular members of the armed forces for that task. Leopoldo López Coujil, the Chief of the Bureau of Investigations of the Army betrayed me, joining Batista at the last moment. If were not for him, Batista would be in jail right now.»

His mumblings were interrupted by a maid who brought a glass of *Courvoisier L'Essence de Courvoisier*. Ambassador Coquet knew it was Prío's favorite brandy. After sipping it briefly Prío continued his musings.

«About ten days ago, at Palacio, I met with generals and colonels,» he fibbed to himself, «who had direct command of troops; I told them that I had heard rumors and occasional news of conversations within the troops about uprisings and to be alert and investigate. They replied there were no problems; some mentioned that in every Army center, as elsewhere, there were individuals who liked to talk too much but that they were alert in case there was a real threat of revolts.»

After a brief pause he questioned himself, «How is it possible that this could be happening now?»

And he continued his lonely monologue. «Just yesterday's morning Grau called me to get together and clear out all misunderstandings among us. I told him to stay at home and not get involved in any way on what was happening, since the party needed a head in case something happened to me!»

As he was ready to continue his soliloquy, Mary and Marian appeared in the room and Prío returned to reality. He embraced his wife and child and asked for María Elena, who had stayed at the suite after fallen sleep. Mary was shedding tears in silence. Marian was simply happy to see her dad.

Prío's wife was dressed in a simple but beautiful Christian Dior dress. He dreamed that he would ask her to take that dress to Europe with the girls, on what he hoped would be a second memorable excursion on board the *Queen Mary*.

«As soon as we would get settled in exile we will return to Europe,» he thought.

At the time, the Queen Mary was the pride of the Cunard Line and Mary —he believed— would again be dressed with her best jewels and a different outfit every night, from New York, to Cherbourg to Southampton.

«Next year would be the tenth year the *Queen Mary* would win the *Blue Riband* [115] and Mary's photos would make all the papers in Europe,» he anticipated.

His wife, in this moment of absolute distress, would be pleased to know she deserved and —once more— would be wearing the best.

Prío tightly embraced Marian and Mary with all his strength. They all knew that difficult years were ahead. They had never had a moment for themselves and now too many hours of privacy were in their future. They cried in silence for a while and then fell into a looming silence where only the motions of their eyes confirmed their being alive.

Photo above:
No Hard Feelings. Havana, Cuba: President Fulgencio Batista of Cuba (right) shaking hands with **Benito Coquet**, personal representative of the Mexican President to Batista's 1954 inauguration, during a palace reception. The two men appeared friendly, even though it was Coquet, who as Mexican Ambassador to Cuba, granted asylum to President Carlos Prío Socarrás and his family in March 1952, when Batista deposed the last constitutional president of Cuba via a *Coup d'État*.

---

[115] The term was borrowed from horse racing (winner of the blue ribbon); it was an unofficial accolade given yearly to the passenger liner crossing the Atlantic, in regular service, with the fastest speed. By 1950, 13 Cunard ships had been awarded the prize. A series of photos in the main dining room of the ship displayed the most beautiful lady in the traversy on each of the prize-wining years. The 1951 photo showed **Mary Tarrero de Prío** in her full beauty and radiance. Carlos Prío had proudly displayed the picture on the main staircase of the Presidential Palace. The picture is shown at the bottom of page 176.

Photos, left to right, top to bottom:
President Prío and family arriving in Mexico City in 1952; The deposed president of Cuba as he boarded the plane in Havana; the elegant class and beauty of **Mary Tarrero de Prío** in 1951.

III The Aftermath

«For almost 18 years I fought Batista. When he assumed power on March 10th, the CTC decreed a general strike. Soon people assured me that Batista would respect all proletarian conquests. When I personally interviewed Batista, I realized that I was wrong opposing him.»

EUSEBIO MUJAL BARNIOL, SECRETARY GENERAL OF THE CONFEDERATION OF CUBAN WORKERS (CTC), IN DECLARATIONS TO THE MAGAZINE *MAÑANA* (MEXICO CITY), PUBLISHED ON MAY 17, 1952.

«I recommend for your consideration the continuation of diplomatic relations with the Batista Government in Cuba. Batista's revolution had no resistance. Ten countries of Latin America and France, Switzerland, Spain and China have already recognized Batista. The United Kingdom, Canada and Austria have asked to be given advance notice of our action.»

MEMORANDUM WRITTEN BY SECRETARY OF STATE **DEAN ACHESON** AND TRANSMITTED ON MAR. 24 TO **PRESIDENT TRUMAN** AT KEY WEST, FLORIDA. THE DEPARTMENT RECEIVED THE PRESIDENT'S APPROVAL OF THIS RECOMMENDATION ON MAR. 27, 1952.

«You planted the indiscipline and discontent within the armed forces, promoting paniagudos (sycophants) without merit or professional capacity, suspending advancement through competition, depriving officers of their right to improve themselves by their own efforts, and dismantling our normal functioning. You even promoted to first lieutenant of the National Police a member of my own household, the cook.»

FRANCISCO TABERNILLA DOLZ, IN A LETTER TO BATISTA DATED AUGUST 4 1960, AFTER CASTRO HAD TAKEN OVER FOLLOWING BATISTA'S FLIGHT FROM CUBA.

28

The March 10 Coup and the Press
Tuesday, March 11, 1952, 6:45 AM, third of the ***Three Days in March***.

THE SUCCESSFUL MARCH 10, 1952 military coup by Fulgencio Batista, with the collaboration and support of many active duty and retired Army officers, the National Police and the Navy, surprised President Carlos Prío and most Cuban society.

A *Coup d'État* was not the palliative solution that people expected or deserved to do away with the mobster groups and the corruption of two consecutive *Auténtico* governments. Most Cubans did not support a break from constitutional government. It was true Cuba had a fragile social, economic and political situation. Yet Cubans could not understand the inertia of the Prío government — in spite of multiple warnings by friends and enemies. They were surprised and disheartened by the lethargy of Carlos Prío at the time of defending the democratic progress the Cuban people had made since 1944. Few knew there was little else Prío could have done.

Children were returned to their homes after classes began to be cancelled in most schools. They found their mothers crying and their fathers on the verge of despair. Rumors began to circulate through the main provincial capitals. Some people were sure there had to be some fighting in the military strongholds. Others felt there must have been some violent reactions to the actions of Batista and his accomplices. Radios were turned on but were only transmitting music. The newspapers did not publish until late in the afternoon and people were snatching them from newsstands, anxious to know what was exactly happening all around Cuba.

The self-appointed dean of the press in Cuba, the *Diario de la Marina*, ignored "120 years of service to the general and permanent interests of the nation," and in a lengthy editorial entitled "Regime Change" justified the *coup*. It was explicit:

«It is not reasonable to believe that this extensive subversion of the established regime was produced by whim or appetite for power. We must accept that there were extreme and grave conditions known to the military but not to public opinion and the press. They must have posed a terrible and imminent threat to the Republic and we believe the Cuban army had to proceed fast and silently to apply this radical remedy that stops the progress of 20 years of Cuban political life. In short, the putsch against the extant government was justified: any other action could not have been expected.»

As one of the papers that routinely defended the policies of the government of Carlos Prío and the candidacy of Carlos Hevia, the newspaper *El Mundo* lashed out against the coup. [116] As always, it tried not being sensationalist or an open opposition vehicle but it published an editorial were it included statements by the *Federación Estudiantil Universitaria (FEU)* against the coup; the editorial skillfully expressed their outrage without analyzing the events or the context in which they occurred.

«While the Cuban people were democratically prepared to go to the elections on June first, which would have elected the new

---

[116] The newspaper **HOY** adopted the same position and criticized the action and extreme and radical measures taken by Batista. It said the only thing to do was to «defend the Constitution and fight for democracy and the unity of workers' and the people.»

rulers of the country, General Fulgencio Batista has produced an unexpected and surprising *coup* that leads him to assume the supreme command of the nation. We hope the nation will continue on a road of peace and order.»

As a mouthpiece of the Liberal Party, the *Excelsior* published an economic-type review of public management conditions, defending the security needs of businessmen. It clearly showed the interest of the paper's owner, Senator Alfredo Hornedo, also owner of the *El Pais* newspaper and the *Mercado Unico* (Havana's Produce Market). The review carefully posed:

«If the seriousness shown by the people is combined with the minimal show of force shown yesterday, we believe that —in spite of all political contingencies— it is possible to sustain a much needed sanity at this time, since in doing so hangs the balance of the nation's economic order and composure.»

The newspaper *Prensa Libre*, loyal defender of the *Auténticos*, did not editorialize; its position in many similar situations was to prepare the road to move to the side of the strongest politicians; its director, Sergio Carbó, proved to be a virtuoso in that shrewd and artful skill.

In a not too transparent attempt to be neutral, the newspaper *Información*, well known for its conservative tendencies, did not issue an editorial opinion. In its first edition after the *Coup d'État* it inserted pictures of the new masters of Cuba, with only undefined and uncompromising factual information; it decided to wait for another day to see which way the wind was blowing.

EL CRISOL

The newspaper *El Crisol* began its first editorial after the *Coup* with a cautious exploration of political positions, like other newspapers were doing across the island; it was a banquet —some enemies called it a diarrhea— of words intended to say much without expressing anything concrete; not a core belief that would have meant risk and commitment. It simply appealed for sanity and common sense. It was inconsistent in that it refused to examine what happened, to define its value or to ascertain opinions or define options for its readers.

Alerta

The newspaper *Alerta* had been originally owned by *Diario de la Marina*. Its top journalist was Ramón Vasconcelos. He wrote on March 11 an article entitled *"El Madrugón del Lunes"* (the early morning surprise on Monday), with probably the best appraisal of the situation in Cuba.

«I expected with anxiety some explanations from General Batista and his unexpected military rebellion and subsequent decapitation of Congress. Our legislators, after all, represented the people's sovereign will, freely chosen in legal elections; the broadcast presented by all radio stations yesterday in the afternoon disappoint the hopes of the citizens. I expected stronger statements and more precise plans; specific and ready to be applied measures necessary to purge our political life and liquidate the plague of gangs that have been among us for too long, the greatest threat and embarrassment of the country.»

BOHEMIA

The magazine *Bohemia*, directed by Miguel Angel Quevedo, in an editorial *"Ante el Hecho Consumado"* (Given the facts), in the edition of March 16, 1952, characterized the military coup as a mistake that would lead the country into a constitutional crisis; it suggested, however, that it would be accepting the facts and even cataloged the *Coup d'État* as "potentially revolutionary."

> «The government of President Prío, because of its fundamental mistakes, its banality and its lack of moral authority, is largely responsible for the events that we now have to mourn and support, God only knows for how long. We believe that the vices of a regime should not be countered by the violent solution that has been given, especially when the government that has just been overthrown by force, would have been removed through the democratic popular voting process.»

After March 10th, the magazine **Carteles** limited itself to publish countless photo essays of the *Coup*, many of which were under the heading:

> «General Fulgencio Batista, the head of the revolutionary movement and Prime Minister of the new Government ...»

Many journalists took a valiant position against Batista and his military band of warriors, regardless of the position taken by the newspapers, radio and TV directors in their editorials. On many levels they were willing to risk their lives. Scholarly authors like Jorge Mañach and Herminio Portell Vilá assumed a belligerent stance, criticizing —from the start of the *Coup*— the crime that was being committed against the republic.

The press outside Cuba, however, was very critical of Batista, particularly in Mexico. The newspaper **Excelsior**, for instance, condemned the *Coup*, explaining in so many words...

> «Batista has attempted against a government that was in power after Cubans exercised their right to a free vote.»

The Mexican magazine **HOY** (not related to Cuba's Communist newspaper **HOY**) declared that the coup was unjustifiable,

> «General Fulgencio Batista had won an enviable place in Cuban history, indeed in the history of America, and lost it all in a moment of fatal obfuscation. It is sad, very sad, that the military man who handed over his power to a political opponent in 1944 —

earning the admiration of all Latin countries— now contradicts his gallant attitude with yesterday's *Coup*.»

The Mexican diplomatic good will and admiration for Batista ended with Batista's *Coup*. A report dated December 1952, showed the change in attitude of the Mexican government toward Cuba. In 1949, Batista had been acclaimed in Mexico as he wielded the tenets of the Mexican Revolution and showed his sympathy for many of the Mexican government measures at a dinner in his honor at the Chapultepec Palace and at a celebration in the Zócalo which brought a 20,000 crowd, organized by the President of Mexico. Three years later, as reported by Don Gilberto Bosques, when he left for Havana on a diplomatic mission, the same President, Adolfo Ruiz Cortines, said good-bye to him with these words:

«Be careful how you treat the Cuban dictator».

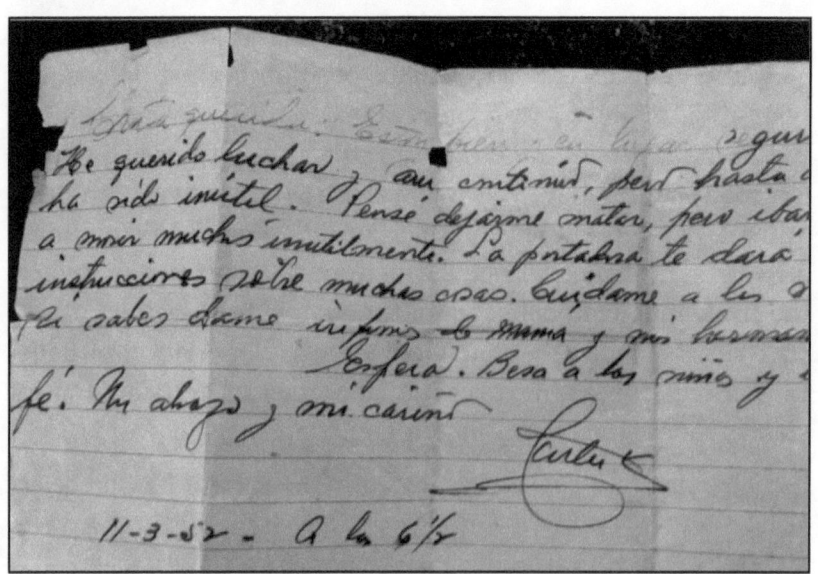

An emotional letter from Carlos Prío to his wife Mary on March 11, 1952

Carlos Prío was a good-hearted and sentimental man, even under stress and in the most difficult situations. His first letter to his wife as he arrived in exile read:

Chata Querida: Estoy bien en lugar seguro (NR: Miami?). He querido luchar y aun continuo, pero hasta ahora ha sido inútil. Pensé dejarme matar, pero iban a morir muchos inútilmente. La portadora te dará instrucciones sobre muchas cosas. Cuídame a las niñas. Si sabes, dame informes de mamá y mis hermanos. Espera. Besa a las niñas y mucha fé. Un abrazo y mi cariño.
Carlos   11-3-52 – A las 6 1/2

Photos, top to bottom, left to right:

Miguel Angel Quevedo, director of *Bohemia* magazine in 1952;
General **Francisco Tabernilla** acclaimed by the military at *La Cabaña* fortress in Havana;
Santiago Rey Perna, a solid Batista follower after surviving an attempt on his life; The *Ortodoxos*, meeting in vain to explore what to do in the face of Batista's Coup in 1952. Shown inside circles, **Roberto Agramonte** and **José Pardo Llada**.

29

The CIA knew Things that Prío Didn't
Tuesday, March 11, 1952, 9:45 AM, third of the **Three Days in March**.

ON THE EARLY HOURS in the morning of March 11, 1952, Albert Foster transmitted to the US Embassy in Havana what would be one of his last reports about Prío, Batista and the complexities of change in the Cuban political scene.

«All military forces in Havana went over to Batista immediately. Before the night was over, the rest of the country joined them. No fighting took place anywhere, except early in the Presidential Palace, almost by mistake. Junior officers that joined the movement were promoted. Pay of the army enlisted men, the policemen, the navy men and the *guardia rural* were raised to a minimum of $100 a month.

«Prío attempted to convene the Legislature in the early morning hours but desisted in his intent after he realized all newspapers, radio and TV stations and telephones were in the hands of Batista's men. All important power centers were taken early in the day: the Presidential Palace, all garrisons and military installations, the CTC headquarters, the main harbors and customhouses, all police stations, *Ayuntamientos* (City Halls), and the like.

«Prío is now at the Mexican Embassy with his Ministers of State (Aureliano Sánchez Arango), Defense (Rubén de León) and Interior (Segundo Curti). Batista has given them freedom to seek shelter at their convenience. Some of Prío's refugee friends from Latin American countries also sought asylum in embassies: former Venezuelan president Rómulo Gallegos is now inside the Guatemalan embassy; also there is Juan Bosch from the Dominican Republic. Both are trying to get to Mexico; Rómulo Betancourt took refuge in the embassy of Costa Rica, hoping to get to the US.

«Late last night, some *Auténticos* tried to contact Batista to ask him to re-instate the Legislature. Batista's response was that it was too early for that decision. They offered to obtain a letter of resignation from Prío but Batista replied he did not need that. Vice President Alonso Pujol insisted he would resign formally anyway and then left for the US.

«In his announced 6:00 PM address to the people (which occurred at almost 8:00 PM), Batista committed to stay in power only until peace and stability returned to Cuba. As of now he controls the army, the executive and legislative powers, and perhaps the judicial branch of government. To soften the blow to the legislators, he offered all members of Congress that they will be receiving their regular pay without the need to hold sessions. Congressional immunity, however, has been suspended.

«No elections will be held on June 1st of this year.

«Our man in Santo Domingo has informed us that the government of Rafael Leónidas Trujillo has recognized the Batista legitimacy. We have reasons to believe that Venezuela and Nicaragua will soon do the same.

«Colonel Eulogio Cantillo has been promoted from Chief of the Army Air Corps to Adjutant General of the Army. Retired Navy Commander José Rodríguez Calderón, now a Rear Admiral, is the new Chief of the Navy. His right hand man is former *Alferez de Navío* Antonio Arias Echevarría; Arias had been Director of the Naval Academy in 1934-1935, and was expelled from the force after he became involved in the 1944 theft of Navy funds. Colonel Manuel Larrubia, a retired Army Major, has been designated Chief of the Army Air Corps, although he has never flown *solo*.

«Batista is planning to install himself in the Presidential Palace and has already received several requests for meetings of solidarity and support from the National Association of Sugar Cane Planters, the Havana Stock Exchange, the National Association of Manufacturers, the Produce Exchange, the Cuban Chamber of Commerce and the Havana Clearing House. José Ignacio de la Cámara, on behalf of these institutions, has sent Batista the following message:

«We are working normally and will come to offer you our respects and to say that we will continue to work, as always, for the good of the country and for the national economy.

«There will be a first meeting of the Council of Ministers on Wednesday, March 12th. It is expected that he will appoint a good and trusted friend of his, Amadeo López Castro, as president of the National Development Commission.»

As he finished his transmission to the US Embassy, Foster descended —radio in hand— from the roof of the apartment building at Escobar Street; he found Tomás, his neighbor and owner of the furniture store at 621 Neptuno Street, waiting for him at the small terrace that provided access to all four 4th story apartments. They chatted briefly and Foster promised Tomás he would visit him at the store's *tertulia* the next day. He got word from Tomás that Santiago Rey had pledged he would bring Gastón Baquero to the meeting.

«There is no way we can escape the Batistianos now,» Tomás thought for himself.

He was very fond of Baquero, however, and was a regular reader of his column in the *Diario de la Marina*. He immediately felt sorry for Aureliano and Menelao —now running for their freedom and perhaps their lives— and could not think of anyone else that could defend the constitutional position in future *tertulias*. Tomás and Foster departed and went to their homes, exhausted by the psychological impact of the day's happenings.

Downstairs, on the second floor of the apartment building at 525 Escobar Street, Juan Marinello and Salvador García Agüero, the two "brains" of the Cuban Communist party, and Carlos Márquez Sterling, the man who presided over the 1940 Constitutional Convention, were still discussing the happenings of the day at 1:00 AM on March 11th. They were uncertain about the future of all parties, particularly the PSP, now that Batista, a "born again anti-Communist," had full powers in Cuba.

«No doubt Cuba lacks a democratic tradition,» were the words of Marinello as he tasted a sip of *Fundador* Brandy.

«The feudal political traditions of Spain were planted in Cuba, and what Cubans have always liked is a strong, centralized government in the hands of a *caudillo*; one single leader solving all public problems is ingrained in the Cuban *ethos*.»

«I fully agree,» was the comment from Márquez Sterling.

«In the history of Cuba, one of the principles that most stand out is the reliance on a *caudillo* and its acceptance even by the Cuban intellectuals. The principles and traditions of a representative form of government were never presented or supported under Spanish rule. Never mind that Cuba was 70 years late in achieving its independence in spite of having quite a few *caudillos*; we were ill prepared to assume the responsibilities demanded by a democratic society. The trend of these 50 years of republican life has been authoritarianism, corruption, violence and finally, the demise of an elected government.. 16 changes of leaders in 50 years of the republic; 7 uprisings, of which 3 were from the military. Our only peaceful times have been during the occupations by the US. What a poor track record!»

«Incredibly poor record,» admitted García Agüero. «For years, most of our people —unlike in the rest of Latin America— have enjoyed their lives well beyond the subsistence level of income. I chaired one of the Commissions at the meeting of the International Bank for Development last year. They reported: The general impression of members of the mission, from observations in travels all over Cuba, is that living levels of farmers, agricultural laborers, industrial workers, storekeepers and others are higher all along the line than for corresponding groups in other tropical countries, and in nearly all other Latin America countries. This does not mean that there is no dire poverty in Cuba, but simply that in comparative terms Cubans are better off, on the average, than people of these other areas.»

«Why was it then that Cubans were so angry and disenchanted that they ignored the defense of the constitution and submitted in silence to the assault of Batista?," asked Marinello.

«Could it be that the middle class in Cuba found itself virtually disenfranchised *viv a vis* the *políticos*? Was it that Cubans have such a short attention span that the calamities in the Grau and Prío's governments made them forget the sacrifices of three wars to achieve a free and democratic society?»

«Take Batista,» remarked Márquez Sterling. «What made him believe he was the best man that could implement social and economic reform in Cuba? Why was he willing to betray the ideals embodied in a 1940 Constitution that he had been instrumental in creating? We all know the allegations of Prío's *auto-golpe* are a pure fantasy. Didn't he realize that Cubans would react to his Coup with stunned disbelief?»

Such questions kept these three men awake until early in the morning. There were no answers to any of their inquires. Like most Cubans, however, rich or poor, educated or illiterate, young or old, in public or private life, they continued pondering these enigmas *ad infinitum*. If there was something that all Cubans know how to do, is to argue, dispute and debate. It has been a national pastime since the first Cuban-born child learned how to talk.

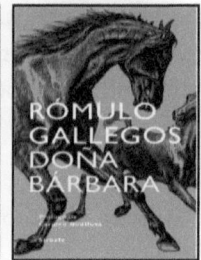

Photos above, left to right:

One of the extraordinary virtues of the Carlos Prío presidency was to provide refuge and security to political exiles from Hispanic America; two notable examples were the shelter provided to **Rómulo Gallegos**, from Venezuela, and **Juan Bosch**, from the Dominican Republic; one from the political right and the other from the left.

```
                    RESTRICTED              DO NOT TYPE IN THIS SPACE
    Air Pouch      SECURITY INFORMATION
       PRIORITY       (Security Classification)    737.5512/4-1752
         FOREIGN SERVICE DESPATCH                  XR 837.43

FROM  :    Earl T. Crain        1715
TO    :    THE DEPARTMENT OF STATE, WASHINGTON.— 1 Enc.  April 17, 1952
REF   :    April 10, 1952                         APR 22 1952
                                                  DEPARTMENT OF STATE
    ACTION      DEPT.                             BUREAU OF
For Dept.  ARA*    1  REP  DCR  OLI  E  IFI  IBS  IRS  ITA  INTER-AMERICAN AFFAIRS
Use Only   REC'D      OTHER                            APR 24 1952
   DB    AIR 24       LAB  FSA

SUBJECT:   Government Raises Pay of Armed Forces and Teachers
```

The BATISTA Government raised the pay of the Army, National Police, the Navy, and of Cuban teachers in a series of decrees published in the <u>Official Gazette</u> of April 3, 1952. The range of the new salaries is outlined as follows:

	New Salary	Old salary
	(Dollars per month)	(Dollars per mo.)
Army		
Major General	$525	$350
Private	82	25
Private, Rural Guard	85	27
Military Emergency Service		
Colonel	315	200
Private	60	12

Civilian employees, under classification of Administrative Chief, Second Class, raised one grade

Navy		
Commodore	535	385
Seaman, Second Class	82	26

Civilian employees, under grade of Administrative Chief, Third Class, raised one grade

National Police		
Colonel	500	325
Policeman (<u>Vigilante</u>)	150	96

These raises were made in accordance with promises Batista made shortly after the March 10 <u>coup</u> and are apparently designed to gain a broad base of support in the rank and file of the armed forces and the Cuban educational system.

A copy of the <u>Official Gazette</u> giving the complete pay scales is enclosed.

                                          For the Ambassador:

Enclosure:
<u>Gazette</u> of April 3, 1952   Earl T. Crain
                                          Acting Counselor of Embassy

Photo:

The report to the **CIA**, from the **US embassy** in Havana, indicating the raises in salary that Batista had granted the Cuban armed forces —to secure their loyalty and adhesion— after the *Coup d'État* of March 10, 1952.

30
Money and Loyalties flowing after March 10
Late March to early May 1952.

ON MARCH 28, 1952, Albert Foster reported to the US Department of State, through the US Embassy in Havana, about the way things were turning out in Cuba. This time his report was ample and detailed and surprised no one at State.

«CTC's Secretary General Eusebio Mujal, as predicted, has joined forces with Batista after renouncing his membership in the *Auténtico* party. The feeling persists that in certain labor quarters some present union officers are in disagreement and will be replaced by leaders with firm Batista convictions and loyalty.

«Most unions have openly declared their approval and adhesion to Mujal; he is, as usual, in this opportunistic game he has been playing with Batista. In private Mujal has stated that he hopes labor will somehow be crucial in bringing back constitutional rule to Cuba. The constitutional guarantees, however, have been suspended and strikes are strictly forbidden. Any labor meetings must request permission from the police force five days in advance. Unconfirmed rumors have it that Mujal is considering the organization of a labor political party. Batista is viewing this with calm and a bit of disinterest. Mujal seems to ignore that the 1940 Constitution does not allow for political parties to be based on ethnic, sexual, religious, wealth or class lines.

«One labor leader, Marco Antonio Hirigoyen, Secretary General of the transportation workers —and a loyal Mujal follower— has declared against such party formation; this corroborates rumors that Hirigoyen and Mujal are at odds with each other. The rumors include difficulties between Mujal and the leaders of the electric plant's workers (Angel Cofiño) and the telephone workers (Vicente Rubiera).

Labor leaders are very reticent to declare openly against Batista, knowing as they do that the General can be ruthless.

«On another level, the CTC announced on April 8 their support to the *Estatutos Constitucionales*, even if it meant no May 1st celebration this year; it is expected that Batista would let Mujal know pretty soon. Mujal is trying now to get permission for an indoor meeting of labor leaders at the auditorium of the *Palacio de los Trabajadores*, at San Carlos and Peñalver Streets in Havana; he had hundreds of cards printed with his name and phone number [117] to be distributed at all union offices, asking common workers to get in touch with him, apparently in an effort to by-pass competing labor leaders. The *Organización Regional Interamericana del Trabajo (ORIT)* and the *Central Latinoamericana de Trabajadores (CLAT)* have both criticized Batista and have been disavowed by Mujal. The *ORIT* leaders have commented «this is how far Mujal has bent to Batista's wishes; it is sickening.» So far, Batista has not recognized the labor leaders of the tobacco, agro and industrial businesses.

«There are significant rifts in the labor movement about the inclusion of labor leaders in the *Consejo Consultivo*. Conrado Rodríguez Sánchez, Assistant Secretary General of *FNTA*, [118] appointed to the *Consejo* after a recommendation of Miguel Suárez Fernández, former *Auténtico* Senate President, now devotedly loyal to Batista, turned down the honors with a public statement denouncing the very existence of the *Consejo*.

«Batista's forces do not yet have absolute control of the labor forces. The military in Camagüey, for instance, has taken over the CTC offices and are holding them until the Minister of Labor decides who takes them over. The new "official" CTC is asking Batista to increase wages in all industries that could afford them, increase pensions and respect all labor contracts retroactive to March 9, 1952. Such demands were never made of Prío's government and Batista detests public pressure on him. We have reasons to believe that Batista will use Mujal until he becomes unwelcome, at which time he will be discredited and cast aside.

---

[117] Phone 7-4901 of the *Confederación de Trabajadores de Cuba*.

[118] *Federación Nacional de Trabajadores Azucareros*. Conrado Rodríguez felt he could not renounce to his belief in the *Ortodoxo* party.

«Batista is feeling so secure that he will discontinue the financial aid given by Prío's government to the CTC; that will translate into severe salary reductions (perhaps as much as 50%) to its Executive Board members, Mujal included.[119] Batista was not even paying attention to serious conspiracies sponsored by Prío and Aureliano Sánchez Arango, based out of Miami, Florida.»

On May 1, 1952, finally, the CTC had its rally at the *Palacio de los Trabajadores*. All industrial and commercial facilities were closed in most of the island. Batista was represented at the CTC indoor rally by his Minister of Labor, Jesús Portocarrero, who assured the workers that «all your acquired rights and conquests will be respected.» Batista's name was widely cheered and applauded every time his name was mentioned. He was not flinching in his opposition to Communists participating in the labor movement. The CTC issued a manifesto with 250 demands, of which it was said Batista had accepted 125 for consideration —not necessarily for approval. In the end he consented on half a dozen only. There had been not a calmer Labor Day in many years of republican life.

In spite of the overwhelming acceptance of Batista as Cuba's new strong man, there were dissenting voices. *El Mundo* newspaper referred to the *Consejo Consultivo* as:

«A caricature of legislative procedure, down to the President's message. This Council can act fast since it does not have to answer to a confused electorate.»

All over Cuba, on the other hand, *Ortodoxo* and *Communist* Concejales and Alcaldes were either swearing allegiance to Batista or leaving office. Those who did not act on their own were simply removed without notice. In Havana, 7 of 27 concejales were dismissed; Herminio Portell Vilá and José Morales Gómez were two of them.

---

[119] Foster was well informed. The ***CTC***, by the end of May, cut about $10,000 of its operating budget, including salaries, gasoline allowances, unneeded personnel, fewer activities, and to top it all, Mujal's salary, with the reasoning that he was already being paid as a Senator. From there on, work was carried out in a very desultory manner all across the ***CTC***. Unknown to the membership, Mujal began to privately "beg" Batista for the reinstallation of subsidies, arguing that he should be more generous and thus command more loyalty than Carlos Prío. Batista paid deaf ears to Mujal's prayers.

The Cuban press, in the meantime, did not report on conversations between Batista and Elliott Roosevelt, son of FDR and former First Lady Eleanor Roosevelt, a graduate of *Groton School* and *Princeton*. He had been involved in the US in the infamous D-2 purchasing scandal. [120] After a Batista-Roosevelt meeting on early May, 1952, Roosevelt invested a vast sum of money in an assembly plant for TV receivers in partnership with DuMont Electronics and a packaging plant for pharmaceuticals in partnership with McKay-Davis Chemicals. When this was finally disclosed in 1957 Batista expressed ...

«Elliott was desirous of investing in Cuba because he wanted to use our country as a launching pad to further investments in South America.»

It was the first of many transactions through which Batista enriched himself after March 10, 1952.

A final and important reaction to Batista's *Coup d'État* came from the Catholic Church. Manuel Cardenal Arteaga, Archbishop of Havana, issued a pastoral letter days after the *Coup d'État* in which he said:

«Although Catholics have the prerogative to exercise their political rights freely, they should not involve the Church in political campaigns. We have been upholding the "apolitical" character of the Church for many years; we hope the present government will accomplish its proclaimed objectives and will lead Cuba to democracy and the reunion of those divided politically.»[121]

---

[120] In 1943 the US was looking for a replacement of its **Lockheed P-38** aircraft. Roosevelt recommended the *Hughes D-2s* after numerous parties financed by a Hughes Aircraft publicist. The parties, in Hollywood and Manhattan, included dalliances and frolicking with actress Faye Emerson (at the time the First Lady of TV), as well as his giving her $132 worth of nylon stockings, paid by Howard Hughes. Ladies' stockings were a rare treat during the prevailing 1943 wartime rationing. Roosevelt married Emerson in 1944 and divorced her in 1950.

[121] Within a little more than a year, on August 12, 1953, as the police was looking for fugitives under the protection of the Church after the 26 July assault on the Moncada Barracks in Santiago de Cuba, **Cardenal Arteaga** was assaulted by Batista's police and suffered a head contusion requiring 20 stitches. The Cardenal never commented on the affair and two weeks later baptized Batista's son in Havana's Cathedral.

Photos, top to bottom, left to right on the right:

Top, **Elliott Roosevelt** in 1952; **Manuel Cardenal Arteaga**, Archbishop of the Catholic Church in Cuba in March of 1952. He silently condemned the *Coup d'État*. Months later, a military gang irrupted in his home and seriously beat him;

Center, an ad for the famous **Dupont Television Corporation**, manufacturers of TV sets and proprietors of a TV network popularized by Archbishop Fulton Sheen's series *Life is Worth Living*. Elliot Roosevelt was a mayor stockholder and Batista facilitated his heavy investment in an attempt to control television in Cuba;

Below, the *New York Times* reporting on the D-2 Pentagon purchasing scandal involving Roosevelt; **Cardenal Arteaga** baptizing Fulgencio (Papo) Batista in 1953.

Photos, top to bottom, left to right:

Newspapers in Havana reported in detail the movements of Carlos Prío and his followers after 1952. According to the **Diario Alerta**, Prío had spent $2 million in counter-revolutionary activities (purchase of armaments, planes and ships in Baltimore) that were being readied in Mexico, Guatemala, Belize and other Republics in the Gulf area. The military leader would have been Aureliano Sánchez Arango. Prío characterized these charges as "absurdities and lies."

31
The Final Withering Away of the Republic
Mid to late 1952

IN AN EDITORIAL IN ITS MARCH, 1952 issue, *Bohemia* magazine declared:

«We are deeply embarrassed; as a publication of incorruptible Cuban ancestry, we regret and despise the capitulation of the entire government of Carlos Prío. We both look anxiously at the triumphant *Coup*, and condemn the cowardice of the civilian leaders who made it possible. We expected from them a more dignified and honorable posture in defense of our civil institutions. We had the right to demand that they had to fall with honor, with gallantry, and without dragging through the ground the flag of civility; instead, they allowed the mandate conferred to them by the people to fall from their hands, without glory. It has been an inexcusable example of cowardice.»

Batista, in his first statements to the press, had declared a moratorium on violence:

«There will be no persecution or hatred towards anyone.»

A few hours later he dismissed his archenemy Nicolás Castellanos as Mayor of Havana and replaced him with an old esteemed friend, Justo Luis del Pozo y del Puerto. Justo Luis del Pozo had been one of the men that entered Columbia with Batista on March 10, on a car that also brought Andrés Domingo y Morales del Castillo, to provide moral support for the General since only Batista carried weapons. They were appropriately rewarded with important positions in the government. Batista proceeded to abrogate the 1940 Constitution and the Electoral Act 1943, replacing them with his own *Estatutos Constitucionales*.[122] Batista then suspended all radio programs of his opponents and charged the Ministry of Information to establish press censorship. The offices of the *Partido Socialista Popular* (*PSP*, Communists) were raided and all manifestations of the *Orthodoxo* Youth movement were outlawed.

Auténtico and *Ortodoxo* leaders complained; they issued manifestos of protest but did nothing concrete, apart from ignoring the calls for unity that the PSP emitted after the coup. The Liberal Democrats, faithful *Auténtico* allies until March 9, quickly went to Batista's side; among them Eusebio Mujal and his unionists, now turned against the labor movement. Havana Mayor, Nicolás Castellanos, and ousted VP Alonso Pujol were dismissed from the Cuban National Party; the party's congressmen and political activists defected and joined Batista. On his way to exile, Alonso Pujol prophesied:

«Batista is an arrogant man of overbearing pride and haughtiness; dictators behave like this in their hours of power and only become humble and sad when they experience their inevitable downfall and defeat.»

Following the predictions made before the *Coup d'État* by Albert Foster, the Chief CIA man in Havana, in a report to the US ambassador Willard Beaulac, Batista proceeded immediately to reorganize Cuba's armed forces.

Brigadier General Francisco Tabernilla Dolz, Colonels Carlos M. González Cantillo, Aquilino Guerra González and Manuel Larrubia Paneque, and Captains Martín Díaz Tamayo, Pilar D. García, Ramón E. Vidal Cruz and Roberto Fernández Miranda, among others, were returned to active service. Francisco Tabernilla Dolz, was promoted to Brigadier General; Colonel Eulogio Cantillo Porras to be Adjutant General of the Army, Captain Luis Robaina Stone advanced in rank to Inspec-

---

[122] They were proclaimed on April 4, 1952 in an extraordinary edition of the *Gaceta Oficial*; their formal name was **Estatutos Constitucionales del Viernes de Dolores.** Their first paragraph read: «Fieles al espíritu de la Revolución y recogiendo los más hondos anhelos del pueblo Cubano...» The Estatutos were written by Colonel Arístides Sosa de Quesada with the indirect participation of Senator Santiago Rey Perna.

tor General and Martin Díaz Tamayo to Quartermaster General.

Other promotions to higher rank were dispensed to Commanders Aquilino Paneque Larrubia and Manuel Guerra González, Captains Alberto del Río Chaviano, Ramón E. Cruz Vidal, Dámaso Sogo Hernández, Leopoldo Pérez Coujil, First Lieutenant Pedro A. Rodríguez Avila, Commanders Joseph C. García and Manuel Aguiar Larrubia Paneque, Captains Felix E. Montoya Pérez, Cándido F. Hernández, Pilar D. García García, Victor M. Robert and Julio Sánchez Dueñas Gómez, and First Lieutenant Fermín Cowley Gallego.

By Decree No. 95, Batista sent into retirement a group of officers who did not join the *Coup* or did not enjoy his personal sympathy: Major General Ruperto Rodríguez Cabrera, Generals Otalio Sosa Llanes, Quirino Uría López, Francisco Alvarez Margolles, Colonels José Acosta de la Fuente, Eduardo Martín Elena, Urbano Matos, Gil Rodríguez and Epifanio Hernández, among others. In total, 77 officers were removed from the service: one Mayor General, three Brigadier Generals, seven Colonels, 22 Lieutenant Colonels, 11 Commanders, 10 captains and some others from lower ranks. It meant the loss of important professional cadres in the army, which aggravated the ineptitude and inability within the Cuban military establishment. Once more in Cuba, blind loyalty prevailed over professional capacity, a symptom of organizations condemned to mediocrity and eventual widespread truancy and malfeasance.

Batista felt all along he could make his new regime palatable if he offered an alternative to the 1940 Constitution. Through his *Estatutos Constitucionales* he pretended to assume power under the mantle of legality and protection of the law. He tried to sell it to the citizenry as an example of civic participation the like of which had never been seen in Cuba.

In his fantasies, or in his Rabelaisian self-importance, Batista believed that most Cubans watched with relief the new order through which he would end gangsterism, corruption, impunity and the public insecurity that prevailed under the *Auténtico* governments. He was sure the students, the banks, as well as all agricultural, industrial and commercial institutions were giving him a vote of confidence to inaugurate a regime that would bring stability to Cuba.

The names of políticos and public men he was able to recruit for his *Consejo Consultivo* tended to reinforce his illusion.[123]

There were elected Senators like Miguel Suárez Fernández, member of the 1940 Constitutional Convention, President of the Senate (1945-1950) and Foreign Minister (1951) in the Prío Cabinet; Carlos Miguel de Céspedes Ortiz, Minister of Public Works (1925-1929) during Machado and member of the Havana Yacht Club, the Vedado Tennis Club, the Miramar Club, and the Marianao Country Club; Members of the House of Representatives like Jorge García Montes Hernández, son of a 1898 exile during the War of Independence, member of the Liberal Party, exiled during the Machado presidency, elected to the House from Santa Clara; Generoso Campos Marquetti, last man promoted to General in the War of 1898, prominent nationalist veteran elected member of the House of Representatives in 1906; Carlos Saladrigas Zayas, former Senator (1936-1940), Minister of Justice (1934), Foreign Minister (1940-1942), Prime Minister (1940-1942) and former candidate to the presidency (1944), and Ramón Vasconcelos Maragliano, prestigious journalist, Machadista in the 1930s, Batistiano in the early 1940s, Ortodoxo in the late 1940s and Batistiano again in the 1950s, the man who wielded the function of censor for Batista after 1952.

Other members of Batista's *Consejo Consultivo* in 1952 [124] were labor leaders like José Luis Martínez Alvarez, from the

---

[123] A complete list of members of the **Consejo Consultivo** was reported to the US embassy by the CIA on May 1st 1952, a full week before it appeared in *Cuba's Official Gazette*. A photocopy of the CIA report is presented on page 244 of this book.

[124] Batista's regime as President of Cuba was scheduled to end December 31, 1958. The new slate of President-Vice President was scheduled to take possession on February 24, 1959. The elections had taken place on November 3, 1958, the vote was compulsory. The presidential candidates by different parties and coalitions had been:

  • ***Andrés Rivero Agüero*** and ***Gastón Godoy and Loret de Mola*** for the National Progressive Coalition, which included four parties: Progressive Action Party, Liberal Party, Democratic Party and Radical Union Party. >>>

Federación Nacional de Trabajadores Azucareros (FNTA) and Eusebio Mujal Barniol, from the *Confederación de Trabajadores de Cuba* (CTC); journalists like Miguel de Marcos, the man who best captured the humor of political Cuba, in the words of Jorge Mañach, winner of the Justo de Lara literary prize in 1938 and the Juan Gualberto Gómez prize in 1950; scholars like Claudio Benedí, member of the Cuban Economic Commission and Minister of Foreign Relations; Rafael Esténger Neulín, member of Cuba's National Academy of Arts and Letters; Gastón Baquero Díaz, journalist, poet, member of *Orígenes*, *Jefe de Redacción* of *Diario de la Marina*, winner of the Justo de Lara literary prize in 1944; powerful and rich people like **Alfonso Fanjul**, heir to the New York-based Sugar empire *Czarnikov-Rionda Company*. Also, Manuel Aspuru San Pedro, sugar baron, owner of Centrales *Toledo* and *Providencia*, Fernando García Tuñón, *Marqués de las Regueras*, a Spanish title given to his family by Alfonso XIII in 1898, and Gastón Godoy y Loret de Mola, lifetime friend of the Batista family, who ran for VP with presidential candidate Andrés Rivero Agüero in the suspended elections of 1958. Years later, upon General Batista's death on August 6, 1973, Gastón Godoy presented his eulogy at the family pantheon in the Cathedral of San Isidro, in Madrid.

The *Consejo Consultivo* ran from April 28, 1952 to January 28, 1954. No one ever questioned Batista's right to anoint himself as President of the Republic.

While this was taking place, the reactions of the traditional political parties and civil and religious organizations was weak and in some cases openly supportive of the military coup. Occasional weak denunciations of the *Coup* were issued with demagogic and hesitant statements, full of political cowardice

---

- **Ramón Grau San Martín** and **Antonio Sánchez Lancís** ran for the Cuban Revolutionary Party (*Auténticos*).
- **Carlos Márquez Sterling** and **Rodolfo Méndez Peñate** were the candidates of the Free People Party.
- **Alberto Salas Amaro** and **Miguel Angel Céspedes** ran for the Cuban Union Party.

and no real intention of creating popular mobilization.

The Cuban Catholic Church had to choose to support the authoritarian regime of Batista —in order to maintain some level of influence— or to assume a role of moral and political opposition. The Church hierarchy's strategic decision was to mobilize lay organizations of men, women, workers and students, collectively known as *Acción Católica*,[125] trusting that they would provide the patriotic response to the *Coup*. As an institution, the Church itself decided to remain silent. Its thinking was that social and political engagement were a Christian duty but one that was conditioned to personal initiative.

The Communist Party (*PSP*), opposed Batista's suspension of the 1940 Constitution in principle but, having lost much of its influence in the labor movement and the popular classes since the 1930s, it decided not to mount any significant resistance. The *PSP's* prestige during the rest of the 1950s was marginal because of frequent struggles against Batista since the fall of Machado

The *CTC*, led by Eusebio Mujal, initially called for a general strike but later, before 72 hours had passed, gave its endorsement to the Coup.

The Cuban Revolutionary Party (*Auténticos*), came out against the *golpe* and called the *Coup d'État* unconstitutional; like Prío, however, its senior leaders rushed to foreign embassies in search of exile. The Republican Party praised Batista and

---

[125] ***Acción Católica*** had its origins in the 1920s when a Belgian priest of working class tradition, **Joseph Cardijn**, founded the Catholic Youth Workers Movement with the blessing of Pope Pius XI. The Pope had lamented that the Church had lost the allegiance of the youth, particularly the young workers. Pope Pius XI's successor, Pius XII, allowed the creation in France of a similar movement to proselytize the young workers, the **Prêtres Travailleurs** (working priests). It was eventually a fiasco as many young priests, fully integrated to the working world and without the protection of the convents, succumbed to the temptations of the flesh. The *Prêtres Travailleurs* were heavily influenced by **Jacques Maritain**, a close friend of Pius XII, **Yves Congar, OP**, the biblical scholar, and Cardinal **Henri de Lubac, SJ**, the foremost Catholic Theologian of the times and *peritus* of the II Vatican Council. Their ideas were seminal for the foundation in Cuba of **Juventud Católica** and **Agrupación Católica Universitaria**. Interestingly, Father Cardijn was in Havana in February of 1952, to give the keynote address to the first *Congreso Regional de la Juventud Católica* that brought together similar movements from the Caribbean and Central America. A few weeks later Batista produced his *Coup d'État*.

criticized the ousted regime. The Liberal and Democratic parties hesitated at first but later praised the *Coup*; before the end of the year they had pacted with Batista. The *PPC* (*Ortodoxos*) did not oppose Batista in a determined and effective way; they only made statements condemning the *Coup*, with empty, ineffectual and vain slogans of moral condemnation.

Photos, left to right, top to bottom:
El Mundo newspaper, reporting a march in Central Park, Havana, to symbolically "bury" the 1940 Constitution; **Bohemia** magazine, endorsing the *Coup d'État*; **Diario de la Marina**, calling attention to the proclamation of the *Estatutos Constitucionales*; **7 Días**, a supplement of *La Marina*, presenting a bio of the General.

The best known Cuban personalities that agreed to be part of Batista's *Consejo Consultivo* in 1952

Photos, left to right, top to bottom:

First Row: **Claudio Benedí**, scholar; **Alfonso Fanjul Sr.** and **Lillian Rosa Gómez Mena**, sugar barons; **Luis Ortega Sierra**, journalist; **Josefina Mosquera**, director of *Vanidades* magazine.

Second Row: **Santiago Rey Perna**, governor of *Las Villas*; **Miguel de Marcos**, journalist; **Anselmo Alliegro**, Senate president; **Radio Cremata**, Congressman.

Third Row: **Ramón Vasconcelos**, journalist; **José Luis Martínez**, labor leader; **Gastón Baquero**, journalist; **Rafael Esténger**, author, diplomat.

Fourth Row, **Carlos Saladrigas**, Prime Minister, **Carlos Miguel de Céspedes**, Minister; **Jorge García Montes**, Prime Minister, **Miguel Suárez Fernández**, Senate President.

Photos, left to right, top to bottom:

Monseñor **Alberto Dalmau**, Bishop of *Las Villas*, the only high ranking Cuban ecclesiastic openly sympathetic to Batista;

A photo from 1955, showing evidence of Batista's acceptance by the US. From the left, Batista, Marta Fernández, his wife, Mrs. Andrés Domingo, Bishop Alberto Müller, Prime Minister Domingo Morales del Castillo, Mrs. and Mr. Nixon;

Batista meeting with **labor leaders** after the March 10 *Coup d'État* in 1952. The man in the left circle is **Eusebio Mujal Barniol**, formerly loyal to the *Auténticos*. The man to his left is **Angel Cofiño**, president of the *Federación de Trabajadores Eléctricos*. Cofiño was later fired as labor leader by Batista in 1957, which caused his severe denunciation of Mujal's divisionism;

Finally, a photo published in the newspaper *Prensa Libre*, showing policemen inside the **University of Havana** in 1952, in clear violation of its autonomy.

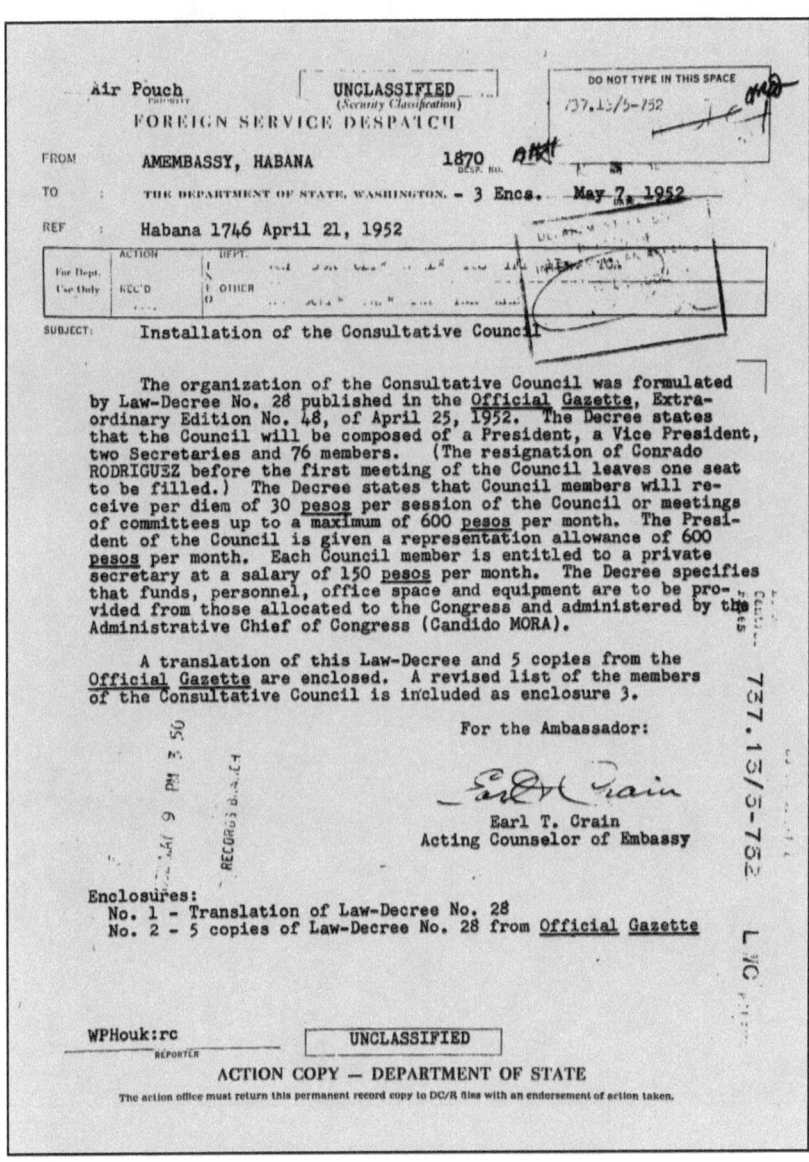

A document with news that reached Washington earlier than Havana:

The successful and swift establishment of a *Consejo Consultivo* gave Batista his first recognition of some legitimacy by the *políticos* in Cuba. Immediately after the publication of the Council list, the *Ortodoxos* expelled from their ranks three important figures that accepted participation in Batista's plans. They were **Ramón Vasconcelos**, director of the newspaper *Alerta*, **Lelio Alvarez Ramírez**, leader of the farmer's organized labor union and **Conrado Rodríguez**, Vice President of the *azucareros*. They responded by accusing Roberto Agramonte of ineptitude and having the weakness of a "*masa fofa*" (flabby mass). **Eduardo Ochoa** (Mayor of Holguín, brother of Emilio Ochoa) was also censured for having visited Batista in early April, 1952. It began to show deep dissentions within the *Ortodoxo* party.

Photos above, top to bottom, left to right:

Students from the University of Havana during a manifestation against the *Coup d'État* by Batista in March of 1952;

A 1949 group cartoon from *David,* published weeks before the *Coup.* It included several cabinet members and supporters of President Carlos Prío: **VP Guillermo Alonso Pujol** (flying on top), **Eusebio Mujal Barniol** (smiling on the left with a loose tie), **Orlando Puente** (behind Mujal), **Lincoln Rodón** (to the right of Mujal in the cartoon), **Antonio Prío Socarrás** (dressed in black), **Rubén de León** (to the right of Antonio Prío), **Segundo Curti** (to the left of Antonio Prío), **Ramón Vasconcelos** (lower left corner), **Manuel Antonio (Tony) de Varona** (back of Carlos Prío), **Santiago Rey Pernas** and **Pelayo Cuervo** (left and right of President Prío). **Carlos Prío** —seasoning bottle in hand— is happily tending to a roasted pork. All participants are extending their plates hoping to receive good portions.

32

The Final Meeting of the Tertulia at 621 Neptuno
Late in the Summer of 1952

THE DAY FINALLY ARRIVED when Tomás Fernández eagerly waited for the presence of Santiaguito Rey and Gastón Baquero on the long rows of rocking chairs in his store. One by one, most of the regulars —after knowing the programmed events of the day— arrived at their seats. Radio Cremata showed up early with Albert Foster and his wife Ruby Alonso. Karl Zimmerman crossed the street as soon as he saw them occupy their back seats.[126] Mariano Armengol, for the first time, showed up in his military uniform, a way of showing off his recent promotion to captain. Those present stood up and applauded as he entered the store, in typical Cuban teasing jocularity. Menelao Mora and Aureliano Sánchez were not expected and, of course, did not show up. Juan Marinello had been warned of the invited guest and showed up, taking the seat normally occupied by Primo Carnera, who was out of the country. Finally Santiago Rey entered the store and introduced Gastón Baquero to the group. No clients had showed up in the morning hours and none were expected in the afternoon. The convulsion of March 10th was still instilling fears in the minds of women, who were the deciding buyers in the furniture business. To warm up the audience Albert Foster was the first to speak. Few in the normal visiting crowd suspected he was a

---

[126] The seats at the end of the rows were the best in the house since you could see everyone (at least their backs) from your position.

CIA man and he had no qualms about projecting his pro-American positions. In fact, it was a subterfuge he enjoyed since most people would reason that no CIA operative could be so openly pro-Yankee:

«This sorry event in the history of Cuba has to be understood in the context of Cuba's relations to the US,» he declared. Policymakers in Washington have always complained of Grau's narrow economic *nacionalismo* and Prío's unpredictable pro-labor legislation. Washington has always favored non-confrontational negotiations, particularly when it comes to the recurrent problems affecting the operations of American companies in Cuba. With Grau and Prío it was very difficult to resolve differences; it became a structural problem forced by one-sided statutes and jurisprudence.»

«You must agree, however,» interrupted Marinello...that none of the two *Auténtico* governments failed to develop a US-compatible foreign policy; their stance at the UN and all international forums have never collided with American interests; on the contrary, they always lended their support when it was required by policy makers in Washington. Cuba, in fact, has been too cooperative with the US for too long.»

It was now Santiago Rey's turn to speak:

«The important issue is that the US has now given Batista a royal welcome. They expect Batista to discreetly restrain the organized labor movement and greet with pleasure the investment of foreign capital in Cuba. This will bring a long awaited prosperity to the island.»

Marinello interrupted.

«What Cuba needs the most is less corruption in government, as well as a fairer re-distribution of wealth, more regulations that will prevent abuses by the rich and wider availability of public services like housing, health and security.»

«But you are not addressing the question of why, after eight — perhaps twelve— years of elected governments, Cuba lost again its constitutional path,» moved Santiago Rey.

Marinello reclined his head on the back of his chair and provided the type of answer a well educated man would do.

«What we are experiencing in Cuba today is the logical consequence of our Hispanic tradition. We are not the heirs of Montezuma, Atahualpa or Hatuey. We have inherited the blood and character of Pizarro, Velázquez and Tacón. Our life today is imprinted by the cultural residues of Spain's last four hundred years of intrigue, struggles and civil wars. Spain's failure to maintain their control of America resulted in the birth and growth of an anarchical inheritance of *caudillismo*. On both sides, by the way. The governments are in the hands of military *caudillos*, the remote parts of the countries are in the hands of rural *caudillos*. On both sides we have the descendants of former *caudillos* and they will breed children with the gens of future *caudillos*. All of these extemporaneous warriors have ornate and bombastic self-bestowed titles and preposterous uniforms. It has been happening in Cuba, Argentina, Bolivia, Perú, Chile, Brasil, Haiti, the Dominican Republic, since the times of the collapse of the Spanish empire. There have been too many Bolívars and Trujillos and very few Sarmientos and Martís. What our peoples have not realized is that militarism and revolution lead to underdevelopment and instability.»

After a pause, Marinello ended up by saying,

«These *coups* and *Counter-Coups* have increased the military appetite but have done nothing for the people's hunger.»

Marinello's words produced a chilling effect on the group. Finally, Gastón Baquero spoke, with the same professorial timbre that Marinello had. No one was expecting an apology for the March 10th indignity when he began to speak. Baquero's words, however, proved to be insightful and prophetic.

«First of all let me anticipate that the US will be one of the first countries that will recognize Batista's government. Cuba, in its trust on the US, is ripe for a new *caudillo* that would replace the failed leaderships of Grau and Prío. For Americans, this man is Batista. It is true that March 10th broke the democratic process and re-opened an era of uncertainty and frustration. The truth is, however, that even though Batista does not have the popularity he had in 1944, [127] this blow to our constitution has been received by Cubans without much of an opposition; the only exception being the University students who have fallen in the hands of criminal elements like Rolando Masferrer and Fidel

---

[127] **Fulgencio Batista** had been elected Senator from Las Villas in 1948 without campaigning or even returning to Cuba from his self-exiled mansion in Daytona Beach.

Castro. Some young people, with the fever of their patriotism, are condemning this *golpe*, but others and their parents are watching with relief that a new order has come that will end the public insecurity of the last two *Auténtico* governments; now the impunity, the tolerance to gangsterism and public corruption that *auténtico* leaders came to enjoy, are probably gone forever.»

As some members of the tertulia tried to speak, Baquero continued his reflexions.

«Cuba has had worse violations of their constitutions. Mario García Menocal produced a *brava electoral* (electoral fraude) in 1917 and retained the presidency in 1917 for four more years. It led to the *Chambelona* uprising. Gerardo Machado extended "legally" his first mandate and it resulted in our worst constitutional catastrophe. So, to a certain extent, we survived them and will survive this present discontinuity in our national life.»

After a brief pause he continued.

«I am sure there are some *políticos* that would look the recent event with gentler and perhaps tolerant eyes, even if they disagree with it.»

«Who?,» all asked almost in unison.

«To give you some names, people like Manuel Benítez, Francisco Grau Alsina, Miguel Suárez Fernández, Eduardo Suárez Rivas, Arturo Hernández, Julio Tarafa Tellaheche, Conrado Rodríguez, Juan Amador Rodríguez, and even José Pardo Llada, Manuel Bisbé and Aramís Taboada. In fact, I would not discount that eminent Cubans like Cosme de la Torriente and Jorge Mañach, without going to Batista's side, would see that it is better to speak to the enemy instead of unrealistically ignoring its power.»

«Are you suggesting that, with Batista, it would be business better than usual, just as if he had been elected?»

«No. If violent opposition ruffles Batista's feathers, he will respond to terror with more terror. He can be a very brutal and hostile man. Acknowledging any abuses on his part, he will claim that they are necessary and have even been requested by law-abiding citizens ready to pay any prize to control political violence. I hope it does not happen; we could protect the republic with a precarious democracy for the duration of Batista's messianic illusions. His legitimacy should be questioned but not challenged; that's not the way military men yield their power. Batista, after all, has a fairly good public record to watch over and protect from dishonor.»

The words of Baquero were followed by a long silence. He took the opportunity to continue.

«Batista is a very smart man. He will make a serious attempt to regain and maintain support from the population. Count on well publicized public works, social programs [128] that the Grau and Prío failed to provide and overt intimidations [129] to keep everybody away from supporting his opposition. If things come to worse, Batista will tolerate opposition but not insurgency. If he has to, he will strengthen his power by artful manipulation, bribes, graft and cruelty.»

These words of Baquero were interpreted by some in the group as imbued with the arrogance of the victorious; yet, they were not contested. They all knew Baquero, a man they all admired, had a history of unquestioned loyalty to Batista. As he had himself expressed in *La Marina*, when it came to loyalty to the man of September 4th, he was *nulli secundus* in his fervor.

As the *tertulia* broke up close to 4:00 PM, on a day where the streets were almost empty, to many of those present the worst part of it was not that Batista had produced a *Coup d'État* but that the citizenry had proved to be so hurt and violated by previous governments that they reacted with indifference at the destruction of constitutional life in Cuba. That, they felt, would take years or perhaps generations to remedy.

---

[128] Many **social programs**, prophesized by Baquero in 1952, were implemented in the next few years for the benefit of *campesinos*, in an attempt to win their loyalty. They did little but enrich the military men managing them.

[129] During the Batista regime that started in 1952, a citizen detained and interrogated by the **SIM** (*Servicio de Inteligencia Militar*) or the **BRAC** (*Bureau Represivo de Actividades Anti-Comunistas*) knew that he would be subject to psychological and physical tortures if deemed necessary. Batista's henchmen best deterrent to prevent involvement in the active opposition was to leave on any street corner, on any city or town, the tortured dead body of a known member of the opposition. It so happened, years later, to **Pelayo Cuervo Navarro** as both a warning and a revenge for the 1957 unsuccessful assault on the Presidential Palace. There are serious doubts that Batista originated or approved these tactics, but the facts are that they were committed by men he had placed in positions of power.

Photos, top to bottom, left to right:

Gaston Baquero at a funeral ceremony in Havana's cemetery;
Salvador García Agüero and **Juan Marinello** in Senate Chambers in Havana;
Santiago Rey Perna in the comfort of his home.
Cosme de la Torriente; **Jorge Mañach**.

33

Were there ever any Good Politicians in Cuba?
A look back to May 1947

FOUR YEARS AFTER THE DEATH of Manuel Fernández Supervielle (1894-1947), a solemn Mass took place at Havana's Cathedral. President Prío was in attendance, as well as Eddy Chibás, Ramón Grau San Martín, Aurelia Palacios (Supervielle's widow), most of President Prío's Cabinet, the top brass in the Cuban military and, of course, Albert Foster, his wife Ruby Alonso, and several members of Havana's US Embassy. In a New York Times reportage by Richard Pack,[130] the world knew of a brief incident at the church entrance in which Mrs. Palacios had screamed into Grau's face «*You were responsible. You are the only one responsible for Manuel's death.*» Indeed, an urgent telegram had arrived at the time of Supervielle's death, on May 4th, 1947 at the Department of State in Washington, DC; it read:

«Habana's Mayor Supervielle died this morning at 8:05, result of a self-inflicted revolver shot one hour earlier. It is generally believed, and even commented over radio, that action was taken as a consequence of despondency over frustrated endeavors to carry out a campaign promise to supply Havana with adequate water works. (Signed) NUFER.»

---

[130] Richard Pack was a NYT correspondent who followed Cuban politics frequently and had characterized Eduardo Chibás as «*a reporter, crusader, gossip and muckraker, who treats listeners to a weekly half hour dose of verbal fireworks.*»

On a second telegram, the following day, the Ambassador reported:

«Great weight public opinion, as openly expressed, blames Grau and administration for death, holding that honest honorable official was hampered in fulfillment waterworks campaign promises by venality of politicians and Supervielle preferred death to dishonor.»

Supervielle had been elected to the House of Representatives in Cuba for the *Partido Demócrata Republicano* and had served as Treasury Minister during the Grau government. In September of 1946 he became Mayor of Havana on a campaign promise to build a new aqueduct for the city. He was supported by a coalition of several political parties, including the *Auténticos*. At the time Havana had a population of 600,000, and the old aqueduct inherited from colonial times had a capacity to deliver water for 150,000 residents. Upon assuming his post, Supervielle had asked his municipal engineers to draw plans for the aqueduct and had resolved the issue of financing the works with a loan of $6 million from the Sugar Workers Retirement Fund; both José Morell Romero, president of the fund, and Jesús Menéndez, president of the National Federation of Sugar Workers, had signed on the project.

Soon, however, the aqueduct proposal was thrust into a political maelstrom. A commission of legal experts was convened to examine the financial issue. A committee of engineers was appointed to search for design flaws. A panel of financiers was asked to analyze costs. The president of the Sugar Workers Retirement Fund, all of a sudden, developed a case of cold feet and began to ask for more time to consult «*trabajadores, colonos y propietarios,*» as the main stakeholders of the fund. They had so many objections and doubts that Supervielle decided to seek a different source of funding.[131] Late in February of 1949,

---

[131] On the January 26 issue of *Bohemia* magazine, an anonymous article disclosed «*shady deals in the municipal council, with aldermen opposed to the Mayor demanding a "slice" of the $6 million funds if their vote was to be in favor of the project.*»

Supervielle began to investigate the possibility of seeking funds from a foreign bank. [132]

An unexpected threat put additional pressure on Supervielle's project. On March 17, 1947, Segundo Curti, majority leader of the House, submitted on behalf of President Grau a proposal that would transfer the aqueduct negotiations to the Ministry of Public Works. Curti's on-the-record reasoning was that Supervielle had proven to be a failed, incompetent, inept and clumsy public servant. Curti's words were instantly rebated by Manuel Bisbé, an *Ortodoxo* representative, but Supervielle failed in his request to strike Curti's words from the record. He knew Grau was speaking with Curti's voice and it devastated him.

From there on, Supervielle became a frustrated, perplexed, and taciturn man. Political enemies began to follow and accost him everywhere, chanting ¡agua!, ¡agua!, ¡agua!. He began to disguise his appearance when attending the *Rex Cinema* with his wife; it completely spoiled his favorite pastime. Whenever his image appeared on a newsreel, the theater was stormed with hissing, booing and derisive whistling.

Finally on Sunday May 5, at 7:30 AM, Supervielle awoke early, took a bath and shaved. He walked to the garage of his house in *Miramar* and greeted Sergio Alvarez, his chauffeur.

«Sergio, your revolver is old and ugly. I will replace it soon with something newer and better. Let me see it.»

Sergio, unsuspectedly, handed Supervielle his .38 caliber revolver. Supervielle examined the weapon and insisted it was not of his liking. Suddenly, the mayor pointed the weapon to his chest and fired one shot. One hour later, as his body laid motionless at the *Hospital Calixto García*, Aurelia, his wife of 18 years, retrieved a note from the interior pocket of his coat.

---

[132] Once again **Bohemia** commented on the financing of the aqueduct, this time throwing doubts about Supervielle's integrity: «*There are speculations as to the identity of the next fortunate mortal that, within a week's time, will enter into negotiations with the mayor; it is suspected that the mayor will accommodate whomever crosses his path next.*»

«I have decided to deprive myself of life,» the note said. «In my efforts to resolve the water problem for those who elected me, I have found many obstacles beyond my control. I could have solved some of these impediments by compromising my conscience, but I decided not to do that. This has been for me a political failure since I have left unfulfilled a promise I made our people. I hope that, in spite of it, they would believe I have always tried to do my best.»

Photo:
Manuel Fernández Supervielle, during his anguished times as Mayor of Havana in 1947.

Even his closest friends, Manuel Bisbé, Eduardo Chibás, Roberto Agramonte, Pelayo Cuervo Navarro, Guido García Inclán, Jorge Mañach, Felipe Pazos, Miguel Mariano Gómez, Miguel Coyula and Cosme de la Torriente, always addressed him as "Dr. Supervielle."

The history of Cuba, before and after March 10, 1952, has been full of good people; noble, selfless, generous people who took care of the helpless, who continued to push when the world said retreat, which embodied the better angels of our nature. What follows is a very shortened list of good Cuban people from the 1950s, many of whom joined in the 1960s the gatherings of exile; it is a small sample of men and women who, by virtue of their skills, character and deeds, made honor to Cuba, made their compatriots happy to have known them, and made them thankful for having done what they did. Today's Cubans are pleased that they were successful; each of them possessed exceptional talents and, of course, each also satisfied two special necessities: all Cubans would have been pleased to meet them; all Cubans would have been happy to trust them with their most dear possessions.

Carlos Hevia y de los Reyes-Gavilán (1900-1964), was President of Cuba for less than three days. During the third week of 1934, Hevia was President from 5:00 p.m. on Monday, January 15, until 1:20 a.m. on Thursday, January 18. Cuban junta leader Fulgencio Batista had obtained the resignation of Hevia's predecessor, Ramón Grau. The choice of Hevia was unpopular with the military, and by Wednesday, Hevia was asked to resign. He was replaced by Manuel Márquez Sterling.

Huber Matos Benítez (1918-) is a Cuban dissident activist and writer. Formerly, he was a revolutionary who assisted Fidel Castro, Che Guevara and other members of the 26th of July Movement (M-26-7) in successfully overthrowing the dictatorship of Fulgencio Batista. Matos had opposed Batista since the general's *Coup d'État* in 1952, which he regarded as unconstitutional, but became increasingly critical of Castro's after his shift towards Marxist principles, and his ties to the Communist Party of Cuba. Convicted of "treason and sedition" by Castro, he spent 20 years in prison (1959–1979) before being released in 1979.

José Miró Cardona (1902-1974) was a Cuban politician who served as Prime Minister for a period of six weeks in early 1959, following his appointment by President Manuel Urrutia on January 5, 1959. On February 13, 1959, Miró unexpectedly resigned and was replaced by Fidel Castro. Miró was a lawyer and professor at the University of Havana and had become a notable leader in the civil opposition to President Fulgencio Batista. He had inspired students to work for the Cuban Revolution. Following his brief spell as Prime Minister of Cuba, Castro designated Miró ambassador to Spain in May 1960, but by July he had rejected the policies of Castro, resigned his post and sought refuge in the Argentine Embassy. He entered the United States as an exile in the winter of 1960.

Pedro Luis Díaz Lanz (1926-2008), joined Fidel Castro's rebel group in Santiago de Cuba in the late 1950s. He was employed as a commercial pilot with *Aerovías Q* airline. He later acted as head of the *Revolutionary Air Force*, and during 1958 he smuggled weapons and ammunition from Costa Rica and Florida into Cuba by air. After the Cuban Revolution, on 1 January 1959, he was confirmed as head of the Cuban Air Force as well as Castro's personal pilot. Within months, he became vocal about his opposition to the influence of communists on the new revolutionary government and, on 29 June 1959, Fidel Castro relieved him of his post.

Guillermo Cabrera Infante (1929-2005), was a Cuban novelist, essayist, translator, screenwriter, and critic; in the 1950s he used the pseudonym *G. Caín*. A one-time supporter of the Castro regime, Cabrera Infante went into exile to London in 1965. He is best known for the novel *Tres Tristes Tigres* (literally "three sad tigers", published in English as *Three Trapped Tigers*), which has been compared to James Joyce's *Ulysses*.

José Ignacio Rivero (1920-2011) was a Cuban exile and journalist, born in Havana, Cuba. He was the grandson of Don Nicolás Rivero, who in 1832 founded the newspaper *El Diario de la Marina*, and the son of Pepín Rivero, who took over the newspaper upon the death of Don Nicolás in 1919. In 1960 the Cuban government confiscated the newspaper and José Ignacio Rivero left into exile where he continued his journalistic career in Spain and the United States. A rally in Rivero's honor, was held on November 17, 1963 by Dr.Emilio Núñez-Portuondo in preparation for a visit by John F. Kennedy to Miami. The visit, which was aimed at dialoguing with members of the Inter-American Press Association, was able to generate an audience of approximately 6,000 to 8,000 Cubans, according to United States Secret Service estimates. Rivero lived in Miami, Florida where he wrote for the Spanish language newspaper *Diario Las Américas* until his death on August 3, 2011.

Mercedes García Tudurí (1904-1997), educator, poet and philosopher. At age 17 she graduated in Arts at the University of Havana, obtaining doctorates in Philosophy and Letters (1925), Pedagogy and Political Science, Social Sciences and Economics and a BA in Diplomatic and Consular Law. She was president of the Section of Philosophy at the *Ateneo de La Habana*, president of Cuba's Board of Education, member of the Council of Social Defense of the Republic and the National Council of Education and Culture of Cuba and presided over the Cuban Society of Philosophy.

Jorge Mañach y Robato (1898-1961), was a Cuban writer and attorney, considered among the most distinguished of his time. His studies of José Martí, the Apostle of Cuban Independence, are thought to be among the best political and literary interpretations of Martí. He was educated in Cuba, Spain, the United States and France. He graduated from Harvard University in 1920, with a B.A. in Philosophy. From there he continued his higher education studies at the *Université du Droit et de la Santé de Lille* in Paris, and finally, at the University of Havana in Cuba.

Elena Mederos (1900-1981), was a woman of extraordinary character, accomplishments and political experience, who was a major force in promoting human rights work in Cuba.

Pedro Luis Boitel (1931–1972) was a Cuban poet, student leader at the University of Havana and a dissident who opposed the governments of both Fulgencio Batista and Fidel Castro. In 1961, Castro sentenced him to 10 years in prison. Boitel died during a hunger strike in 1972, while serving a sentence handed down by the communist regime.

Olga Serra Schweyer (1924-) is an extraordinary Cuban woman; born in Matanzas from a prestigious and wealthy family with roots in Cataluña and Germany. Her literary and political tertulias in her ancestral home at Playa 111, Matanzas, hosted by both she and her husband Samuel Nodarse, were attended by some of the most important figures in the island. She was desolate upon knowing of the March 10 *Coup d'État* in 1952 and actively began her fight to restore democracy in Cuba, securing arms to the rebels and providing shelter in her home. After the 1959 take-over by the Communists in 1959, she became again a defender of freedom, organized *Operación Pedro Pan* in central Cuba and was imprisoned, like her husband. She went into exile after her husband escaped from prison. Nodarse became one of the first *balseros* who took to the waters, risking his life on a perilous trip to Key West.

Ernesto Lecuona y Casado (1895-1963) was probably the best contemporary Cuban composer and pianist of his time. He was born of a Canarian father and a Cuban mother, and achieved worldwide fame during his lifetime. He composed over six hundred pieces, mostly in Cuban rythms, and was a pianist of exceptional skill.

Gonzalo Roig (1890-1970) was a worldwide known Cuban musician, composer, musical director and founder of several orchestras. He was a pioneer of the symphonic movement in Cuba. In 1931, while participating in the creation of the National Theatre, he composed and premiered his zarzuela *Cecilia Valdés*, a typical example of the Cuban lyric theatre.

Julián Orbón (1925-1991) was a Cuban composer who lived and composed in Spain, Cuba, Mexico, and the US. Aaron Copland, more than once, referred to Orbón as «Cuba's most gifted composer of the new generation.»

Lydia Cabrera (1899-1991) was a Cuban anthropologist and poet, an authority on *Santería* and other Afro-Cuban religions. During her lifetime she published over one hundred books; her most important book is *El Monte*, the first major anthropological study of Afro-Cuban traditions. She made valuable contributions in the areas of literature, anthropology, and ethnology. In 1930 she met Federico García Lorca in Cuba; the poet dedicated his poem *"La Casada Infiel"* to Lydia. For many years, she stated her dislike for the Revolution and socialist-Marxist ideology and moved to Spain first and later to Miami, where she died.

Marta Pérez (1924-2009) was an extraordinary mezzo-soprano and the first Cuban to sing in Milan's famed *La Scala* Opera House, which she did in 1955, at age 31, in the role of *Preciosilla* in Verdi's opera *La Forza del Destino*. She shared the stage with Renata Tebaldi and Giuseppe di Stefano. By age 13, she began to perform as a soloist with the Philharmonic Orchestra of Havana. She was mentored by Cuba's greatest musicians of her time: Ernesto Lecuona and Gonzalo Roig. In 1961, she went into exile in Miami and performed nationally on The Ed Sullivan Show. In 1967, she co-founded the *Sociedad Pro Arte Grateli*, which stands for *Gran Teatro Lírico*.

Fernando Bujones (1955-2005) was an American dancer, born in Miami, Florida to Cuban parents, regarded as one of the finest male dancers of the 20th century and hailed as one of the greatest American dancers of his generation. In 1967 he won a scholarship to the School of American Ballet, the official school of the New York City Ballet Company. He joined the American Ballet Theatre (ABT), one of the world's preeminent dance companies, in 1972 and by the following year, became a soloist; in 1974, at 19, he was not only one of the youngest principal dancers in the world, but the youngest principal male dancer in ABT's history. It was during that period that Mikhail Baryshnikov defected from the Soviet Union and joined ABT in 1974. They worked together as dancers for six years, after which Bujones worked under Baryshnikov's artistic direction. Bujones died of malignant melanoma at age 50, and was buried at Caballero Rivero Woodlawn North Park Cemetery and Mausoleum in Miami.

Adolfo Domingo De Guzmán Luque (1890-1957), was an early 20th century Cuban starting pitcher in *Major League Baseball*. Luque was inducted into the Cincinnati Reds Hall of Fame in 1967. A native of Havana, Luque played winter baseball in the Cuban League from 1912 to 1945. He was also a long-time manager in the league. He was elected to the Cuban Baseball Hall of Fame in 1957.

Saturnino Orestes Armas "Minnie" Miñoso Arrieta (1925-), was born in Havana, Cuba. He is one of the famous Major League Baseball players from Cuba. A left fielder and third baseman, he played 7 different positions on 4 teams, for 17 seasons beginning in 1949 and ending in 1980. He received The Sporting News Rookie of the Year Award in the American League for 1951, and received one of the 9 original Rawlings Gold Glove Awards in 1957. Miñoso was signed by the Cleveland Indians as an amateur free agent in 1948. Between 1949 and 1964 he played for the Indians, the Chicago White Sox, the St. Louis Cardinals and the Washington Senators.

Ignacio Jacinto Villa, aka *Bola de Nieve* (1911-1971), was a successful Cuban singer-pianist and songwriter, whose round, black face earned him the nickname by which he was always known. Villa was born in Guanabacoa, and studied at the *Mateu Conservatoire* in Havana. He worked as a chauffeur and played piano for silent films until his friend *Rita Montaner* took him on as her accompanist in the early 1930s. He was an elite rather than a popular figure, a sophisticated cabaret stylist known for ironic small talk and subtle musical interpretation, with a repertoire that included songs in French, English, Catalan, Portuguese and Italian. He toured widely in Europe and the Americas; his friends included Andres Segovia and Pablo Neruda.

José Lezama Lima (1910-1976) was a Cuban writer and poet who was considered one of the most influential figures in Latin American literature. Born in *Columbia*, the military camp close to Havana, where his father was a colonel, Lezama lived through some of the most turbulent times of Cuba's history, fighting against the Machado dictatorship. His literary output includes the semi-autobiographical, baroque novel *Paradiso* (1966), the story of a young man and his struggles with his mysterious illness, the death of his father, and his developing sensuality and poetic sensibilities. Lezama Lima also edited the magazines *Verbum* and *Orígenes*, presiding as the patriarch of Cuban letters for most of his later years. He died in 1976 at age 65 and was buried in the Colon Cemetery, Havana. Twenty-three years after condemning his "anti-revolutionary activities", the Cuban government paid homage to Lezama Lima through the release of a film, Strawberry and Chocolate, in 1994. In the film, Lezama is a model to Diego, a wayside gay intellectual.

Aurelio de la Vega (1925-), was born in Havana, Cuba in 1925. After studying at the University of Havana (Ph.D. in Law), at the *Conservatorio Ada Iglesias* (Ph.D., Music Composition) and also with Fritz Kramer (Havana), and Ernst Toch (Los Angeles), he settled in California in 1959 and became Distinguished Professor of Music and Director of the Electronic Music Studio at California State University, Northridge. He has been a prolific award-winning musician, who has written 70 works for symphonic orchestras and chamber groups, including pioneer forays into electronic music, none performed in Castro's Cuba. Until recently, and for 53 years, Aurelio de la Vega has been among the top Cuban composers outside his native Cuba but dead to the Communist regime.

Cubans with great achievements in the Cuba of the 1950s and later in Exile

Photos, top to bottom, left to right:
Carlos Hevia, Huber Matos Benítez, José Miró Cardona, Pedro Luis Díaz Lanz, Guillermo Cabrera Infante, José Ignacio Rivero, Mercedes García Tudurí, Jorge Mañach Robato, Elena Mederos.

Cubans with great achievements in the Cuba of the 1950s and later in Exile

Photos, top to bottom, left to right:

Pedro Luis Boitel, Olga Serra Schweyer, Ernesto Lecuona y Casado,
Gonzalo Roig, Julián Orbón, Lydia Cabrera,
Marta Pérez, Fernando Bujones, Adolfo Luque,
Orestes "Minnie" Miñoso, José Lezama Lima, Aurelio de la Vega.

Photos above, top to bottom, left to right:

A distinguished group of Cuban intellectuals that made their names in Cuba during the generations of 1933 and 1952:

1 **Gaspar Agüero**; 2 **Joaquín Llaverías**; 3 **Emilio Roig de Leucheswring**; 4 **Carolina Poncet**; 5 **José María Chacón y Calvo**; 6 **Francisco González del Valle;** 7 **Fernando Ortiz**; 8 **Francisco de P. Coronado**; 9 **M. Pérez Beato**; 10 **Antonio Iraizoz**; 11 **Mariano Brull**.

The last democratic change of government in Cuba, in 1948, as **Ramón Grau San Martín** welcomed **Carlos Prío Socarrás** at the Presidential Palace in Havana.

A promising 1933 generation of Cuban politicians was entirely wiped out on the 10th of March of 1952
(continued)

Photos, top to bottom, left to right:

José Raimundo Andreu Martínez, Prío's Minister of Commerce;
José (Lolo) Villalobos, Mayor of Guabanacoa;
Francisco González Orue, Mayor of Marianao;
José Manuel Casanova, Senator, President of the *Hacendados*;

Manuel Febles Valdés, Prío's Minister of Public Works;
Francisco Grau Alsina, Prío's Minister of Agriculture;
Manuel Antonio de Varona, Prío's Premier;
Rubén de León, Prío's Minister of Interior;

Aureliano Sánchez Arango, Prío's Minister of Education;
Antonio Prío Socarrás, Prío's Minister of the Treasury;
Virgilio Pérez López, Prío's Minister of Communications;
Ramón Corona, Prío's Minister of Justice.

A promising 1933 generation of Cuban politicians was entirely wiped out on the 10th of March of 1952
(continuation)

Photos, top to bottom, left to right:

Orlando Puente, Prío's Secretary of the Presidency and the Council of Ministers;
Edgardo Buttari; Prío's Minister of Labor;
Mariblanca Sabas Alomá; Prío's Minister without Portfolio;
Ramón Vasconcelos, Prío's Minister without Portfolio;

Primitivo Rodríguez, Prío's Minister without Portfolio;
Eduardo Suárez Rivas, Ex-President of the *Liberal* Party;
Santiago Rey Pernas, Republican Party leader in the Senate;
José Miguel Tarafa Govín, leader of the Democratic Party in Matanzas;

Armando Codina Subirat, leader of the *Auténticos* in Oriente Province;
Pelayo Cuervo Navarro, Senator and founder of the *Ortodoxo* Party;
Segundo Curti Messina, founder and leader of the *Auténtico* Party;
Pastor del Rio Carrillo, leader of the Democratic Party in the House.

A promising 1933 generation of Cuban politicians was entirely wiped out on the 10th of March of 1952
(continuation)

Photos, top to bottom, left to right:

Manuel Bisbé, founder of the *Auténtico* Party, then leader of the *Ortodoxos*;
Armando Caiñas Milanés; leader of the Democratic Party in Oriente Province;
José Suárez Rivas; former Minister of Labor and leader of the House;
Sergio Mejías, former Mayor of Matanzas and member of the House;

Noel del Pino, founder of the *Auténtico* Party;
Emilio (Millo) Ochoa, leader of the *Ortodoxo* Party;
Rafael Guas Inclán, lifelong Liberal, former Governor of Havana;
Luis Casero Guillén, Mayor of Santiago de Cuba, Prío's Minister of Public Works;

Lincoln Rodón, President of the House of Representatives in 1948;
Miguel Suárez Fernández, President of the Senate in 1948;
Manuel Dorta Duque, founder and leader of the *Ortodoxo* Party;
Radio Cremata Valdés, Senator and leader of the *Liberal* Party.

Epilogue
The Lessons of March 10, 1952

> *Quis custodiet ipsos custodies?*, (Who will guard the guards?)
> ROMAN POET JUVENAL, ***SATIRES***, SATIRE VI, LINE 347.

WHY WAS IT SO DIFFICULT for Cuba to have a stable civilian government free from the influence, interference or intervention of the military? Cuba, after all, was in 1952 one of the most progressive countries in the Americas, second to none among the Spanish-speaking peoples on a per-capita basis, with the possible exception of Argentina. In 1952, its standard of living, again, on a per-capita basis, was higher than most European countries, and all Asian, Middle Eastern and African countries, bar none. Other statistics were very favorable: 80% of Cubans could read and write, it had more physicians than most countries in Europe, 33% of Cubans were in the middle class, 24% of the labor force was working in industries and the island had more consumption of electrical energy than any country in Latin America. It was true that this progress was due to the singular exploitation of sugar cane by over 160 sugar mills,[133] but the wealth this solitary crop created was enough to pro-

---

[133] In the 1950s Cuba produced over five million tons of sugar per year, three million of which were exported to the US under very favorable conditions.

duce a pleasant life for many Cubans, even though most of them knew a considerable underclass was being left behind.

Cuba, like most of Latin America, was an island of politicized soldiers and army-friendly politicians. The military institution was always considered in the context of its political functions: a stabilizing force, an arbiter of internal disputes, the protector of the constitution, the ultimate guardian of democracy and freedom. For some politicians, it was considered an indispensable source of leadership that would remedy the weakness of social structures and lack of discipline. The m ilitary, of course, never had any foreign or extra-national relevance. As in most of Latin America, Cuba was never under serious threat from abroad. [134]

The armed forces, since independence in 1902, dominated Cuban political life. Unfortunately, the top ranking Cuban patriots in the Wars of Independence did not live to see an independent Cuba.

José Martí, the inspiration of all patriots in 1895, died in *Dos Rios*, days after going ashore in Cuba in 1895;

Antonio Maceo, the leader of the East-West invasion force, died near Punta Brava, near Havana, in 1896;

Ignacio Agramonte, the leader of the furious and heroic charge that rescued Manuel Sanguily, died in Jimaguayú, in his native Camagüey, during the war of 1868-78;

Vicente García, a General in the 1868-78 War, hero of Las Tunas and dozens of battles, was assassinated by the Spaniards in Venezuela in 1888.

Ramón Leocadio Bonachea, the last rebel that rejected the *Pacto del Zanjón*, was captured by Spanish forces and executed in 1885;

Flor Crombet, the General who fought on the three independence wars, was killed in *Altos de Palmarito*, near Baracoa, as the final war got started in 1895;

---

[134] With the exception of laughable occasional risks of war with Rafael Leónidas Trujillo, the Dominican dictator.

Bartolomé Masó, the man who first proclaimed the independence of Cuba in Bayate in 1895, elected President of the Republic at Arms in 1897, opposer of the Platt Amendment, retired presidential candidate against Estrada Palma in 1901, died in 1907.

Calixto García, also a General on the three independence campaigns, died of pneumonia in Washington DC, in 1898, before the proclamation of the Republic.

And so on for other great leaders. Who was left to govern Cuba upon the advent of the Republic? Generals and military men from the second tiers of leadership during the wars:

José Miguel Gómez, head of the Sancti Spíritus brigade, who fought under Serafín Sánchez and Máximo Gómez, a prominent and not inglorious record that did not prevent him from voting for the *Platt Amendment* in the 1901 Constitutional Assembly.

Mario García Menocal, the Cornell graduate who commanded the artillery in the takeover of Victoria de las Tunas under Calixto García. He had spent most of his youth in Tabasco, Mexico, in the sugar industry. Upon joining the War of 1895, he fought under Máximo Gómez, Antonio Maceo and Calixto García and was heavily influenced by José Miguel Gómez. He had no major leadership functions during the independence wars.

Gerardo Machado y Morales, one of the youngest Generals in the 1895-1898 War of Independence, who fought in Las Villas side-by-side with José Miguel Gómez, who used to kid him at times saying «Machado had been our best cattle-rustler against the Spanish Army.»

Carlos Mendieta Montefur, Villareño, physician, whose most important contribution to the independence of Cuba was a mission to the US with Brigadier General Bernabé Boza to coordinate the joint operations of the Cuban and the US armies during the American army invasion in June of 1898. He obtained the rank of Colonel after bringing to Cuba a large shipment of medical supplies through *Punta Alegre*, in the north of

Camagüey, but never led an important battle and never was a leader of men.

Add to the scarcity of top leaders at the start of the republic, the fact that Cubans reached their independence with an absolute lack of experience in governance.

During the XIX century, native Cubans had no participation of any relevance in the power structure of the island. Early (1810) in the century, for instance, Havana's *Cabildo* (a 13 member municipal council) designated 3 candidates for Deputy to the Spanish Courts. Three illustrious criollos were chosen, *Francisco de Arango y Parreño*, *Andrés de Jáuregui* and *Pedro Regalado Pedroso*, of whom de Jáuregui was elected to the *Cortes*. Later, in 1822, during the years of Fernando VII in the throne of Spain, *Félix Varela* was elected to represent Cubans in the Courts. During Napoleonic times, *Joaquín de Santa Cruz*, father of Joaquín de Cárdenas Santacruz, Count of Jaruco, and *Juan Clemente Núñez del Castillo y de Molina*, Count of Castillo and Marquis de San Felipe, were elected to be Deputies at the Cadiz Court. In 1837 *José Antonio Saco* was elected Deputy to the Courts. In 1878, after the Pacto del Zanjón, a March 1, 1878 proclamation granted Cubans representation in the Courts of Spain. In all of these cases, however, Cuban deputies before the Spanish Courts played no role beyond those of mere straw men. In the words of Enrique José Varona in 1921,

«Cubans were kept obedient under the saber of the men from the Spanish crown. They even feared freedom and for that reason, when the continent was up in arms, Cuba remained submissive, paying taxes without electing representatives with any power, buying the right to have servants at the expense of their right to dignity.»

The unchallenged hegemony of military men in the first years of the Republic was easy to understand in the context of the exclusivity in organizational know-how of the Cuban Independence Army. For the first 40 years of republican life, it was impossible to eliminate the linkage of political life and militarism. More so since there was always a close tie between armies, power and civil society in the Spanish world. That link age was apparently broken in Cuba after the election of Ramón Grau San Martín to a military-free presidency in 1944 and it was confirmed with the Prío presidency in 1948. Was the rise of *Generalísimo* Franco in Spain after the 1936-1939 Civil War what gave Batista the green light to resurrect the authority of the Army in Cuban life? Why did the norms of Spanish *falangismo* prevailed in Cuba over the codes of American liberalism so close and successful in the north? Did the collapse of colonial status produced in Cuba the same ill-fated brooding of *caudillos* as in the rest of Latin America? Was the discipline of the military a pre-requisite for the upper classes to be comfortable enough to bring on capital formation and general prosperity?

In Cuba, for a long while, people trusted that with economic development and a more modern social structure, there would be fewer opportunities for the armed forces to intervene in political life. Batista destroyed that expectation; he was aided by the prevailing corruption and social unrest brought about by gangsterism during the Grau and Prío governments. It was also facilitated by a fashionable anti-imperialism in the intellectual classes of Cuba and the discrediting diatribes of deranged leaders like Eduardo Chibás.

Batista's [135] intervention in Cuba —under the premise of restoring order— produced a *de facto* government that forever

---

[135] A little known episode in Batista's life made his fate very close to that of **Maximilien de Robespierre** during the French Revolution. Robespierre, the strong man in Paris that had turned into a dictator after the Reign of Terror, was interrupted by one of his enemies during a speech at the *National Convention* on July 28, 1794. Jean-Guillaume Tallien, a fellow delegate, accused him of treason. In spite of his public speaking ability, Robespierre hesitated a moment and several co-conspirators of Tallien began to shout «*the blood of Danton is choking him!,*» at which point Robespierre ran away from the meeting and took refuge at Paris' *Hôtel de Ville*, from where he was taken to the guillotine and executed by his enemies.

Years later, in the midst of the 1933 Cuban revolution, **Fulgencio Batista** was invited to a meeting at the home of Sergio Carbó, director of *Prensa Libre* newspaper; Carbó was one of the members of the *Pentarquía* (the government by five), and the man who had promoted Batista to General and chief of the Cuban Army. A group of students, fed-up with Batista's ambitions, had arranged for one of them to accuse the General of treason; that would have been followed by a group of students, led by Carlos Prío, taking him directly to a firing squad in Columbia. The key to the ambush was the consent of Grau San Martín; he had agreed to confirm that Batista had become a traitor. All was arranged so that a student would then shout «Death to the traitor!». At the precise moment when Grau had to join the accusing chorus, he changed his mind and said nothing. It gave Batista an opportunity to escape and go directly to Columbia, where he consolidated his leadership over the army. Two almost identical stories with very different outcomes.

and irreversibly limited people's participation in the governance of the country. In the mid 1950s, twelve of twenty Latin American republics were in the hands of military dictators. By the end of the decade only two persisted: Paraguay's *Alfredo Stroessner* and Cuba's *Fidel Castro*. Argentina's *Juan Domingo Perón*, Nicaragua's *Anastasio Somoza*, the Dominican Republic's *Rafael Leónidas Trujillo*, Venezuela's *Marcos Pérez Jiménez*, Haiti's *Paul Magloire*, El Salvador's *José María Lemus* and Colombia's *Gustavo Rojas Pinillas*, in a few glorious years, were assassinated or escaped with their pilfered plunderings. Not so in Cuba. Batista's legacy was a broken nation; it could not have been more offensive.

Photo:
Fulgencio Batista in *Columbia Camp*, March 10, 1952, with his famous Colt .45 ACP, 5" 8-round weapon under his leather jacket.

Appendices

**I - The Presidential Cabinets
before and after March 10, 1952**

**II - Arguments before the US Department
of State by Supporters and Opponents
of the March 10 *Coup d'État***

**III – Important World Events
during the Year 1952**

**IV –Cuban Military participating
or leading in the 1952 *Coup***

V — *Consejo Consultivo* 1952

**VI – Main Characters at the times of the
of the March 10, 1952 *Coup d'État***

VII —Alphabetical Index

I – The Presidential Cabinets
before and after March 10, 1952

Carlos Prío's Last Cabinet *

Oscar Gans	Prime Minister
Luis F. Casero	Minister of Public Works
Eduardo Suárez Rivas	Minister of Agriculture
Ramón Zaidín	Minister of Commerce
Félix Lancís	Minister of Education
Sergio M. Mejías	Minister of Communications
José R. Andreu	Minister of Health
Rubén de León	Minister of Defense
Angel Manuel Ferro	Minister without Portfolio
Antero Rivero	Minister without Portfolio

*   Most of the Cabinet resigned in order to run for elective office on June 1, 1952, according to the *Gaceta Oficial* on March 7, 1952.

Fulgencio Batista's First Cabinet **

Miguel Angel de la Campa	Minister of State
Miguel Angel Céspedes	Minister of Justice
Ramón Hermida	Minister of Interior
Marino López Blanco	Minister of Finance
Oscar de la Torre Reyné	Minister of Commerce
Andrés Rivero Agüero	Minister of Education
Alfredo Jacomino	Minister of Agriculture
Jesús A. Portocarrero	Minister of Labor
Pablo Carrera Jústiz	Minister of Communications
José A. Mendigutía	Minister of Public Works
Enrique Saladrígas Zayas	Minister of Health
Nicolás Pérez Hernández	Minister of Defense
Ernesto de la Fé	Minister of Propaganda
María Gómez Carbonell	Minister without Portfolio
Julia Elisa Consuegra	Minister without Portfolio
Justo Salas Arzuaga	Minister without Portfolio
Santiago Alvarez	Minister without Portfolio
Leonardo Anaya Murillo	Minister without Portfolio

** The Cabinet was appointed through a series of Decrees issued by Fulgencio Batista as Prime Minister, as per the *Gaceta Oficial* on March 11, 1952.

II - Arguments before the US Department of State by Supporters and Opponents of the March 10 *Coup d'État*

In 1952, the Cold War tension between the US and the USSR was escalating rapidly. US Senator Joseph McCarthy of Wisconsin launched the congressional investigations into Communist spies in the US government. The country was in the midst of a recession, the US was heavily involved in the third year of the bloody and indecisive Korean War (June 1950-July 1953) and the Department of State was alarmed by the 1950 election of Jacobo Arbenz Guzmán (a leftist) in Guatemala. It was in this context that Fulgencio Batista produced his *Coup d'État* in Cuba. Whether or not Batista could be trusted as an anti-Communist became the most important parameter in the decision of the US to accept or oppose his newly formed government. In the end, and in light of the *Truman Doctrine**, the US accepted Batista. What follows are the arguments on both sides of the issue.

Supporting Fulgencio Batista and the Coup

- From day 1, Batista has given public and private statements concerning its intention to control international Communism in Cuba.
- On June 12, 1992, for instance, he stated he would «*fight Soviet ideology with the same energy as that with which he previously fought Nazi-Fascism.*»
- The Cuban delegation to the UN has consistently aligned Cuba with the US.
- On April 3, 1952, the Batista government broke relations with the Soviet Union, and refused to allow USSR diplomats to enter Cuba.
- On May 22, 1952, Cuba's *Consejo Consultivo*, on its first session, approved a bill to investigate Communist activities in Cuba.
- During 1953, Batista's administration has changed the electoral code to require 4% signatures of the electorate (rather than 2%) in order to register a party, thus making it almost impossible for the PSP (Communist Party) to qualify for the 1954 elections.
- The CTC (Cuban Confederation of Labor) has been cleaned of Communists by the Batista government.
- The *Hoy* newspaper has consistently attacked Batista since March 10, 1952; Communist sympathizers have been arrested, Communist establishments have been raided and Communist meetings have been broken up or denied permits to hold gatherings.

- Batista's *PAU* (*Partido Acción Unitaria*) has been reorganized as the *PAP* (*Partido Acción Progresista*) and all Communist infiltrators have been left behind in May of 1953.
- In the opinion of the US Department of State, «the available evidence does not support the allegation that Batista is pro-Communist,» according to a Memorandum of June 16, 1953. In Havana, the *El Mundo* newspaper, on July 19, 1953, carried a story on its front page under the headline "*US denies that Batista is pro-Communist.*"

Opposing Fulgencio Batista and the Coup

- Batista has maintained close relations with Cuban Communists and there are Communists in important positions in his government.
- Batista is a close friend of Communist leader Juan Marinello, who has a strong influence in the Ministry of Labor.
- Batista gave legal status to the Communist party in 1938, and was elected President in 1940 under a coalition that included the Communists, and official propaganda that exhibited the "*hammer and sickle.*"
- In 1940 Batista gave absolute control of the CTC (Cuban Confederation of Labor) to the Communists and included them in his Cabinet.
- In the last free elections in Havana (June 1, 1950), Batista allied his party (PAU, Partido Acción Unitaria), to the PSP (Popular Socialists Party).
- Under Batista, in 1952, Communists have been elected to the Executive Committee of the CTC (Cuban Confederation of Labor).
- On March 9, 1952, the Communist newspaper *HOY* called for the organization of a "*popular front*" to defeat Carlos Hevia (the candidate of the PRC, Partido Revolucionario Cubano (Auténticos), as «*the candidate of imperialism and the reactionary middle class.*»
- Batista's Coup breaks a still young Cuban tradition of selecting presidents by popular vote and will undermine Cuba's democracy with a return to the times of the military *caudillos*.
- The military *Coup d'État* undoes more than a decade of constitutional development.

---

* Truman argued that the US could no longer stand by and allow the forcible expansion of Soviet totalitarianism into free, independent nations since US National security depended upon more than just the physical security of American territory. The **Truman Doctrine** committed the US to actively assist nations to preserve their political integrity when it was threatened by Communism and it was in the best interest of the United States to take an active role.

III – Important World Events during the Year 1952

- King **George VI** of England died and his daughter **Elizabeth** was proclaimed Queen of England.
- **Joseph Stalin** ruled the USSR and, in Egypt a military coup overthrew **King Farouk**.
- For the first time, the US detonated a **Hydrogen Bomb**. The United Kingdom announced it had an **Atomic Bomb**.
- In science: the **contraceptive pill** became available, the **Polio vaccine** was developed and **transistor radios** went on sale.
- **Pius XII** was Pope. **Winston Churchill** was Prime Minister of the United Kingdom. **Vincent Auriol** was President of France. **Konrad Adenauer** was Chancellor of West Germany.
- **Eva Perón** died in Argentine.
- *I Love Lucy* was tuned in by 10,000,000 US viewers.
- The US flied the **B-52** for the first time.
- **Ernest Hemingway** published *The Old Man and the Sea*.
- In México the **Paricutín Volcano** exploded burying the town of San Juan Parangaricutiro.
- The **Mau Mau** rebellion started in Kenya.
- On Nov. 4, **Eisenhower** defeated Stevenson, and became President of the US.
- On March 20, **An American in Paris** earned the Oscar Academy Award.
- **Puerto Rico** became a self-governing US Commonwealth.
- The **UN building** in New York was built.
- The **Winter Olympics** were held in Oslo, Norway; the Summer **Olympics** in Helsinki, Finland.
- The NY Yankees won the **World Series** beating the Brooklyn Dodgers 4 games to 3.
- In boxing, **Jersey Joe Walcott** defeated **Ezzard Charles** on June 5 and was later defeated by **Rocky Marciano** on September 23 for the World Heavyweight Championship.
- The price of a loaf of **bread** was $0.16; Sears was selling good **rayon shirts** for $3.66; a **Magnavox TV-Phonograph-Radio** was $595; a two-door Buick sedan was $2,200.
- Batista made the cover of **TIME** magazine on April 9.
- The **Communist party in Cuba** registered less than 50,000 voters.
- Batista published a new **Constitutional Code**: anyone wishing to organize a party had to gather 5,000 signatures and, after January 1953 parties could act normally, preparing for the elections in November 1953.

IV – Cuban Military participating or leading the 1952 *Coup dÉtat*

Alberto del Río Chaviano.
Antonio Blanco Rico.
Aquilino Guerra González.
Arístides Sosa de Quesada.
Carlos E. Pascual Pinard.
Carlos M. Cantillo González.
Carlos Tabernilla Palmero.
Dámaso Sogo Hernández.
Fermín Cowley Gallego.
Florentino Evelio Rosell Leiva.
Francisco Tabernilla Dolz.
Francisco Tabernilla Palmero.
Ignacio Leonard Castell.
José Fernández Rey.
Juan Rojas González.
Julio Sánchez Gómez.
Leopoldo Pérez Coujil.
Luis Robaina Piedra.
Manuel Ugalde Carrillo.
Martín Díaz Tamayo.
Pedro A. Barreras Pérez.
Pedro A. Rodríguez Ávila.
Pedro A. Valdivia Romero Armengol.
Pilar García García.
Ramón Cruz Vidal.
Roberto Fernández Miranda.
Víctor M. Dueñas Robert.

V — *Consejo Consultivo 1952*

SENATORS:
Miguel A. Suárez Fernández, Carlos Miguel de Céspedes Ortiz, Eusebio Mujal Barniol, who declined at the last minute. [136]

MEMBERS OF THE HOUSE OF REPRESENTATIVES
Jorge García Montes, Luis Lima Delgado, Carlos M. Ferreti Vidal, René Gregorio Ayala, Mario Cobas Reyes, Ignacio Alonso Lorenzo, Jesús Villa Suárez and Radio Cremata Valdés.

FORMER CONGRESMEN:
Ricardo Eguilior Vinent, Generoso Campos Marquetti, Carlos Saladrigas y Zayas, Aquilino Lombar, Leonardo Anaya Murillo, Justo Salas Arzuaga, Martín A. Iglesias Abreus, Ramón Vasconcelos Maragliano, Walfredo J. Rodríguez, Santiago C. Rey Pernas, Gustavo Gutiérrez Sánchez, José Pardo Jiménez, Germán López Sánchez, José Elías Olivella, Desiderio Sánchez Varela, Ernesto Rosell-Leyte Vidal, Manuel García Herrera, Julián García Benítez, Wilfredo Albanés Peña, Anselmo Alliegro Milá, Pedro Cuní Estorino, Luis Loret de Mola, Angel Pardo Jiménez and Alberto Aragonés.

LABOR LEADERS
Mercedes Chirino Chapotín, José Pérez González, Conrado Rodríguez Sánchez (resigned on 22 May 1952), Alfredo Haydar Mata, José Ribalta, Raquel Valladares, Felipe Savigne, José Luis Martínez Alvarez and José M. Vázquez Prieto,

JOURNALISTS
Armando Maribona, Gustavo E. Urrutia, Miguel de Marcos, David Grillo, Angel C. Artola, Rafael Esténger, Luis Ortega Sierra, Gastón Baquero, Regino Díaz Robainas, Josefina Mosquera and Raúl Lorenzo Ruiz.

OPINION MAKERS
Claudio Benedí, Octavio Montoro, Evelio Govantes, Zoila Leiseca, Hortensia Llamazares, Julia Elisa Consuegra, Carlos M. Raggi Ageo, José R. García Pedroso, José Manuel Carbonell, Gastón Godoy-Loret de Mola, Carlos Bustamante Sánchez and Raúl López Ibáñez.

POWERFUL AND RICH
Comandante Manuel Varona Guerrero, Justo García Rayneri, Francisco de Pando, Burke Hedges, Alfonso Fanjul, Manuel Aspuru, Fernando de la Riva, Jorge Barroso Piñar, Pastor Torres Sánchez, Guillermo de Zaldo Castro, Santiago Alvarez Rodríguez and Guillermo Aguilera Sánchez.

---

[136] **Eusebio Mujal**, decided to serve Batista as General Secretary of the *Confederación de Trabajadores de Cuba (CTC)*, rather than at the Consejo.

SENIOR ADVISORS

Antonio Alonso Avila, Arturo Pérez Heredia, Ricardo Ferrera Ortega, Juan Bautista Diago, Justina Hernández, Carlos Fernández Campos, Humberto García Riverto, Rafael Miquel, Mario Torres Menier, Pedro Montano Bofill, Ricardo Torres de Navarra, Manuel Quevedo Juarézagui, Jorge Herrera Morales, Miguel Saludes Gutiérrez, Francisco Díaz Silveira, Armando Aguilar Bencomo, Hatuey Agüero, Fernando García Tuñón, Guillermo Mestre Fernández, Arturo Fernández González, Lelio Alvarez, Juan B. Columbié, Mario Leyva González, Luis Oliva Pérez, David Quinta, José R. Pérez Magariño, Arsenio González, María Teresa Díaz de Villegas, Manuel Soto Fraga, Avelino Pascual López, Eduardo Dumois Cárdenas, Manuel J. Villar Melens, Heriberto Madrigal Ramírez, Alfredo Valmaña, Fernando de la Cruz and Emilio Maza.

EXECUTIVE MEMBERS OF THE CONSEJO

Rotating Presidents, Carlos Saladrigas y Zayas, Gastón Godoy-Loret de Mola, Justo García Rayneri and Generoso Campos Marquetti; Vice President, Jorge García Montes; Secretary, Walfredo J. Rodríguez, José Elías Olivella Lastra.

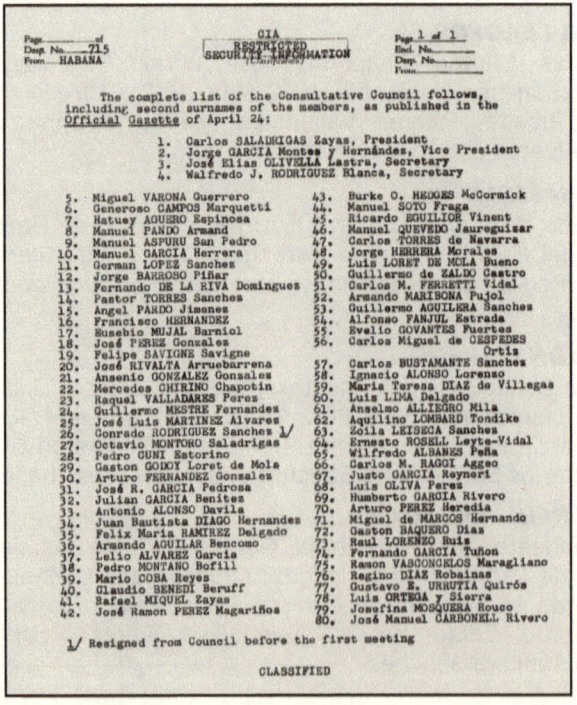

Document above:

A copy of the **CIA report** listing the members of the *Consejo Consultivo*. It reached Washington, DC, two days before it was published by the papers in Havana.

VI – Main Characters at the time of the March 10, 1952 *Coup d'État*

Dean Acheson (1893-1971)

    Secretary of State during the Truman Presidency. An alumnus of both Yale and Harvard and a lifelong Democrat. Designer of the Marshall Plan and founder of NATO. In 1950 he was blamed for the "loss of China." He persuaded Truman to get into the Korean War in June of 1950. During the presidency of Kennedy he was an advisor in the Missile Crisis. He was considered by Republicans as being "soft on Communism."

Roberto Agramonte (1904-1995)

    Dean of the School of Philosophy and Letters of the University of Havana; Ambassador to México, Vice-Presidential Candidate with Eduardo Chibás as President in 1948; Presidential candidate for President in 1952; taught at the University of Puerto Rico after 1960; died in exile in Miami in 1995 at age 91.

José Braulio Alemán (1864-1930)

    Former Brigadier General during the War of Independence in 1895. He was a lawyer and newspaper owner. In 1896 he was the leading author of the Constitution of *La Yara* and was a firm opponent to the Platt Amendment during the 1901 Constitutional Assembly. During the Republic he served as Senator, Minister of Education and Ambassador to Mexico and was very involved in the modernization of the University of Havana.

Anselmo Alliegro (1899-1961)

    Mayor of the town of Baracoa; member of the Cuban Congress in 1925, 1940 and 1945; Prime Minister in 1944; President of the Cuban Senate in 1954-1959; several times member of the Cabinet; served as President of Cuba for one day after Batista left the country on January 1, 1959; died in exile in Miami at age 61.

Ruby Alonso (1928-1999)

    She was Secretary at the Presidential Palace in Havana, and a graduate of the University of Pennsylvania with a Master Degree in English. She became the favorite secretary of President Carlos Prío in dealings with international correspondence and issues. Married Albert Foster, the top CIA man in Havana in the early 1950s and was probably a CIA operative herself. She died in Miami in 1999 after leaving Cuba as an exile in 1960.

Manuel Alvarez Margolles (1905-1964)

    He was a Colonel in the Cuban Armed Forces and during the Prío government was the top army official in the Oriente province. He resisted the *Coup d'État* and decided to stay in Cuba. He became involved in the "30 de Noviembre" conspiracy (MRR, MRP, DRE, FAL, etc.) and was captured together with hundreds of conspirators. He was shot by a firing squad in 1964 at *La Cabaña*.

Fulgencio Batista y Zaldivar (1901-1973)

    Rose to power in the 1933 rebellion of the Sergeants; he was elected President for four years in 1940; returned to the presidency after a *coup d'état* in 1952. Batista took refuge in the Dominican Republic in 1959 after being overthrown by Castro's revolution. Found political asylum in Portugal; he died of a heart attack in 1973 while visiting Marbella in Spain at age 72.

Gastón Baquero (1918-1997)

    Baquero was a notable journalist and poet. He was born in Banes, Oriente and graduated as an agronomist from the University of Havana. He dedicated his life to poetry, translations of poems and journalism. Was Editor in Chief of *Diario de la Marina* since the 1940s. Went into exile in 1959 and died in Madrid.

Willard Leon Beaulac (1899-1990)

US career diplomat and writer, graduate from Brown University, a devout Catholic, served in the Navy in WWI, born in Rhode Island, former ambassador to Paraguay, Colombia, Cuba (1951-1953) and Argentina. Retired in 1960 and taught at the Universities of Southern Illinois and Ball State, died in Washington, victim of Alzheimer disease.

Manuel Bisbé Alberni (1906-1961)

Bisbé was one of the founders of the University Reform movement and of the first Federation of University Students (FEU) in Cuba. He graduated as doctor in Public Law, Civil Law and Philosophy; served as professor at the Escuela Normal de Matanzas and the Secondary School in Havana. Member of the opposition movement to the dictatorship of Gerardo Machado; was expelled from Cuba in late 1930. In 1944 he was elected member of the House of Representatives by the Cuban Revolutionary Party (*Authénticos*). In May 1947 participated in the founding of the Party of the Cuban People (*Orthodoxos*). Bisbé was a candidate for the Senate in the 1952 elections, frustrated by the *coup* by Fulgencio Batista. He died in New York in 1961 while serving as ambassador to the UN.

Ruperto Cabrera Rodríguez

Cabrera was a professional soldier who on August 24, 1949, replaced General Genovevo Pérez Dámera as Chief of the Army in Cuba. He was appointed by Carlos Prío, who promoted him from Brigadier General to Mayor General. During Batista's *Coup d'État* he was retired from the army according to *Decreto 94* of March 10, 1952. Also retired on that day were Generals Otalio Soca Llanes, Quirino Uría López and José H. Velázquez Perera, as well as Colonels Francisco Alvarez Margolles, José Acosta de la Fuente, Eduardo Martín Elena, Urbano Matos Rodríguez and Epifanio Hernández Gil, among others, leaving the Cuban army devoid of know-how, leadership and professionalism. Ruperto Cabrera was asked by Batista to join the March 10, 1952 conspiracy; he refused to cooperate but did nothing to stop it, according to some of his peers. He was arrested at his home at 3:00 AM on March 10, 1952.

Eulogio Cantillo Porras (1911-1978)

Cuban military man who became Chief of the Army in Cuba under General Batista on March 10, 1952. He had been the top student in the military academy, with Ramón Barquín his second. He had been Chief of the Military Aviation when Batista appointed him to the top military post in 1952. During the last days of Batista in 1958 he had a meeting with Castro and helped Batista to flee to the Dominican Republic. He went to prison for 15 years after January 1, 1959 and before completing his sentence was freed and went to exile in Miami, where he died in 1978.

Sergio Carbó Morera (1892-1971)

Carbó was a journalist at the newspapers *El Fígaro, La Discusión, La Prensa, El Día* and, *Prensa Libre*. He was a member of the *Pentarquía*; In 1933 he was instrumental in appointing Fulgencio Batista as General. He earned the Justo de Lara Prize in Cuba (to top journalists). His son was a member of the 2506 Brigade against Castro in 1961.

Pablo Carrera Jústiz

Carrera Jústiz was Minister of Communications in Batista's first Cabinet in 1952. He had been a professor at the University of Havana and a Secretary of the Presidency.

Luis Casero Guillén (1902-1978)

Casero was a former Mayor of Santiago de Cuba; he was arrested during the attack to the Moncada Barracks. He also served as Minister of Public Works in the government of Carlos Prío; became notable for his plan of 60 public works completed in 60 days, a promise he carried to the end. Casero was one of the most outstanding public servants in Cuba during Republican times. He was a member of the *Organización Auténtica* and left Cuba after the triumph of the revolution.

Nicolás Castellanos

Castellanos was a former president of the City Council of Havana. A handsome truck driver that became mayor in 1950 opposing Antonio Prío, the president's brother who was an odds-on favorite to win. Castellanos was supported by Fulgencio Batista, Grau San Martín and the Communist Party, one of the strangest political alliances in the history of Cuba. His campaign was based almost exclusively in providing plenty of water for the capital. Time Magazine called it the "Bathtub Election."

Edmund A. Chester (1897-1973)

A highly respected journalist, senior VP of CBS radio and TV, Bureau Chief for Latin America for Associated Press. In the late 1940s Mr. Chester emerged as the director of News, Special Events and Sports for the CBS Television Network; it included direction of the first televised session of the United Nations General Assembly in November 1949. He was a good friend of General Batista and wrote the book "*Un Sargento llamado Batista*" in 1954. He wrote speeches for Batista, lived in Havana for many years and died of Alzheimer's at age 76.

Eduardo René Chibás (1907-1951)

Chibás was a life-long politician, radio personality and founder of the *Ortodoxo Party* in Cuba in 1947 as a splinter of the Grau and Prío *Partido Auténtico*. He denounced corruption and gangsterism; as an anti-Communist Senator he warned his followers of Batista intentions of producing a *Coup d'état* in 1952. He shot himself during his weekly radio program and, after 11 days of intensive care, died in a hospital. His funeral was attended by thousands.

Carlos Miguel de Céspedes Ortiz (1881-1955)

He was a descendant of a cousin of Carlos Manuel de Céspedes del Castillo, the father of the Cuban Nation. He was a lawyer and politician, born in Matanzas, a law graduate from the *University of Havana;* Secretary of Public Works (1925-1929), Justice (1929-1930), Education (1930-1932), and Senator from Camagüey and Matanzas. Nicknamed "The Dynamic" because of the many works that he inspired and supervised during the Machado government. His residence was destroyed at the fall of Machado and in its place was built the *Church of Corpus Christi* in Miramar. He died of sadness at age 74, shortly after the death of his wife Margaret.

Carlos Cantillo González

He was one of the officers from the Cuban Armed Forces who collaborated with Batista in the *Coup d'État* of March 10, 1952. With Colonel Roberto Fernández Miranda, Colonel Carlos Cantillo González took over the military aviation camp in Columbia. After January 1, 1959, he stood on trial accused of treason. General Cantillo was accused of having "betrayed Fidel Castro," when he failed to deliver his troops to the rebels in Santiago Cuba, as he had promised.

Angel Cofiño García

Angel Cofiño García was a Secretary General of the *Confederación General de Trabajadores de Cuba (CGT)*. He was a reformed Communist, having left the party in 1940. The *CGT* was formed in 1949 through a split that was legally recognized as a faction of CTC. The split had its epicenter in the telephone and electricity workers' unions. *CGT* was led by Angel Cofiño, but later reunited with the legal CTC after a short period of existence. Angel Cofiño, as head of the electrical workers union had numerous conflicts with Eusebio Mujal. They ended when Mujal —who blindly supported Batista on March 10, 1952, removed Cofiño from office. In exile, Cofiño was a member of the *Frente Cívico Revolucionario Democrático*. He died in Miami at age 68.

Benito Coquet

Benito Coquet was a personal representative of the Mexican President to Batista's inauguration on February 27,1955; he was the same man who in March of 1952, as Mexican Ambassador to Cuba, granted asylum in Mexico to President Carlos Prío Socarrás and his family when Batista deposed Prío via a *Coup d'état*. Coquet became Secretary to the Presidency in Mexico and was campaign manager for José

Vasconcelos. His son was taken to court by the government of Michoacán for profiting, as Michoacan's Secretary of State, from the distribution of Taxi licenses in the state.

José Manuel Cortina y García (1880-1970)

Cortina was a Cuban politician, lawyer and journalist; one of Cuba's most outstanding orators and diplomats. He graduated from the *University of Havana* as a lawyer in 1903 and for more than half a century wrote for several important cultural magazines in Cuba. He was a member of the Cuban House of Representatives and the Senate since 1906. He acted as President Alfredo Zayas' Secretary of the Presidency and President Miguel Mariano's Foreign Minister; was a delegate to the *League of Nations* in 1927. Cortina was instrumental in the elimination of the *Platt Amendment* in the early 1930s. He died in exile in Miami at age 90.

Ajejo Cossio del Pino (1906-1952)

Former member of the Republican Party in Cuba in the 1950s, who was murdered on 11 February 1952 at the *Restaurant Strand*, in Belascoain and San José Streets. At the time of his death he owned *Radio Cadena Habana* and the *Restaurant Topeka*. Followers of Emilio Tró had written his name in Tró's tomb to warn him that the *Union Insurreccional Revolucionaria (UIR)* had placed a bounty on his head. Cossio was a follower and friend of Mario Salabarría (Salabarría and Tró participated in the *Orfila* massacre). He was shot by four gangsters that hit him 16 times. Cossio had been Minister of the Interior during Grau's government and had promised «*Se acabaron las Pistolas.*» (This is the end of weapons). Cossio turned out to be the Calvo Sotelo that Batista was missing in Cuba. It was rumored at the time –with no proofs- that Batista had paid the assassins of Cossio del Pino.

Fermín Cowley Gallego

A Cuban military man accused of many crimes committed during the Batista 1952-1959 government. On March 10, 1952 he had been a First Lieutenant in an infantry battalion in Santiago de Cuba. Once it was clear that Prío had fled the Presidential Palace in Havana, Cowley arrested Colonel Margolles, the military chief in Santiago, and facilitated the release of the new military chief, Alberto del Rio Chaviano. It got Cowley a promotion to Lieutenant Colonel, as well as his appointment to the second highest position in Santiago. In 1956 he was transferred to the top position in Holguín, where he was responsible for the "*pascuas sangrientas*" on that year (23 youngsters killed in anticipation of a revolt in northern Oriente to support the landing of Castro in the south). In retribution, Cowley was murdered by William Gálvez on November 23, 1957 at an airport in Holguín.

Radio Cremata Valdés (1904-1972)

Cuban Senator and attorney, born in Santiago de las Vegas, died in Miami, after 40 years in exile. He was one of the most popular young members of the House of Representatives in Cuba; leader of the Liberal Party and scion of one of the most illustrious families in Havana.

Gustavo Cuervo Rubio (1890-1978)

Cuban physician and politician. VP from 1940 to 1944 under Batista, after he was unsuccessful in 1936 as a VP candidate under Grau San Martín. He was a member of the 1940 Constitutional Assembly. In 1959 went into exile and died in Miami at age 88.

Segundo Curti Messina (1910-2000)

Curti had been a student leader against Machado, Minister of Interior in the government of Grau San Martín, and a former student in the College of Architecture of the University of Havana. He was a founding member of the PRC (A) and Minister of Defense in the government of Carlos Prío after having served in the House of Representatives for two periods. Curti went into exile in 1952 after the *Coup d' État* of Batista and returned to Cuba in 1959 where he died at age 90.

Rafael Díaz-Balart (1926-2005)

Cuban politician that served as majority leader, Minister of the Interior and Senator during the second presidency of Fulgencio Batista. In 1955 he opposed the amnesty granted by Batista to Castro (his former brother-in-law) after the attack on the Moncada Barracks. He was the son of a representative of the same name elected to the House in Cuba in 1936. After his exile in 1959 he lived and prospered in Spain and served as a diplomat for several Latin American countries. He died at age 79 in Miami after a prolonged battle with leukemia.

Martín Díaz Tamayo (1928-1995)

General in Batista's government; Batista appointed him director of the Bureau for the Repression of Communist Activities (BRAC) in July of 1955. He had been apparently falsely accused of carrying an order from Batista in 1953, during the Moncada attack, to «kill ten prisoners for each dead soldier.» In 1957 he was promoted to Major General and appointed chief of the *Servicio de Inteligencia Militar (SIM)*. In 1958 Díaz Tamayo was found to be conspiring against Batista and was retired from the Cuban army. He was allowed to go into exile in March of 1959 and died in Miami.

Eduardo Martín Elena

Colonel Martín Elena was a popular military chief at the Goicuría Barracks in Matanzas, Cuba, at the time of the March 10 *Coup d'État* by Batista. He was never a politician but a true democrat, rejecting Batista's promises to promote him to the rank of General. After the successful *Coup*, he requested to be discharged from the army and –thanks to his strong engineering credentials- became manager and CEO of *Rayonera de Matanzas*, one of the largest textile companies in Cuba in the 1950s.

Rafael Esténger Neulin (1899-2003)

Cuban poet, diplomat, writer, biographer and lawyer; member of the Machado government, founding member of Cuba's *Colegio Nacional de Periodistas*. Over the years he wrote for *Letras, El Fígaro, Cuba Contemporánea, Alerta, Avance* and *Bohemia*. Went into exile in 1959.

Manuel Fernández Supervielle (1894-1947)

Cuban Lawyer and politician, a graduate of the University of Havana. Member of Congress from the *Partido Demócrata Republicano* in 1940. Joined the Auténticos and was Minister of the Treasury. Mayor of Havana in 1946. Died in Havana in 1947 of a self-inflicted gunshot when he could not fulfill his promise to bring water to the city.

Orestes Ferrara Marino (1876-1972)

Naturalized Cuban military man, politician, diplomat, university lecturer, writer and journalist of Italian origin. He was a member of the Cuban Liberation Army (colonel under Calixto García and Máximo Gómez) and one of the leaders of so-called historical liberalism. House Representative for various periods, Secretary of State in the government of Gerardo Machado, a member of the 1940 Constitutional Assembly and Cuba's ambassador to UNESCO in 1955. Author of numerous papers and studies on history and international relations. Ferrara was fired from all his positions in 1959, moved to Rome and Paris, and died in exile.

Albert Foster (1918-1998)

Former CIA chief in Havana in the 1950s. Graduated from Johns Hopkins School of Advanced International Studies in Washington, DC. Lived in Cuba with his wife Ruby Alonso, secretary in the Presidential Palace. After leaving Cuba in 1957 was appointed chief of European operations for the CIA. Retired in Miami in 1962 and lived there for the remainder of his life.

Oscar Gans López-Martínez (1903-1965)

Cuban attorney and politician. Served as Foreign Minister, Cuban ambassador to the US and Prime Minister in Prío's government. Member of the *Partido Acción Unitaria* and later a good friend of General Batista.

Rafael García Bárcena (1907-1961)

Poet, philosopher and Cuban revolutionary. Graduated in Philosophy and Letters from the University of Havana in 1938. Maintained an active opposition to Gerardo Machado; was a member of the first University Student Directory in 1927, and in 1930, directed his press agency *Cuba Libre*, writing proclamations against Machado. One entitled "To arms" called to rebel against injustices of Machado; as a result he was imprisoned in the *Castillo del Príncipe* in Havana. On September 4, 1933 he signed with others, including Sergeant Batista, the proclamation establishing the *Pentarchy*. He was involved in the founding of the *Partido Revolucionario Cubano (PRC)* in 1936. He was also one of the founders of the Cuban Society of Philosophy. On April 5, 1953 he was arrested along with other young students and was accused of organizing and leading an attempt to take by assault the fortress of *Columbia*; he was tortured and sentenced to two years in prison on the Isle of Pines. Seriously ill in 1961, he died of a stroke on June 13, 1961, at age 54.

Armando García Sifredo (1917-2004)

Journalist, author, broadcaster and founder of two newspapers in exile in Miami: *Patria* and *La Nación*. As a young man he became popular as the voice of *Radio Cadena Azul*. He was a member of the *Auténticos* and served as Senator during Grau's presidency, when he was the youngest member of the Cuban Congress. He strongly condemned the March 10 1952 *Coup* of Batista. In 1959 he was arrested and deported into exile under a threat to his life. For health reasons he moved to Sparta, South Carolina in 1998, where he died. He asked to be cremated so that his remains could be returned some day to Cuba.

Jorge García Tuñón (1913-2003)

Important military figure in Cuba. After the *Coup d'État* by Batista he was promoted from Captain to *Brigadier General*. He has been identified as the military man who initiated the *Coup* in Cuba before Batista committed to it. In 1952 Tabernilla was designated Chief of the Army and García Tuñón, according to many «the real mastermind of the *Coup*,» was only appointed Chief of Columbia Camp. Jorge García Tuñón and his brother Roberto entered Columbia on March 10 1952 in the second car of a caravan of three. In the first was traveling Batista with Tabernilla Dolz and Roberto Fernández Miranda.

Rafael Guás Inclán (1896-1975)

Former Senator (1940-1944), governor of Havana (1944-1948), Minister of Communications (1953-1954) and VP of Cuba (1954-1958); son of Carlos Guás Pagueras, a Cuban Senator and General from the 1895 Independence War. He became involved in politics during the presidency of Menocal and in 1925 was the youngest elected member of the House of Representatives. Guás went into exile in Miami in 1933 and again returned as an exile to Miami in 1959. He was a member of the 1940 Constitutional Convention. He was elected VP in the dubious elections of 1954 when Batista was declared elected. A street mob vandalized and burned his office on January 1st 1959 as he left for exile in Miami. Volunteered for the 2506 Brigade but was rejected because of his age. His son died during the Bay of Pigs invasion.

Ramiro Guerra Sánchez (1880-1970)

Historian, economist and teacher. Graduated from *Colegio La Luz* in Batabanó in 1898 and participated in the Summer School for teachers at Harvard University sponsored by the US intervention government. Doctorate in Pedagogy in 1912; director of Havana's Normal School for Teachers in 1915. General Superintendent of Schools in Cuba in 1926. Founder with Arturo Montori of the magazine *Cuba Pedagógica*. Director of *Diario de la Marina* from 1943 to 1946. Died in Havana at age 90.

Muchachos del Gatillo Alegre (Trigger Happy Boys)

The most important of these gangster groups in Cuba were the *Movimiento Socialista Revolucionario (MSR)* under the control of Rolando Masferrer, Manolo Castro, Fabio Ruiz and Mario Salabarría, the *Unión Insurreccional Revolucionaria (UIR)*, led by Fidel Castro and Emilio Tró, and the *Acción Revolucionaria Guiteras (ARG)* led by Eufemio Fernández and Jesús González Cartas, alias *el Extraño*.

Ramón Grau San Martín (1887-1969)

Cuban physician, professor of Physiology at the University of Havana and author of several books in his specialty. He was appointed provisional president in 1933 and elected to the presidency in 1944. Son of a prosperous tobacco grower from Pinar del Río; travelled extensively through Europe for several years until 1921. Because of his support of the university students he was imprisoned in 1931 and upon release went into exile. Except for accusations of allowing corruption, nepotism and violence, he has been considered a good president of Cuba. He died in 1969, at age 82, poor, desolate and feeble after the dissolution of the Cuban Republic in 1959.

Fabio Grobart, aka Antonio Blanco, aka Abraham Simjovitch (1905-1994)

Poland born communist of many aliases that, as a tailors' assistant, became a founding member of the Cuban Communist Party in 1925, with Julio Antonio Mella and Rubén Martínez Villena. For decades he served as a party ideologue and was the man who introduced both Fidel and Raúl Castro at party meetings. He was deported from Cuba in 1930 by Machado and in 1948 by the Prío government; recruited by Ernesto (Ché) Guevara, he returned in 1960 as top party planner. His role in Cuba after 1960 has never been fully documented. It is known, however, that he was the highest ranking representative of the Third International in Cuba. He died in Cuba in 1994 at the age of 89.

Carlos Hevia y de los Reyes (1900-1964)

Cuban surgeon, a graduate from the US Naval Academy at Annapolis in 1919. President of Cuba for three days (January 15 to January 18, 1934) after Fulgencio Batista removed Grau San Martín from the Presidency at the request of the military after the fall of Machado. He had been Minister of Agriculture under Grau. After lots of protocol, including a 21 gun salute during his inauguration, and after been sworn in by his father-in-law (Chief Justice Juan Federico Edelman) Hevia resigned in favor of Carlos Mendieta. During the administration of Carlos Prío Hevia served as Foreign Minister and was the 1952 candidate for president from the *Auténtico* Party. Died in 1964.

Marcos Hirigoyen

One of the top labor leaders in the 1950s in Cuba, member of the AFL-CIO International; he was first a Communist and later a rabid anti-Communist. He was Havana's transportation (bus drivers) labor boss and had links with *Acción Revolucionaria Guiteras (ARG)*. During the March 10 1952 *Coup*, Hirigoyen went to the University of Havana with Pascasio Linares and Calixto Sánchez –other important labor leaders- to resist Batista. He assured Mujal (the top CTC leader) that the transportation sector would join the general strike against Batista. He was arrested; Mujal joined Batista's forces after the General promised to respect all labor laws.

Mario Kuchilán Sol

Cuban journalist who had a regular column in *Prensa Libre* under the heading "Babel." He was also a master caricaturist, publishing his drawings in *La Semana, Karikato, El Mundo, Prensa Libre* and other political newspapers of the times. He had no reservations condemning the Batista followers for their support of the *Coup* on March 10, 1952. He was punished by his adversaries by bringing him out of his home and viciously torturing him. After 1959 he joined the Castro regime, became the occupying director of *Prensa Libre* and continued writing in support of the revolution.

Félix Lancís Sánchez (1900-1976)

Cuban physician, writer and politician, three times Senator, Minister of Education and twice Prime Minister from 1944 to 1945 and 1950 to 1951. Founder of the *Partido Auténtico* in 1934. During the government of Carlos Prío he was his right hand supporter in Congress. He was jailed after the end of the Republic in 1959 but never left Cuba. Died in Havana, childless, soon after the death of his wife Carmelina Barba de Lancís at the age of 76.

Jorge Mañach y Robato (1898-1961)

Cuban attorney, political analyst and writer, educated in Cuba, Spain and France. Harvard graduate in 1920 with a degree in Philosophy. Taught at Columbia University. Member of the *Grupo Minorista*; participated in the *Protesta de los Trece* and in the 1933 revolution. Mañach was one of the founders of the *Revista de Avance* and was Cuba's Foreign Minister in 1944. His most important essays and books were *La Crisis de la Alta Cultura* (1925), *Indagación del Choteo* (1928) and *Martí el Apóstol* (1933). Mañach was forced by Castro into exile and died in Puerto Rico in 1960 at the age of 62. See page 225.

Juan Marinello Vidaurreta (1898-1977)

Marinello was a lawyer and a leading Cuban communist intellectual and politician. In 1923 founded the *Falange de Acción Cubana*, a Marxist organization, with Rubén Martínez Villena. Later the same year he participated in the *Protesta de los Trece*. With Julio Antonio Mella he joined the *Movimiento de Veteranos y Patriotas* in 1923 during the government of Alfredo Zayas. Machado sent him to exile in Mexico. He was a propagandist for the Republican cause in the Spanish Civil War of 1936. He died in Havana at the age of 79.

Carlos Márquez Sterling Guiral (1898-1991)

Cuban attorney, diplomat, writer, politician and professor of law and economics at the University of Havana, where he founded the School of Journalism that bears his uncle's name. Member of the Cuban House of Representatives; Minister of Education and Labor; President of the 1940 *Constitutional Assembly*. He was detained many times by the Batista government before he ran for President in 1958. Al the closing of the Republic he went into exile and died in Miami at age 93. See page 77.

Joaquín Martínez Sáenz (1902-1974)

Cuban lawyer, economist and politician. He served as Senator, Minister of the Treasury, Minister of Agriculture and President of the *Banco Nacional* in 1952. In September 1931 he founded the *ABC*, a right-leaning movement that contributed to the fall of the Machado government. He became famous in the US for a .38 caliber pistols duel with his nemesis Oscar de la Torre where both men ended up firing into the air. Martínez Sáenz was a member of the 1940 Cuban Constitutional Assembly. He died in exile at age 72.

Rolando Masferrer Rojas (1918-1975)

Cuban politician, congressman, newspaper editor of *El Tiempo* and bona fide gangster; he was an early member of *Joven Cuba*, the far-left organization founded by Antonio Guiteras in 1934. Masferrer participated in the Lincoln Brigades during the Spanish Civil War in 1936 and was a member of the Cuban Communist Party. In 1975 he wrote an editorial in his Miami newspaper *Libertad* condoning terrorism. He died at age 57 in Miami, victim of a bomb placed in his car.

Salvador Massip Valdés (1891-1978)

Eminent geographer; Doctor of Pedagogy and Philosophy at the University of Havana and Master of Arts from the Faculty of Pure Sciences of Columbia University; Professor Emeritus at the University of Havana. In 1912 he began his teaching activities as an assistant professor of anthropology at the Faculty of Sciences of the University of Havana and later as Professor of Geography at the *Instituto de Matanzas*, the Faculty of Arts at the University of Havana and Smith College in Puerto Rico. For his part in the strike of March 1935 he was arrested and deported to Mexico, where he served as Professor at the National Autonomous University. At the fall of the Gerardo Machado government he was appointed Ambassador of Cuba in Mexico. He died in Havana at age 87.

Sergio Mejías Pérez

Close collaborator and supporter of President Carlos Prío. Member of the Cuban legislature –which he occasionally presided- representing the province of Matanzas. On March 10, 1952, with Diego Vicente Tejera, accompanied President Prío in his quest for support in Matanzas. They returned to Havana empty handed. He had been appointed Minister of Communications by the deposed president.

Otto Meruelo

Journalist and TV personality in Cuba during the government of Batista after the March 10, 1952 *Coup d'État*. After the fall of Batista on January 1, 1959, Meruelo began to hide until he was found and betrayed by Antonio Nuñez Jiménez, an old friend and devoted revolutionary. He was taken to court on April of 1959 and condemned to 30 years (Cause 351 of that year). He served 20 years, one month and 11 days and went into exile in Miami.

José Miró Cardona (1902-1974)

Cuban lawyer, professor of the Universities of Havana and Puerto Rico, civic leader of the opposition against Batista in the late 1950s, Prime Minister briefly in 1959 and Ambassador to Spain in 1960. After breaking with Castro, he sought refuge in the Argentine embassy in Havana and went into exile in early 1961. He was a liaison between Cuban rebels and the US during the Kennedy administration and the Bay of Pigs invasion. As the invasion failed to achieve its objectives, Miró —whose son had disembarked in Cuba— denounced the CIA and John F. Kennedy for their failure to provide the promised support. He died in San Juan, PR, at age 72.

Menelao Mora Morales (1905-1957)

Cuban lawyer and politician. Fought against Machado and became a militant of the ABC. Participated in the 1935 strike; he was detained, accused of terrorism and sent into exile in the US. In Cuba he was secretary and chief executive of the *Cooperativa de Omnibus Aliados* (Havana public transportation buses). He became a member of the PRC (A) and served several periods as Representative. Mora was killed in Havana during the attempted magnicide (an assault on the Presidential Palace) against Batista on March 13, 1957.

Andrés Domingo Morales del Castillo (1892-1979)

Cuban lawyer, judge and politician; Senator from 1944 to 1952, Minister of the Presidency, Justice, Housing, Defense and Foreign Relations, and temporary President in 1954, when Batista wanted to run for President under very questionable circumstances. He was to be the last candidate for President in Cuba under even more problematic elections in 1959, when the insurgents were coming down from the *Sierra Maestra*. Morales never married and died in exile in Miami at age 87.

Eusebio Mujal Barniol (1915-1994)

Originally a young Catalonian baker's son from Guantánamo, Eusebio Mujal joined the Communist party in the early 1930s and got to be Secretary General of *Joven Cuba* after he renounced to Communism. In 1938 he left *Joven Cuba* and joined the *Auténtico* party. In 1946 he joined other CTC members of the PRC (A) on a campaign to expel all Communists from the CTC, even though Grau was still in a pact with Cuban Communists (PSP). In 1952 he met with Batista after the General's *Coup* and joined forces with him, cancelling a strike that threatened Batista's grip on the government. When Castro called for the destruction of the 1958 sugar crop in Cuba –a prelude to his defeating Batista- Mujal gave orders to the sugar workers to «stand guard against the torch.» He found asylum at the Uruguayan embassy after the triumph of the revolution and went into exile.

Emilio (Millo) Ochoa y Ochoa (1907-2007)

Cuban politician, dentist and college professor. Member of the 1940 Cuban Constitutional Convention —and its longest surviving signatory. Founder of the *Partido Auténtico* in 1934 and the *Partido Ortodoxo* in 1947. Served as Senator of the Republic from 1940 to 1948. Was arrested 32 times because of his political opposition —first to Batista and later to Castro. Went into exile in 1960; practiced dentistry until 1965; taught in Nebraska and Chicago until 1971 and retired to Miami to live his last days with rather modest means. He was without doubt, one of the most scrupulously honest politicians from Cuba. Died in Miami of cardiac arrest at age 99.

José Pardo Llada (1923-2009)

Cuban journalist, politician, diplomat and radio personality. Attended the *University of Havana* but never graduated. In 1944 became famous while informing the public through CMQ radio of an impending hurricane during three consecutive days. Was a consummate critic of the government of Ramón Grau, every day at 1:00 pm, through *Unión Radio*, at the time the program with the largest audience in Cuba. His most famous slogan was "*iqué desparpajo señores!*" (gentlemen, what a mess!). He was elected several times for public positions in Colombia after leaving Cuba and died in Bogotá as an exile from Castro at age 86.

Leopoldo Pérez Coujil

Colonel in the Cuban Army during Batista's dictatorship after 1952. He replaced Martín Elena in Matanzas on March 10, 1952; he left Columbia on January 1, 1959 at the same time that Batista did. He was considered by the government of Castro one of the main assassins in a group that allegedly included: Esteban Ventura, Pilar García, Hernando Hernández, Julio Laurent, Ángel Sánchez Mosquera, Rolando Masferrer, Conrado Carratalá, Merob Sosa, Alberto del Río Chaviano, Irenaldo García Báez, José María Salas Cañizares and a few others. He died in exile.

Genovevo Pérez Dámera (1910-1970)

Chief of the Cuban army from 1945 to 1949 during the government of Ramón Grau San Martín. He was confirmed in that position but never got along with Carlos Prío and was replaced as Chief of the Army -at the request of a group of officers- by General Ruperto Cabrera. He later became Senator for Pinar del Rio and finally left Cuba and died rather poor in exile.

Colacho Pérez

One of the conspirators that supported Batista in his *Coup d'État* of March 10, 1952. In the 1930s, he had been a member of the *ABC* party, to which Batista also belonged as a young man. Colacho was one of the main civilian participants in the March 10 conspiracy, together with Ramón Hermida and Pablo Carrera Jústiz. It has been said that on Friday, March 7, 1952, Batista was having lunch at his daughter Mirta's house in Havana, when he was visited by three important supporters: Rodríguez Calderón, García Tuñón and Colacho Pérez. They were told –before anyone else- that the Coup would be next Monday, March 10, 1952. See pages 141 to 143 for details on the chosen date.

Antonio Prío Socarrás (1905-1990)

Cuban banker and Minister of Treasury during the government of his brother Carlos Prío. In 1950 ran for mayor of Havana and, in one of the cleanest elections in Cuba, lost to Nicolás Castellanos, who had been Vice Mayor during the time of Manuel Supervielle as Mayor. According to people close to him, Antonio liked parties and money and the two things came together when –still married to Rosario Páez, a beautiful lady- he fell in love with Olga Chaviano, Cuba's foremost exotic dancer; he set her up in a luxurious apartment in Havana, barely a few days after meeting her in person. After the fall of his brother Carlos, Antonio gave Olga a farewell gift which was reportedly an envelope with a large sum of money. Weeks later Olga was about to marry Ramón Antonio Crusellas, heir to Cuba's Colgate, *Jabón Candado* and Dial Soap distributorship, when Norman Rothman, owner of Havana's *Sans Souci* Nightclub, proposed and married her. Antonio left Cuba for exile in 1959 and died in Miami in 1990.

Orlando Piedra Negueruela (1917-

Cuban military man, supervisor of the Secret Police, head of the Police at the Presidential Palace and Chief of the *Buró de Investigaciones*, an organization responsible for flushing out opponents to the Batista government, from 1952 to 1959. He was originally en employee of the tramways in Havana and became a policeman in 1941. During the March 10 *Coup* he became Batista's favorite *guardaespalda* (bodyguard) He fled Cuba with Batista in 1959.

Carlos Prío Socarrás (1903-1977)

Charismatic lawyer and student leader, elected Senator for Pinar del Rio in 1940 and elected President of Cuba in 1948. Served as Minister of Public Works, Minister of Labor and Prime Minister in the Grau government. Lifetime member and founder of the *Partido Auténtico* in Cuba. Presided over a time of constitutional order and political freedom in Cuba. He was called *"el Presidente Cordial"* for his civility, accessibility and friendliness. He was credited by Arthur M. Schlesinger to having said «*They say I was a terrible president of Cuba but I certainly was the best president Cuba ever had.*» In the opinion of many Cubans, this was absolutely true. Prío died in Miami, at age 74.

Herminio Portell Vilá (1902-1992)

Cuban foremost historian in the XX century, particularly Cuban-United States relations. He left Cuba after the Communists seized power in 1959, and died at his home in Miami in 1992. Portell Vilá taught at the *Escolapios* School from 1923 to 1926, became a Guggenheim fellow in 1931 and later taught at the University of Havana until he left Cuba. His political life was limited to being a member of Havana's Municipal Council. In exile in the US, he worked for the Voice of America and wrote incessantly.

Orlando Puente Pérez

Puente was a close friend of Carlos Prío, who appointed him Secretary of the Presidency in 1948 and Minister without Portfolio in 1951. Prior to Prío's government he had been an official of the Labor Ministry during Grau's presidency. His sister was married to Angel Cofiño, anti-Communist leader of the *CTC*. He was reported by *the* CIA to be "charming but incompetent and somewhat arrogant." He ran for the Cuban House of Representatives in 1952 but never made it due to Batista's March 10 *Coup*.

Guillermo Alonso Pujol (1896-1968)

Cuban Politician, Senator and Senate President of the Republic in 1940, founder of the *Republican Party* in 1944; he united his forces to those of the *Auténticos* to elect Grau San Martin in 1944 with the *Coalición Auténtico-Republicana* against Carlos Saladrigas, Batista's candidate. He succeeded as VP candidate with Carlos Prío in 1948 and broke with him almost immediately after becoming Vice-President of Cuba. They defeated Nuñez Portuondo, *the Liberal-Democra*tic candidate and Zoilo Marinello, the *Communist candidate.* Aside from their radical left leaning credo, Zoilo and his brother Juan Marinello were wealthy owners of a considerable fortune in Cuba.

Miguel Angel Quevedo (1896-1969)

Editor and proprietor of the popular weekly magazine *Bohemia*, widely read in Cuba and all Latin America. The magazine had been founded by his father in 1908; Miguel Angel (son) took over in 1927, a year before the death of Quevedo Sr. During the government of Carlos Prío (1948-1952) the magazine became his inexhaustible opponent. Quevedo later joined the cause of Fidel Castro and supported his movement to unseat Batista in 1959. Frustrated by the communist fervor of Castro, who confiscated his magazine in 1960, Quevedo went into exile and took his life at age 73. One of his best friends, Enrique de la Osa, creator of the popular *Sección en Cuba*, betrayed his old boss and became the political *interventor (de facto* manager) of *Bohemia* in 1959.

Juan José Remos Rubio (1896-1969)

Juan J., as he liked to call himself, was an eminent Cuban author and analyst. He graduated from the University of Havana with a degree in *Filosofía y Letras*. Almost immediately –at age 18- he became director of the magazine *Arte* and began to teach at the *Instituto de la Habana*. He eventually became Ambassador to Spain, member of the Cuban Academies of History and Language. With Emeterio S. Santovenia, Ramiro Guerra and José Manuel Pérez Cabrera, Juan J. wrote *Historia de la Nación Cubana*, a masterful and timeless work in 10 volumes. During his senior years he became a consultant to the Batista government and in 1959 took the road to exile, dying in Miami 10 years later.

Santiago Rey Perna (1908-2003)

Rey Perna was a prominent political figure in Republican Cuba. His father was a veteran of the 1895 War of Independence. Santiaguito, as he was known, held the position of Minister of Interior during the Batista 1952-1959 term —he had been his friend since the 1930s, when he was a leading member of the Conservative party. Rey Perna was a member of the 1940 Constitutional Assembly, and was considered as a learned man of exceptional talent, and a known aficionado and expert in Cuban history. After 1959 he went into exile in Mexico and later in Miami, where he lived for 40 years and died of a heart attack at age 95.

Alberto del Río Chaviano

Rio Chaviano was a Cuban military man that became a good friend of Batista when he joined the army in 1933. By 1941 he had been promoted to Second Lieutenant; in 1948 he made it to the rank of Captain. On March 10, 1952, he was Chief of the Guardia Rural in Palma Soriano and he joined the forces of Batista. The assault of the Moncada Barracks in Santiago de Cuba found him Chief of that garrison; under orders from Batista he got to suppress the photos of the massacre, with the exception of those published in *Bohemia*. After commanding the government forces in Oriente, sensing defeat, he left Cuba before Batista and flew to the Dominican Republic.

Andrés Rivero Agüero (1905-1996)

Cuban lawyer, writer and politician, elected president two months before the dissolution of the Republic in 1959. Never took possession. Graduated from the *University of Havana*, member of the *Liberal Party*. In 1940 was Minister of Agriculture; after 1952 Minister of Education, Senator and Prime Minister. After January 1, 1959 he went into exile and died in Miami at age 91.

Carlos Saladrigas Zayas (1900-1956)

Cuban lawyer, politician and diplomat. Served as Senator in 1936, Minister of Justice in 1934, Foreign Minister in 1933 and 1956, Prime Minister from 1940 to 1942 and Ambassador to Great Britain. After serving as Batista's Prime Minister he became the presidential candidate for Batista's party in 1944; he lost to Ramón Grau San Martín and the *Auténticos*. Died at his home in Havana at age 56.

Alberto Salas Amaro

Salas Amaro was the director of the Cuban newspaper *Ataja*, one of the newspapers that most supported Batista during 1952-1959. (The others were Ramón Vasconcelos' *Alerta* and Rolando Masferrer's *Tiempo en Cuba*). Salas Amaro was a good friend and Batista's personal secretary. Together with Andrés Rivero Agüero (*Coalición Progresista Nacional*), Carlos Márquez Sterling (*Partido del Pueblo Libre*), Ramón Grau San Martín (*Partido Auténtico*), Alberto Salas Amaro (*Partido Unión Cubana*) was a presidential candidate in the contrived elections of 1958. He obtained 1.44% of the vote. He was arrested on January 23, 1959 and later went to exile in Miami.

Rafael Salas Cañizares (1907-1956)

Salas Cañizares was a military man promoted by Batista in 1952 from Lieutenant to *Brigadier General*. During the *Coup d'État* of March 10, he took charge of all the police stations in Havana and the National Police Headquarters. As a faithful Batista subordinate he commanded the capture and killing of *el Colorado*, Orlando León Lemus (allegedly carried out by Lutgardo Martín Pérez on February of 1955, at *el Colorado's* home in Durege Street, Santos Suárez, Havana) and personally directed the assault of the Embassy of Haiti on October 29, 1956, where he was killed.

Aureliano Sánchez Arango (1907-1976)

Cuban lawyer, university professor and astute politician. Active during the fights against Machado. Founding member of the *Partido Auténtico*. Minister of Education and Foreign Minister during the government of Carlos Prío. Took the road to exile in Mexico in 1952 and later participated in several underground movements against Batista. In 1958 financed the movement against Batista by Castro and later had to seek asylum in the US. Died of a heart attack in Miami at age 69.

Dámaso Sogo Hernández

Dámaso Sogo was a low level military man in Cuba who became known as the man who –while serving as officer of the day at Columbia Camp- opened the gates of the base to provide access to Batista on March 10, 1952.[137] He was promoted to Brigadier General for this important service. Later, after a 16 day hunger strike by prisoners in 1957, he was appointed director of the *Presidio Modelo de Isla de Pinos*, replacing Colonel Manuel Ugalde Carrillo. In 1958 he was assigned to the *Sierra Maestra*, where he served with Lieutenant General Eulogio Cantillo Porra, Brigadier General Alberto del Río Chaviano, Coronel José Manuel Ugalde Carrillo, and Lieutenant Coronel Merob Sosa.

Policarpo Soler (1908-1961)

Alleged to be the most powerful Cuban gangster (aka Domingo Herrera). He dressed as a police lieutenant throughout the Batista presidency and in 1944 went into exile in Mexico where he met Orlando León Lemus (*el Colorado*), another alleged Cuban gangster, also exiled in Mexico because the events in *Orfila* on September 1947 (see pages 23, 28 and 59). Returning to Cuba in 1948 he participated in numerous attacks as part of the *"muchachos del gatillo alegre."* (the trigger-happy buddies). After he was taken into custody he escaped the *El Principe* prison, traveled to Spain and the Dominican Republic where he was shot in 1961 by Trujillo bodyguards at age 53.

Arístides Sosa de Quesada (1921-2000)

Sosa de Quesada was known as the military-poet in Cuba in the 1950s. He had been born in Limonar, Matanzas, and by 1936 he was Chief of the Military Judicial Service of the Cuban Army's Cultural Section. In 1942-1944 he served as Defense Minister in Batista's first government and began to write frequently. Among his most important productions was the *Estatutos Constitucionales* that Batista instituted on March of 1952, after his *Coup d'État*. It earned him a promotion to General. He was also the founder of *Bibliotecas Ambulantes* with José Angel Buesa, the *Revista Isla* and the *Reediciones Isla*. He went into exile in 1962 and became professor at Dana College in Nebraska. In Miami he founded the *Grupo Artístico Literario Abril (GALA)*.

Francisco Tabernilla Dolz (1888-1972)

El Viejo Tabernilla, as his friends called him, was the first graduate of the *Escuela de Cadetes del Ejercito Cubano* in 1917. One of his first assignments was at *La Cabaña* garrison, where he returned as Chief in 1934-1944. He became a loyal Batista follower during the September 4, 1933 first *Coup d'État* by Batista, and for that reason was licensed from the army by Grau San Martín in 1944. He returned briefly as Chief of *La Cabaña* after Batista's *Coup d'État* in 1952, before he was appointed Chief of Staff of the Cuban Army. With Anselmo Alliegro he witnessed the resignation of Batista in 1959. He departed Columbia ahead of the General on January 1st and broke with Batista during his days in exile. He died in Miami at the age of 84.

Mary Tarrero de Prío (1924-2010)

María Dolores (Mary) Tarrero Serrano was first lady of Cuba from 1948 to 1952, as wife of President Carlos Prío, the last constitutional president of Cuba. She was born in Camagüey and studied stenography at an early age. While working in Cuba's Senate building, she met Carlos Prío and at age 24 became First Lady. She was a beautiful woman and inspired a popular song by Oswaldo Farrés —the author of *Quizás, Quizás*— entitled *Sensación*. With her two daughters and husband she went into exile in 1952 and returned to Cuba in 1956 after an amnesty by Batista. A few months later they returned to exile after Batista found out Prío was financing his opponents. The family returned in 1959 and went back to Miami as exiles at the end of the

---

[137] There is some evidence that Sogo was not on time and on March 10 failed to open the gate of Post number 4 at Columbia; Captain **Jorge García Tuñón**, who was in one of the cars of Batista's caravan, had to step out and remove himself the chain at the gate, risking his life before the surprised eyes of a sentry who had not been warned. Once the chain was dropped, Sogo arrived after a quick sprint that left him out of breath; he confirmed that it was OK to open the gate.

year, after realizing Castro had become a Communist dictator. Mary died of pneumonia in 2010, never having returned to Cuba.

Diego Vicente Tejera y Rescalvo (1914-1992)

Dieguito Vicente Tejera was a Matanzas-born *Auténtico* Cuban Senator (1944-1952), a member of the House of Representatives (1940-1944) and a former Minister of Education. He was accused with ousted president Carlos Prío of conspiring to export arms from the US in 1954. Also arrested at the time were Prío and Segundo Curti, former Cuba's Minister of the Interior. During his arrest in Tampa, Tejera allegedly became irritated for the lassitude and indolence of his Bondsman and peeled a bunch of $100 dollar bills from his wallet and posted his own bond. He left politics on March of 1952 and went into exile in 1959, living most of the time in the Dominican Republic. He moved to Miami shortly before his death.

Cosme de la Torriente Peraza (1872-1956)

Veteran of the War of 1995, under the command of Major General Calixto Garcia. He was elected representative to the Constitutional Assembly of *La Yaya*, where he was very active drafting the constitution which was approved on October 29, 1897. He participated in the siege of Santiago de Cuba and on August 18, 1898 was promoted to Colonel, fighting under the direction of Calixto Garcia. He accompanied García on his trip to Washington to manage the recognition of the House of Representatives of the Cuban Revolution by the U.S. government, as well as to secure a loan to pay the members of the Independence Army. In 1901 he was a judge in the province of Matanzas and in July 25, 1903 was appointed first secretary of the legation of Cuba in Spain. From May 20, 1913 to January 10, 1914 he served as Cuban Secretary of State. In 1934 he was president of the National Association of Independence Army Veterans. He held several political offices during the first years of the Republic. In the 1950's, during the dictatorship of Fulgencio Batista, he chaired the Association of Friends of the Republic, an organization founded to seek mediation between the dictator and the traditional political opposition. He died in Havana in 1956.

Manuel Ugalde Carrillo (1919-1997)

Manuel Antonio Bartolomé Ugalde Carrillo was born in Rodas, Las Villas, in 1919. He joined the Cuban army in 1941, graduated in 1944 and reached the position of Chief of the *Servicio de Inteligencia Militar (SIM)* after Batista's Coup in 1952. During the last years of Batista he commanded an infantry division (about 5,000 men) in the *Sierra Maestra*. In 1959, after the collapse of constitutional life in Cuba, he was characterized by *Bohemia* magazine as «*One of the most prominent murderers of the Batista regime. His time at the Presidio Modelo in the Isle of Pines, as well as in several other military positions can only be remembered by the cruelty, death and torture he sowed.*»

Quirino Uría, M.M.N.P. (1907-1984)

Chief of the Columbia Military Camp during the governments of Grau San Martín and Carlos Prío. In 1949 he was promoted to four-stars Brigadier General and appointed Chief of the National Police substituting José M. Caramés. Uría became famous for his war against gangsterism. Within days of his appointment to the police he arrested members of the *Movimiento Socialista Revolucionario (MSR)* and the *Unión Insurreccional Revolucionaria (UIR)*, led by Policarpo Soler and Orlando León Lemus (*el Colorado*), as well as others in the "most wanted" lists. Uría was asked by Batista to be part of the March 10, 1952 coup and lead the Cuban Army; he firmly declined to betray the 1940 Cuban Constitution and resigned from the army. On the day of the *Coup* he was detained and removed from Columbia camp. Years later, when the Communists toppled Batista's government, he became an exile. He died in the US at age 77.

Manuel Antonio de Varona y Loredo (1908-1992)

Cuban lawyer and politician. Served as Senator and Prime Minister during the Carlos Prío government. Member of *Organización Auténtica*. He was director of the *Brigada 2506* who attempted to overthrow Castro in 1961. In 1961 the New York Times called him "Cuba's perennial rebel." He had been arrested for the first time at 16, for taking part in anti-government activities during the presidency of Alfredo

Zayas. In 1938 he became a lawyer upon graduation from the *University of Havana*. Varona spent time in jail during the governments of Machado and Batista. He was one of the first Castro opponents in 1959 and died in exile in Miami at age 84.

Ramón Vasconcelos Maragliano (1890-1965)

Vasconcelos was a brilliant, controversial and versatile Cuban politician and journalist; a man of fickle and reactionary ideas. He began his political life in the Liberal Party during the government of Major General Mario García Menocal. He fought Gerardo Machado, but then served as his diplomat in Paris. He chaired the Liberal Party (1930 to 1940), served as a Senator (1936 to 1948) and Minister of Education in 1942, but this time for the constitutional government of Batista. He criticized but joined the *Partido Revolucionario Cubano Auténtico (PRC)* and was Minister without Portfolio for Prío. Later he joined the *Partido del Pueblo Cubano Ortodoxo (PPC)* and fought the *Auténticos*. After 1952 he became again pro-Batista. He left Cuba in 1959 but returned in 1964, and died there in 1965.

Ramón Zaydín y Márquez-Sterling (1895-1968)

Cuban lawyer and politician. A very lucid and charismatic professor at the *University of Havana*, cousin of Carlos Márquez Sterling; Prime Minister of Cuba between 1942 and 1944; Member of the *1940 Constitutional Convention*; Senator for Camagüey; member of the Cuban delegation to the UN; VP candidate when Carlos Saladrigas was the presidential candidate in 1944. They lost to the *Auténticos'* Grau San Martín and Raúl de Cárdenas. He died in Madrid at age 73.

VII — Alphabetical Index

1940 Constitutional Assembly, 248, 252
621 Neptuno Street, 65, 70, 166, 188

A

ABC, 23, 24, 25, 66, 252, 253, 254
Acción Católica, 203
Acción Revolucionaria Guiteras, 16, 18, 23, 250, 251
Adolfo Domingo De Guzmán Luque, 223
Albert Foster, 29, 30, 33, 50, 53, 55, 62, 65, 66, 73, 74, 79, 86, 91, 145, 166, 186, 192, 199, 209, 215, 245, 249
Alberto Alvarez-Cabrera, 85
Alejo Cossio del Pino, 22, 90
Alemán, 24, 59, 245
Alerta, 13, 17, 90, 101, 182, 249, 256
Alfonso Fanjul, 202, 243
Alfredo Jacomino, 238
Alfredo Zayas, 252, 259
Alonso Pujol, 13, 47, 48, 100, 103, 109, 187, 199, 255
Alvarez Margolles, 80, 81, 83, 152, 165, 200, 245, 246
Alvarez-Cabrera, 86
Alvaro Barba, 162, 165
Andrés Rivero Agüero, 201, 202, 238, 256
Angel Cofiño, 51, 62, 192, 247, 255
Anibal Escalante, 25, 47, 68, 76
Anselmo Allegro, 101, 245, 257
Antonio Guiteras, 252

Antonio Prío, 24, 47, 75, 160, 247, 254
Aramís Taboada, 212
Arbenz, 36, 239
Arévalo, 36, 59, 108
Armando Caiñas Milanés, 230
Armando Codina Subirat, 229
Aureliano Sánchez Arango, 228
Aurelio de la Vega, 224
Autobuses Modernos, 55

B

Bacardi, 136, 138
Baraguá, 12
Beaulac, 33, 34, 36, 47, 76, 80, 110, 125, 199, 246
Benito Coquet, 173, 247
Benito Remedios, 24, 25
Blanco Rico, 67, 242
Blas Roca, 68, 77, 137
Bloque Obrero Progresista, 54
Bohemia, 13, 101, 182, 198, 216, 217, 249, 255, 256, 258, 268
Bola de Nieve, 74, 223
Botella, 158

C

Cabrera Infante, 220
Cámara de Representantes, 164
Capitol, 14
Caracoles, 141, 142
Carlos Hevia, 22, 73, 74, 91, 95, 103, 107, 160, 180, 218, 240, 251
Carlos M. Cantillo, 67, 242
Carlos Mendieta, 23, 233, 251
Carlos Miguel de Céspedes, 201, 243, 247
Carlos Saladrigas, 100, 201, 243, 244, 255
Carrera Jústiz, 159, 238, 246, 254
Carteles, 183
Cayo Confites, 17, 59, 61
Ceiba del Agua, 30
Central Latinoamericana de Trabajadores, 193
Central Nacional Obrera de Cuba, 54
Chibás, 48, 51, 91, 94, 95, 96, 97, 106, 158, 215, 247
Columbia, 8, 18, 20, 30, 39, 58, 69, 70, 80, 83, 113, 117, 123, 124, 125, 129, 138, 142, 147, 148, 149, 152, 153, 154, 155, 160, 161, 166, 172, 198, 224, 235, 247, 250, 252, 254, 257, 258
Communists, 33, 43, 47, 53, 54, 56, 66, 68, 69, 76, 82, 87, 95, 96, 107, 126, 131, 194, 221, 239, 240, 253, 255
Confederación de Trabajadores de Cuba, 51, 62, 193, 202, 243
Consejo Consultivo, 9, 193, 194, 201, 202, 205, 237, 239, 243
Cooperativa de Omnibus Aliados, 19, 48, 253
Courvoisier, 174
CTC, 51, 53, 54, 55, 62, 69, 77, 82, 113, 137, 154, 177, 186, 192, 193, 194, 202, 203, 239, 240, 243, 247, 251, 253, 255
Cuartel Goicuría, 167
Cuban Communist Party, 68, 251, 252
Cuban-American Cultural Institute, 88

D

Dámaso Sogo, 66, 86, 124, 125, 147, 148, 200, 242, 257
Dean Acheson, 8, 15, 36, 47, 88, 115, 177, 245

Diario de la Marina, 17, 126, 180, 182, 188, 202, 220, 245, 250
Díaz Lanz, 219
Díaz Tamayo, 66, 67, 147, 199, 242, 249

E

Edgardo Buttari, 75, 229
Eduardo Chibás, 8, 13, 51, 90, 91, 94, 95, 96, 97, 106, 107, 158, 215, 235, 245, 268
Eduardo Suárez Rivas, 229
El Crisol, 16, 17, 182
El Mundo, 17, 76, 90, 180, 194, 240, 251
El País, 181
Eleguá, 268
Elena Mederos, 221
Emilio (Millo) Ochoa, 106, 230
Ernesto de la Fé, 238
Ernesto Lecuona, 221, 222
Esso Belot, 125
Estatutos Constitucionales, 110, 193, 199, 200, 257
Eufemio Fernández, 16, 17, 19, 20, 23, 61, 250
Eulogio Cantillo, 52, 155, 161, 187, 199, 246, 257
Eusebio Mujal, 53, 55, 59, 77, 82, 177, 192, 199, 202, 203, 243, 247, 253
Excelsior, 181, 183

F

Fabio Grobart, 67, 68, 251
Facundo Pomar, 53, 56
Federación Estudiantil Universitaria, 162, 180
Federación Nacional de Trabajadores Azucareros, 53, 193, 202
Felipe Pazos, 91, 155
Félix Lancís, 73, 154, 238, 251
Fermín Cowley, 67, 124, 129, 152, 200, 242, 248
Fernández Miranda, 110, 111, 124, 146, 147, 199, 242, 247, 250
Fernando Bujones, 223

FEU, 43, 59, 162, 165, 180, 246
Fidel Castro, 19, 31, 59, 61, 68, 99, 219, 221, 236, 247, 250, 255, 268
FNTA, 53, 54, 55, 193, 202
Foster Dulles, 29, 82
Francisco González Orue, 228
Francisco Grau Alsina, 228
Francisco Tabernilla, 69, 83, 87, 124, 147, 177, 199, 242, 257, 268
Franklin, 266

G

Gangsterism, 23, 59, 82, 86, 87, 89, 90, 96, 156, 200, 212, 235, 247, 258
García Agüero, 76, 137, 188, 189
García Bárcena, 86, 158, 250
García Sifredo, 168, 172, 173, 250
García Tuñón, 86, 110, 159, 202, 244, 250, 254, 257
Gastón Baquero, 126, 130, 188, 202, 209, 211, 243, 245
Gastón Godoy-Loret de Mola, 243, 244
Generación de los puros, 156
Generoso Campos Marquetti, 201, 243, 244
Genovevo Pérez, 15, 16, 17, 18, 19, 29, 59, 96, 246, 254
Gerardo Machado, 40, 43, 212, 233, 246, 249, 250, 252, 259
Goicuría Barracks, 79, 249
Gonzalo Roig, 222
GRAS, 89, 90
Grau, 16, 18, 22, 23, 24, 44, 47, 48, 51, 59, 62, 69, 75, 76, 80, 81, 82, 83, 86, 89, 90, 91, 102, 103, 107, 110, 138, 174, 189, 202, 210, 211, 212, 213, 215, 216, 217, 219, 235, 247, 248, 250, 251,
253, 254, 255, 256, 257, 258, 259
Grupo de Represión de Actividades Subversivas, 89
Guás Inclán, 124, 250
Guatacas, 158
Gustavo Cuervo Rubio, 248

H

Havana Electric Company, 56
Huber Matos, 219

J

Jesús González Cartas, 18, 23, 61, 77, 250
Jimaguayú, 12
Joaquín Martínez Sáenz, 24, 252
Jorge García Montes, 201, 243, 244
Jorge Mañach, 100, 183, 202, 212, 221, 252
José (Lolo) Villalobos, 228
José Alvarez Diaz, 91
José Fallat, 22, 61
José Ignacio Rivero, 126, 220
José Luis Martínez, 53, 55, 201, 243
José M. Alemán, 24
José M. Caramés, 20, 58, 258
José Manuel Casanova, 126, 228
José Miguel Tarafa Govín, 229
José Raimundo Andreu, 75, 228
José Suárez Rivas, 230
Juan Bosch, 36, 186
Juan Francisco Fleitas, 74, 79, 80
Juan J. Remos, 100, 101, 108
Juan Marinello, 30, 50, 68, 69, 106, 188, 209, 240, 252, 255
Julián Orbón, 222
Julio Antonio Mella, 251, 252
Justo Luis del Pozo, 147, 198

K

Karl Zimmerman, 66, 209
Kuquine, 8, 53, 55, 67, 99, 100, 101, 102, 109, 123, 124, 126, 129, 130, 134, 138, 142, 146, 147

L

La Cabaña, 13, 69, 70, 80, 152, 153, 155, 162, 164, 165, 245, 257
La Chata, 13, 18, 101, 158, 160
Lázaro Peña, 137
Leonardo Anaya Murillo, 238, 243
Lezama Lima, 130, 224
Library of Congress, 14
Lincoln Rodón, 230
López Castro, 100, 188
Lopez Coujil, 173
Luis Casero, 91, 95, 107, 246
Luis Casero Guillén, 230
Luis Muñoz Marín, 36
Luis Pérez Espinós, 91, 164
Lydia Cabrera, 142, 222

M

Manolo Castro, 23, 59, 250, 268
Manuel Antonio de Varona, 47, 91, 258
Manuel Bisbé, 25, 48, 212, 217, 230, 246
Manuel Dorta Duque, 230
Manuel Febles Valdés, 228
Marcos Hirigoyen, 55, 192, 251
María Elena, 174
Marian, 174, 175
Mariano Armengol, 66, 67, 69, 209
Mariblanca Sabas Alomá, 229
Marino López Blanco, 238
Mario Kuchilán, 159, 251
Márquez Sterling, 76, 188, 189, 202, 219, 252, 259
Marta Fernández, 124, 146
Marta Pérez, 222
Martín Elena, 79, 80, 81, 82, 83, 110, 154, 155, 166, 167, 200, 246, 249, 254
Marxist, 252
Mary Tarrero, 161, 175, 257, 268
Menelao Mora, 48, 66, 209, 253
Mercedes García Tudurí, 220
Miami, 245, 248, 250, 252, 253, 256, 259
Miguel de Marcos, 202, 243
Miguel Suárez, 193, 201, 212, 230
Miguel Suárez Fernández, 193, 201, 212
Miguelito Uría, 149
Miró Cardona, 219, 253
Modesto Barbeito, 53
Moncada Barracks, 80, 81, 152, 195, 246, 249, 256
Morales del Castillo, 101, 147, 198, 253
Movimiento Socialista Revolucionario, 19, 23, 59, 250, 258

N

New York Times, 258
New York Tribune, 266
Nicolás Castellanos, 47, 48, 51, 198, 199, 247, 254
Noel del Pino, 230
Nuñez Portuondo, 106

O

Olga Serra, 221
Omnibus Aliados, 56
Omo Ti Iansa, 134, 139, 141
Orestes Armas "Minnie" Miñoso, 223
Orfila, 22, 23, 59, 107, 248, 257
Organización Regional Interamericana del Trabajo, 193
Orígenes, 130, 202, 224
Orisha, 140, 141, 142
Orlando León Lemus, 22, 61, 256, 257, 258, 268
Orlando Puente, 62, 75, 229, 255
Oscar Gans, 73, 74, 91, 238, 249
Otilio Soca Llanes, 161
Otto Katz, 69

P

Palacio de los Trabajadores, 193, 194
Pardo Llada, 96, 212, 254
Partido Acción Progresista, 40, 240
Partido Acción Unitaria, 40, 99, 102, 103, 240, 249
Partido Revolucionario Cubano, 22, 43, 240, 250, 259
Partido Socialista Popular, 30, 137, 199
Pastor del Rio, 229
Pedro (Perucho) Formental, 66
Pedro Luis Boitel, 221
Pelayo Cuervo, 76, 90, 107, 145, 213, 229
Pentarquía, 246
Pepe San Martín, 91
Pepín Bosch, 48, 91
Perucho Formental, 70
Pilar García, 67, 102, 113, 124, 161, 242, 254
Policarpo Soler, 22, 61, 257, 258, 268
Portell Vilá, 85, 86, 87, 88, 89, 90, 91, 92, 130, 155, 158, 183, 194, 255
Prensa Libre, 17, 146, 158, 159, 181, 235, 246, 251
Presidente Cordial, 255
Presidential Palace, 18, 30, 62, 70, 73, 80, 145, 146, 148, 154, 158, 159, 164, 165, 166, 168, 172, 173, 175, 186, 187, 213, 245, 248, 249, 253, 254
Primitivo Rodríguez, 75, 229
Primo Carnera, 65, 70, 209
Protesta de los Trece, 252

Q

Queen Mary, 174, 175
Quirino Uría, 18, 29, 58, 59, 60, 63, 70, 110 >

147, 148, 161, 200, 246, 258, 268

R

Racism, 136, 138
Radio Cremata, 25, 66, 209, 230, 243, 248
Rafael Díaz Balart, 99
Rafael Esténger, 101, 103, 104, 202, 243, 249
Rafael Guas Inclán, 230
Ramón Corona, 47, 228
Ramón Vasconcelos, 17, 75, 182, 201, 243, 256, 259
Ramón Zaydin, 259
Rasputin, 8, 94, 96, 97
Raúl de Cárdenas, 259
Republicano, 249
Rio Chaviano, 81, 83, 129, 248, 256
Rivero Agüero, 256
Roberto Agramonte, 22, 76, 86, 101, 106, 158, 245

Rockefeller Group, 34
Rolando Masferrer, 19, 23, 51, 59, 68, 82, 212, 250, 252, 254, 256
Rómulo Betancourt, 186
Rubén de León, 20, 50, 75, 168, 186, 228, 238
Rubén Martínez Villena, 251, 252
Rubio Padilla, 91

Ruby Alonso, 30, 74, 85, 166, 209, 215, 245, 249
Ruperto Cabrera, 16, 36, 101, 110, 147, 148, 161, 246, 254

S

Saladrigas, 256, 259
Salas Cañizares, 83, 109, 110, 111, 125, 145, 152, 167, 254, 256, 268
Salvador Díaz Versón, 113
Salvador Massip, 86, 155, 252
Sánchez Arango, 66, 75, 91, 95, 159, 168, 186, 194, 256
Santeros, 136, 140
Santiago Rey, 66, 188, 199, 209, 210, 256
Segundo Curti, 91, 154, 160, 161, 168, 186, 217, 229, 248, 258
Sergio Carbó, 17, 181, 235, 246
Sergio Megías, 164, 167, 173, 252
Sergio Mejías, 230
Servicio de Inteligencia Militar, 113, 159, 213, 249, 258
Sosa de Quesada, 101, 124, 126, 130, 199, 242, 257
Suárez Rivas, 212, 238
Supervielle, 48, 215, 216, 217, 249, 254

T

Time Magazine, 247, 268
Tomás Fernández, 31, 65, 209
Tropicana, 146, 147
Trujillo, 16, 36, 54, 59, 88, 96, 146, 187, 232, 236, 257

U

Ugalde Carrillo, 66, 67, 102, 113, 242, 257, 258
Unión Insurrectional Revolucionaria, 23
University of Havana, 245, 248, 249, 251, 252, 254, 256, 259
US Embassy, 30, 36, 47, 55, 62, 73, 74, 75, 76, 77, 86, 94, 95, 96, 106, 166, 186, 188, 192, 215

V

Vicente Rubiera, 51, 192
Vicente Tejera, 90, 164, 173, 253, 258
Virgilio Pérez López, 75, 228

Y

Yemayá, 140, 141

The font used throughout the text has been **Palatino Linotype**, one of the classic old style serif typefaces inspired by designs of the 16th century Italian calligrapher **Giambattista Palatino**. The font was reissued in 1948 by **Hermann Zapf** for the Linotype Foundy, the company created by Ottmar Mergenthaler, a German immigrant to the U.S. who invented the revolutionary line typesetting machine that was first used in 1890 by the **New York Tribune**.

The font used in the covers, title pages, headings and ornaments is **P22 Franklin Caslon**, a faithful interpretation of the type used by Benjamin Franklin in the 1750's in his printing shop and particularly in his **Poor Richard's Almanac**. This font was developed in 2006 by the International House of Fonts for the Philadelphia Museum of Art to commemorate the 300th birthday of our most remarkable Founding Father.

The font accompanying the photos and illustrations is **Verdana**; a humanist sans-serif typeface designed by **Matthew Carter** for *Microsoft Corporation*, with hand-hinting done by **Tom Rickner**, then at *Monotype*. Demand for such a clear and easy to read typeface was recognized by **Virginia Howlett** of *Microsoft's* typography group. The name "Verdana" is based on a mix of *verdant* (something green, as in the Seattle area and the Evergreen state of Washington), and *Ana* (the name of Howlett's eldest daughter

Raúl Eduardo Chao received his PhD from Johns Hopkins University at age 25 and after a brief stint in industry spent 18 years in academe, as full professor and Department Chairman at the **Universities of Puerto Rico and Detroit**. In 1986 he founded a very successful management consultancy, assisting companies and government agencies to develop positive work environments and process improvement techniques as the means to secure improvements in productivity and quality.

The Systema Group had as clients many Fortune 100 companies and Federal and State organizations, both in the US and abroad. As its Chairman, Chao has written a dozen books and numerous articles in newspapers and reviewed journals. He and his wife Olga live in Coral Gables, Florida and spend long periods of time in Paris.

Back Cover Photos:
(Clockwise from top left)

1. A poster from the Communist Party supporting Batista for the presidency in 1940.
2. Bastista's favorite photo of himself.
3. A candle for *Eleguá*, the owner of all roads in the *Yoruba* religion. The *Santo Niño de Atocha* or *San Antonio de Padua* under syncretic practices.
4. Police photo of Fidel Castro, accused for the murder of Manolo Castro in 1948.
5. The always elegant first lady Mary Tarrero de Prío.
6. Colonel Rafael Salas Cañizares, Havana's Chief of Police in 1952.
7. An open letter from Eduardo Chibás to Carlos Prío published in *Bohemia* Magazine on May 8, 1949.
8. Havana Carnival poster in 1952.
9. General Francisco Tabernilla Dolz, appointed Chief of the Army by Batista on March 10, 1952.
10. Eduardo Chibás' political poster in 1948.
11. Fulgencio Batista on the cover of Time Magazine on April 21, 1952.
12. Mobsters Policarpo Soler and Orlando León Lemus in 1952.
13. Brigadier General Quirino Uría, the man who patriotically turned down Batista's offer to command the Cuban Army in 1952.
14. Carlos Prío Socarrás, Cuba's *Presidente Cordial*.

www.ingramcontent.com/pod-product-compliance
Lightning Source LLC
Chambersburg PA
CBHW030312080526
44584CB00012B/533